Gender, Sexualities and Culture in Asia

Series editors
Stevi Jackson
Centre for Women's Studies
University of York
York, United Kingdom

Olivia Khoo
School of Media, Film and Journalism
Monash University
Melbourne, Australia

Denise Tse-Shang Tang
Department of Sociology
University of Hong Kong
Hong Kong

The Gender, Sexualities and Culture in Asia book series provides a welcome new forum for monographs and anthologies focusing on the intersections between gender, sexuality and culture across Asia. Titles in the series include multi- and interdisciplinary research by scholars within Asia as well as in North American, European and Australian academic contexts. It offers a distinctive space for the exploration of topics of growing academic concern, from non-normative cultures of sexuality in Asia, to studies of gendered identities cross the region, and expands the field of Asian genders and sexualities by applying a cultural lens to current debates, including rural lives, migration patterns, religion, transgender identities, sex industry and family.

More information about this series at
http://www.palgrave.com/gp/series/15191

Cassini Sai Kwan Chu

Compensated Dating

Buying and Selling Sex in Cyberspace

Cassini Sai Kwan Chu
University of Hong Kong
Hong Kong, Hong Kong

Gender, Sexualities and Culture in Asia
ISBN 978-981-10-6973-4   ISBN 978-981-10-6974-1   (eBook)
https://doi.org/10.1007/978-981-10-6974-1

Library of Congress Control Number: 2017962100

Cover illustration: redsnapper / Alamy Stock Photo

Printed on acid-free paper

This Palgrave Macmillan imprint is published by Springer Nature
The registered company is Springer Nature Singapore Pte Ltd.
The registered company address is: 152 Beach Road, #21-01/04 Gateway East, Singapore
189721, Singapore

CONTENTS

1 Introduction   1

2 Theoretical and Methodological Issues in Researching
Compensated Dating   19

3 The *Brothers*—Part I: Men Who Buy Compensated Dating   47

4 The *Brothers*—Part II: Why Compensated Dating?   77

5 The *Brothers*—Part III: Becoming and Being a *Brother*   105

6 Why Do Girls Engage in CD?   127

7 More than Bounded Authenticity   153

8 Conclusion   187

Bibliography   199

Index   213

LIST OF FIGURES

Fig. 1.1   Police warning on eight online discussion forums between 2009 and 2012   11

Fig. 1.2   A new police warning since 2013   12

Fig. 2.1   Conceptual framework   24

Fig. 2.2   Constructs and content domains   41

Fig. 4.1   Fertility rates at specific ages, 1981–2015 (From Women and Men in Hong Kong Key Statistics (2015: 48) by Census and Statistics Department)   93

Fig.4.2   Women Aged 15 and Above by Educational Attainment (From Women and Men in Hong Kong Key Statistics (2012: 60) by Census and Statistics Department)   94

Fig. 7.1   Original group: Except Sam and Aaron, who had only met online but never offline, the rest of the group had met each other offline previously   170

Fig. 7.2   Final group: Billy introduced Winnie, a CC, to the group. Wendy introduced me to the group. New friendships were formed   171

LIST OF TABLES

Table 1.1   Definitions of key terms used by CD participants   14

Table 2.1   Demographic characteristics of 30 male respondents   36

Table 2.2   Demographic characteristics of 12 female respondents   36

CHAPTER 1

Introduction

Peter, a 36-year-old and well-educated man, married his first and only girlfriend in his late twenties. He has two kids and has been engaging in compensated dating (hereafter known as CD) as a client for three years. He described his behaviors of dating young girls in CD as if a wolf dog hunting for preys in a jungle. Knowing that I had been having a hard time recruiting girls who offered CD for interviews, he referred Jenny, a 19-year-old high school student, to me. Peter told me that he met Jenny online and had been devising a plan to have sex with her for free. Jenny was reluctant to meet me for a face-to-face interview at the beginning but after chatting online for several weeks, she finally let her gurard down, invited me to go to a Taiwanese pop singer's concert with her, and agreed to be interviewed before the concert.

Sitting in front of me was a very shy and polite young girl, who was literally wearing no make-up and just like many other teenagers, she was struggling with breakouts on her face.

Cassini:	*Do you consider yourself as a sex worker?*
Jenny:	*A little bit. Offering CD is probably not a good thing; otherwise, I would have told other people about it. But I do not feel like I am a sex tool because I didn't only have sex with my clients. We talked a lot too. Our dates were never rushed.*
Cassini:	*Where did you have sex with your clients?*
Jenny:	*I went to their apartments.*

© The Author(s) 2018
C. S. K. Chu, *Compensated Dating*, Gender, Sexualities
and Culture in Asia, https://doi.org/10.1007/978-981-10-6974-1_1

Cassini: *Isn't it a bit dangerous to go to the apartments of the clients who are basically strangers?*

Jenny: *I know! I was a little bit wary too. There was a girl being murdered by her client in his apartment a few years ago, right?*

Cassini: *Yes. Since you acknowledged the potential risks, why did you still go to their apartments?*

Jenny: *Because I had chatted with them online for a long period of time before I actually met them and I believed that they were good guys.*

Cassini: *Didn't you worry that your clients might secretly install some pinhole cameras in their apartments and record your sexual encounters?*

Jenny: *Um… one client did video-record our sexual intercourse without recording my face.*

Cassini: *How could that be possible!? Video-recording your sexual intercourse without recording your face?*

Jenny: *Well, I don't know. Just let it be. I trusted him. It's all about trust.*

Cassini: *Didn't you worry that he would upload the video onto the Internet or use it to blackmail you?*

Jenny: *No! He is not this type of person. I really trust him.*

Cassini: *Why do you trust him so much? It was the first time you met him, right?*

Jenny: *Yes. I don't know. I just feel like he is a nice guy, but I am feeling stupid now because I didn't charge him for extra money for the video-recording.*

At the end of our interview, I asked Jenny if she would go on a CD date with Peter. She said she would consider it, but the probability was low because she was not in need of money. Although Peter told me that he was planning a sexual trap for Jenny, the best that I could do was to lay out all the possible risks underlying CD that she might not be aware of, and to remind her to be cautious and be protective of herself at all times. After all, she was already 19. She had the right and autonomy to make her own decisions about her life.

Why do girls like Jenny willingly engage in CD? If girls in CD do not consider themselves as sex workers, even if they are selling sex to strangers, then how do they perceive themselves and categorize their CD behaviors? Why do some girls unquestionably trust their clients? Where does the trust come from? If young girls sell their sex and sexualities not for money, then what for? Meanwhile, why do men engage in CD? If they simply desire for sex, why don't they purchase it from traditional forms of prostitution, which is cheaper, easier to access, and less time consuming?

This book addresses all these questions and other conundrums surrounding CD by studying the lived experiences of individuals who are buying and selling CD. To date, the phenomenon of CD is under-researched. The limited studies on CD have focused largely on young women who provide CD and there is relatively less known about men who seek CD (Ho, 2003; Lam, 2003; Lee & Shek, 2013). By adding the narratives of clients, this study responds to the lack of research on clients and expands our knowledge surrounding CD, and the current commercial sex market.

Despite a small, but growing body of studies on the subject of CD, there is at present little empirical research based on the testimonies of people who are actually involving in the activity. However, to obtain a comprehensive picture of CD, the insider perspectives and experiences are necessary to be revealed and interpreted. This study aptly fills this research gap. It offers invaluable empirical foundation from which to comprehend the operation of CD, the reasoning behind individuals' involvement in CD, as well as the ways they conceptualize their identities and behaviors in relation to sexuality and prostitution. The ethnographic data on CD clients and CD providers offers a precious insider perspective, which will be helpful for policy-makers to develop appropriate social, legal, and educational polices related to CD, online sexual activities, and sexual health. It will also help parents, educators, and people who work with adolescents to foster a positive approach to them and to provide guidance and care in response to their needs and conditions.

Undoubtedly, the Internet has changed the formation of our sexuality and has greatly expanded the organization of the sex market. This book sheds lights on the complexity of the relationships between different aspects of this new world: love, sex, money, and technology. Besides providing a theoretical insight into sexuality in late modern society in a Chinese context, it is my hope that the present findings and analyses will expand feminist discussions on the notion of prostitution and of the authenticity of prostitute–client relationships

The present study documents the lived experiences of male clients and CD providers in Hong Kong. It analyzes how they perceived themselves, their CD behaviors, and their intimate relationships, both inside and outside CD, as well as their coping strategies for the social, moral, and legal stresses associated with their CD behaviors. Finally, it illuminates the emotional and physical impacts of CD on the participants. These analyses are informed by feminists' understanding of prostitution and women who sell sex, Hochschild's (1983) notions of emotional labor and the commercialization of human feeling, Bernstein's (2010) concept of bounded authenticity, Sanders' (2008) discussion on the authenticity of commercial relationships, Giddens' (1990, 1992b) ideas of plastic sexuality, confluent love, pure relationship, and the consequences of modernity, as well as Beck's (1992) conception of modern risk society.

Rather than conceptualizing CD as a monolithic form of commercial transaction, a type of sexual behavior, or a form of sexual exploitation, this study focuses on the reflexive CD processes and the dynamic CD relationships in which men and women conduct and make sense of their intimate, sexual, and gendered lives and identities. The notion of CD is understood here in a larger sociocultural context and a complex hybridization of sexual ideologies, gender structure, paradoxical sociocultural values, as well as the effects and consequences of modernity. Such a perspective helps us rethink a number of aspects: the wider changes in gender relations; what it means to be a heterosexual Chinese man and woman; and how heterosexuality and intimacy are practiced as we enter into the progressively digitalized and modernized world. This study updates the knowledge we currently have about individuals who engage in CD and the sex market as a whole; it also speaks to the broader transformations of some of the key social structures and elements particularly gender and sexualities in the era of late modernity.

OVERVIEW OF CD

CD generally refers to a mutually agreed contract between a female, who is usually a teenage girl, a schoolgirl, or a young woman in her 20s, and a relatively older man. While the girl offers her friendly companionships and possibly sexual favors to the man, the man, in turn, provides monetary and/or social benefits to the girl. The benefits could be in the form of cash, tuition, a nice dinner, temporary shelter, overseas vacation, drugs, or luxury goods such as handbags, clothes, cosmetics, watches, and phones, etc.

The concept of CD originated in Japan in the early 1990s. It spread to Taiwan in 1999, before moving on to Korea and subsequently, Hong Kong. Currently, the phenomenon of CD can also be found in Malaysia, Macau, and some parts of Mainland China such as Shanghai and the Canton province (Anonymous, 2012c). The initial notion of CD did not incorporate the aspect of sexual exchange: Adolescent girls simply provided their companionships to clients. However, the phenomenon of CD has quickly transformed from a nonchalant non-sexual relationship to a relationship in which sex has become the predominant interest. Today, although CD does not automatically equate to sexual exchanges, in many cases, CD does involve a variety of sexual interactions, ranging from kissing, fondling, and oral sex to safe vaginal sex, unsafe vaginal sex, anal sex, and sadomasochism. Therefore, many social and institutional parties in Asia, such as the regional crime prevention department, the police force, parents, teachers, social workers, and the media, generally conceptualize CD as a modern form of sex work (Joshua, 2009; Lai, 2007; S. B. Rubin, 2002). In Japan, the country in which the notion of CD originated, the government now requires the use of the term 'prostitution' to denote any instance of what previously had been regarded as CD (Udagawa, 2007). The Asian Women's Fund also stated that even though sexual intercourse might not take place, CD is fundamentally the same as adolescent prostitution because both areas involve an exchange of sexual services for money (Udagawa, 2007). Similarly, the US Department of State indicated that CD is a mechanism that encourages minors to prostitution in the 2014 annual human trafficking report (Department of State, 2014). Thus, more often than not, the term CD is abstractly considered as an euphemism of teenage prostitution (Ueno, 2003).

Public knowledge surrounding CD comes largely from the media because there is little empirical knowledge in grappling the phenomenon of CD. As such, what and how media interpret and transmit the notion of CD to the wider society is important in shaping the public discourse of CD. It is practically impossible to talk of the media reports as straightforwardly empirically false because they are composed of some factual statements in addition to moral claims; however, the reports are often one-sided, or even distorted, and represent only partial account of the reality. Reports in the media usually feature CD cases that involve underage individuals, coercion, illegal drugs, murder, or other criminal activities (Anonymous, 2011a, 2012b; Yuen, 2009). In the media discourse, men who seek CD are generally regarded as 'predators' while girls who provide CD are portrayed according to two extremes. On the one hand, girls are sometimes depicted as 'innocent victims'. On the other hand, girls are sometimes described as 'vain and morally deprived' individuals (Anonymous, 2009). In general, media representations of CD are highly negative with at least two layers of stigmatization: moral and legal. Such a focus on the immoral and unlawful aspects of CD ignores the link among gender, social class, sexuality, masculinity, and youth culture into consideration. Out of this set of circumstances, there emerged broadly held stereotypes created by the media that clients are predators and oppressors while all girls involve in CD are vain, mercenary, vulnerable, brainless, lazy, and morally deprived individuals who are willingly to sell their bodies, youth, and sexualities to gratify their consumerist desires (Smalley, Contreras, Childress, Bailey, & Sinderbrand, 2003). Based on various interviews and ethnographic data, the present study breaks the myth about CD members and illustrates that sex and materialistic consumption are hardly the only reason for men and girls to engage in CD. Individuals engage in CD for multiple reasons in terms of personal, social, and historical aspects.

Moreover, when the phenomenon of CD becomes 'illegalized' and 'demonized', the phenomenon is defined primarily by criminality—while certain types of young girls, especially girls who already have delinquent behaviors and girls who have psychological vulnerabilities rendering them at risk for developing delinquent behaviors, are at higher risk of being victimized in CD, certain types of men, particularly those who already have sexually deviant tastes and behaviors, are more likely to exploit and oppress young girls in CD. Although such portrayals are misrepresentations of the CD population in reality, these highly negative images force CD participants to relate to one another in very secret and clandestine networks. As a result, the general society has very little opportunity to understand the complexity of this group of people. The ones who are visible are those who display illegalized behaviors, which are taken to be further evidence of the criminal nature of CD. However, based on the ethnographic data of this study, a majority of CD incidents do not involve coercion, drugs, or other illegal dimensions, and therefore are not exposed to the public. It is the aim of this book to reveal, explore, and analyze these hidden CD cases.

In Hong Kong, the female providers are no longer limited exclusively to underage girls, but include a wider age range of young women into their late 20s. Taiwan also has a similar situation such that CD 'has become an umbrella term for all forms of individually-operated sex work in Taiwan' (J. Ho, 2003, p. 331). Despite the similarities between CD and the traditional forms of sex work in their commercial and probably sexual aspects, their connotations are different. While the former insinuates professionalism, the latter suggests amateurish or occasional sexual practitioners. Although most outsiders probably undermine this difference and therefore reduce them to being essentially the same, the insiders often emphasize this differentiation and therefore locate CD as a more valuable and noble form of interpersonal exchange rather than prostitution. The ways that this distinction is being constructed and reinforced will be elaborated throughout this book.

Although prostitution or teenage prostitution is not a new phenomenon, the trend of CD is worrisome for many stakeholders in the society because the way to enter into CD is getting easier and easier, the practice of CD is getting increasingly furtive, and, more importantly, the age of the providers is becoming younger and younger. In Taipei, girls as young as nine years old were already voluntarily offering themselves available for CD (Anonymous, 2011b). Similarly, in Hong Kong it was reported that girls as young as 12 years old were willingly to sell their sexuality for shopping money (Anonymous, 2011a). The fact that the phenomenon of CD uncovered a growing number of young and underage girls who were not only sexually active, but were also selling their sexualities had appalled Hong Kong society, which is, more or less, still affected by the traditional Confucian ideology which tends to repress female sexuality and value female chastity. Moreover, sexuality is traditionally an arena of our most intimate and private expression of self, which ought not to be commodified in the public sphere. The commodification of the sexuality of teenage and underage girls, who have historically been perceived as asexual, provokes even more moral panic. Accordingly, CD is generally perceived as a social illness that reflects the moral decay of modern societies. The society at large not only condemns CD, but also fears it. This fear comes from its threats to sexual morals, standards of behavior, family integrity, and the system of monogamy.

As we have moved into the twenty-first century, these traditional ideologies have been profoundly challenged. The Internet and mobile technologies in modernity have given rise to an unprecedented sexual revolution where individuals, regardless of their sex and age, can explore and experience sexuality freely and anonymously (A. Cooper, David, Griffin-Shelley, & Robin, 2004). Sexual negotiations in the form of CD have become more underground due to the facilitation of various computer-mediated-communications, which have dramatically changed the nature of the commercial sex market and client–provider relations. The anonymous nature of the Internet greatly reduces the stigma and embarrassment during the process of sexual negotiation and CD itself.

The notion of CD is contestable because it raises sensitive and ethical issues around issues such as adolescent sexuality, commercial sex, morality, the misuse of computer-mediated communication, and the risks of cyberspace. The association between economics, sex, and technologies has become increasingly intricate and embedded in modern relationships. Such change has provided new opportunities, but simultaneously generate new ethical dilemmas in contemporary society. While capitalistic features and sexualities are becoming highly clustered in our intimate lives, the seemingly congruent connection between marriage, sex, and romantic love are becoming increasingly fragmented (Giddens, 1992a). Concisely, this book explores the implication of CD, and illustrates how the drastic transformation of various key social institutions, such as sexuality, gender, identity, family, and the economic market have given rise to the phenomenon of CD in the late modern world. Besides addressing the reasons why individuals take part in CD, this book also explores the process of becoming a client or a provider, and the process of developing various forms of client–provider relations which could be seen as a microcosm of gender construction and relations in the wider society. While some individuals rationally and intentionally choose to engage in CD, others come across CD accidentally through referrals, random browsing on the Internet, online chatrooms, online games, and various phone applications designed for social networking. Many of them, especially adolescent providers, are not fully aware of the implications of CD. They tend to underestimate the dangers and consequences embedded in CD while overestimating their self-efficacy in controlling the CD senarios. Unsurprisingly, their self-beliefs are hardly ever completely consistent with the reality (Bandura, 1982). Hence, although individuals may be confident that they are able to direct what would and would not happen in CD, many of them are in fact vulnerable to the sexual, physical, and emotional risks that are latent in CD (see, for example, Anonymous, 2010a, 2012a; M.-S. Chan, 2012; Zhang, 2011). Some psychological harms of CD might not be immediately apparent, but they might have underlying consequences that could be detrimental to the involved individuals in the long run (see, for example, Anonymous, 2010b; Y.-W. Cheung, 2011; Tse & Mak, 2011). So, even though CD might represent a new platform to practice modern intimacies, it can be problematic if it is not practiced responsibly and rationally. It is the aim of this study to provide a more comprehensive understanding of the phenomenon of CD by revealing the variety of CD cases and the diversity of participants who are largely invisible in the general society and the media.

Having said this, it is unrealistic to have an accurate and reliable figure on the number of people involved in CD as many of them cannot be identified. Moreover, the mobility of the CD market is extremely high as individuals can join or withdraw from it at any time. The only pattern that can be discerned is that the holiday seasons seem to be the peak seasons for the CD market (Y.-W. Lam, 2012). There seem to be more adolescents providing CD around Christmas holidays, summer holidays, and Valentine's Days, perhaps for several reasons. First, adolescents do not have school during these holidays, so they have more spare time. Second, they need additional money to hang out with their friends during holidays, or to purchase gifts for their boyfriends/girlfriends. Third, some adolescents who study overseas would return to Hong Kong and engage in CD during holiday seasons. Because the CD market is so fluid and elusive, it is difficult to agree on a precise figure for the CD population. Yet the increasing trend of CD is undeniable. Yang Memorial Methodist Social Service, which has been working with adolescents involved in CD since 2005, reported that the number of the CD cases it was dealing with had increased sixfold between 2007 and 2011. Given the increasing prevalence of CD amongst adolescents, in 2009, the social service center started a Concern Action in Relieving *Enjo-kosai* (CARE) Youth Project funded by The Community Chest to serve adolescents involved in CD and to increase the social awareness of CD on its plausible physical and psychological harm to adolescents, as well as a possible threat to the public hygiene and ethics.[1]

In Hong Kong, prostitution operated individually and privately is not illegal, but a lot of activities related to the coordination of prostitution are (Travis S. K. Kong, 2002). For example, in 2017, 23 people were arrested when police busted a syndicate which had earned HKD20 million between 2012 and 2017 by facilitating CD between male clients and female providers through a website (Mok, 2017). Individuals can possibly be charged for soliciting for an *immoral* purpose in public, causing prostitution, living on the earnings of the prostitution of others, and controlling persons for the purpose of unlawful sexual intercourse or prostitution. Given that some providers of CD are minors, the legal risks with which clients of CD face also include having intercourse with a girl under 13, having intercourse with a girl under 16, causing or encouraging prostitution of,

---

[1] Refer to the CARE project's website. Retrieved on March 15, 2013. (http://careproject.yang.org.hk)

intercourse with, or indecent assault on girls or boys under 16, and indulging in indecent conduct toward a child under 16.[2] As such, although CD is not legally defined in the law, there are many legal constraints and consequences when enacting and negotiating CD.

Since cyberspace is the major platform for CD negotiations in Hong Kong, new legal issues have evolved around the cyberworld. The major questions to ask are: Shall citizens of the cyberspace be subjected to the same legal regulations as citizens in the physical space? Does the virtual world demand different legal regulations from existing ones? Given that cyberspace has increasingly becoming the space for CD solicitation, in 2012, the police force and the Department of Justice began to consider a new definition or at least a clarification of the meaning of 'a public place' such that 'online discussion forums' would be included under the category of the 'public place' (Wong & Cheung, 2012). If the definition were officially adjusted, then soliciting for CD online would be treated as the same as soliciting for prostitution in a public space. In other words, it would be illegal to solicit for CD online. However, it is still contestable whether or not cyberspace will be treated as a public space as it raises other operational difficulties and ethical issues such as privacy.

In the meantime, before any legal principle has been amended to regulate the solicitation for commercial sex in cyberspace, the Hong Kong Police Force had issued a warning message in at least eight CD-related Internet forums since 2009 in the hope to deter young individuals and men from becoming involved in CD (Chung, 2009). A warning message as shown in Fig. 1.1 from the Crime Prevention Bureau will automatically appear before entering into the CD forum. The warning message was in Chinese, which translates to 'Do not sell the body for money. Engaging in CD online will completely ruin your future. Ethical values shall be placed in the first priority. The most practical thing to do is to treasure your dignity.' Follow by the warning was an explanation of the legal consequences related to CD behaviors:

> According to Hong Kong law, any man who engages in sexual behaviors with underage girls, or anyone who solicits other people to involve in unethical acts, is immediately considered as committing serious crimes. Report to the police through e-mail for any information about illegal compensated dating activities.

[2] Social Welfare Department. 2008. "Legal Aspects." Retrieved March 15, 2013. (http://www.swd.gov.hk/doc/fcw/proc_guidelines/childabuse/Chapter03_updated_at_April08.pdf)

警方呼籲

勿爲金錢　出賣肉體
上網援交　前途盡毀
道德價值　應放首位
珍惜自尊　最爲實際

根據香港法例，任何男子與未成年少女發生性行爲；或
任何人唆使他人作不道德行爲，即干犯嚴重罪行。

如有任何關於非法援交活動消息，可以電郵至
crm-kw-rcpo@police.gov.hk
向警方舉報。

西九龍總區防止罪案辦公室

香港警務處 HONG KONG POLICE FORCE

警告：此區只適合十八歲或以上人士進入或觀看 (或合乎你當地的成年合法年齡)。此區內容可能令人反感；不可將此區的內容派發、傳閱、出售、出租、交給或借予年齡未滿18歲的人士或將本網站內容向該人士出示、播放或放映。

本人已年滿十八歲
同意進入

本人未滿十八歲
離開

LEGAL DISCLAIMER WARNING: THIS DISCUSSION BOARD CONTAINS MATERIAL WHICH MAY OFFEND AND MAY NOT BE DISTRIBUTED, CIRCULATED, SOLD, HIRED, GIVEN, LENT, SHOWN, PLAYED OR PROJECTED TO A PERSON UNDER THE AGE OF 18 YEARS OR LOCAL LEGAL AGE.

I am at least 18 years old.
Agree

I am under 18 years old.
Leave

Fig. 1.1   Police warning on eight online discussion forums between 2009 and 2012

Underneath the warning were two self-selected check boxes—'I am at least 18' and 'I am below 18'—in an attempt to screen out individuals below 18 years old from accessing the CD forum. However, it was not a very effective method to verify the age of the users. Because of the anonymous nature of cyberspace, underage individuals could always select 'I am at least 18' to access the CD forum. Even if a user selected 'I am below 18' and thereby he or she would be denied access to the CD forum, he or she

Fig. 1.2   A new police warning since 2013

could immediately return to the screening page to select 'I am at least 18', and accessed the CD forum conveniently without any legal consequences. In 2013, a new police warning sign as shown in Fig. 1.2 was created and replaced the old one in some CD forums. The warning has shortened to 'Do not let money destroy the body. Say no to CD is the most practical thing to do' in Chinese and 'Make the Right Decision Go For Right Direction' in English.

In 2017, an even more simplified bilingual warning without any graphical design has replaced the previous ones in a major CD forum, which says:

Legal Disclaimer Warning: This discussion board contains material which may offend and may not be distributed, circulated, sold, hired, given, lent, shown, played or projected to a person under the age of 18 years or local legal age.

One element that remains the same in all three warnings is the self-selected check boxes regarding the age of the users, which is impractical.

DEFINITIONS OF KEY TERMS

CD participants employ a set of vernacular terms to facilitate their communication, both online and offline. These terms create a social message of inclusion and a feeling of belonging to the CD group such that if a person understands these insider terms, then CD members would know that the person is probably be 'one of us'. Thus, using vernacular terms strengthens a sense of closeness within the CD community and creates a sense of sisterhoods/brotherhoods. It also serves to make CD an exclusive and discreet activity because an outsider overhearing a description or discourse using these vernacular terms could be quite lost.

Some of the most important terms include *Brothers* and *Ching* (師兄), which denote male clients of CD. *Big Brothers* and *Dai Ching* (大師兄) refer to those who have engaged in the CD for a relatively longer period of time. Throughout this book, I will use the term *Brothers* to denote male clients of CD. Another important term is *CC*, which refers to a girl who provides sex in CD. It is derived from a Cantonese term 'C *Chung*' (私鐘), which literally translates to 'private clock'. This term has been used to refer to individually operated sex workers since the 1980s to underscore their flexible working hours and private practice. *PTGF*, a short term for *part-time girlfriend,* refers to a girl who provides CD that does not provide sexual services, but only companionships. *Agent girl* or *A girl* refers to a girl who works for an agent. *A girls* are generally regarded as *pseudo-CCs* because *A girls* act and operate more like traditional sex workers and less like *CCs* (the differences between traditional sex workers and *CCs* will be discussed in subsequent chapters). Last but not least, the word *trade* is

Table 1.1 Definitions of key terms used by CD participants

Terms	Definition
Brother/ Ching	Male client
CC	A girl who provides CD that involves sexual services
PTGF	Short form for part-time girlfriend. This term refers to a girl who provides CD that does NOT involve sexual services
Agent girl/ A girl	A CC who works for an agent
Trade	CD transaction
Q	Male ejaculation. 1q refers to one time of ejaculation. 2q refers to two times of ejaculations and so on.
3P	Sex that involves three players.
69	Simultaneous fellatio and cunnilingus
ML	Make love, sexual intercourse
BJ	Blow job, fellatio
HJ	Hand job, the manual stimulation of a penis
BM	Body massage, usually refers to a CC using her body to perform a massage on a Brother
CS	Camera sex
PS	Phone sex
dom	Condom
ONS	One-night stand
SM	Sadomasochism
PAW	Parents are watching

used to denote CD transaction. For example, if a *Brother* asks a *CC* 'do you have time to trade?', it means 'do you have time to engage in CD?' Table 1.1 provides a list of key terms employed by CD participants.

ORGANIZATION OF THE BOOK

This book is organized into eight chapters. The present chapter provides a background of CD. The next chapter lays out the theoretical framework that was used to analyze the phenomenon of CD and the methodology that was employed to collect empirical data in this study. The chapter describes the process of conducting ethnography and interviews in the virtual world as well as in the physical world. It also discusses the practical and ethical challenges that I encountered during the research process.

Given the relatively scant literature on male clients and rich literature on female sex workers, this book focuses predominantly on male clients and their relationships with *CCs*. Chapters 3, 4, and 5 reveal *Brothers'* journey in CD, Chap. 6 discusses the subjective experiences of *CCs*, and Chap. 7 explores *Brother–CC* relationships. In particular, Chap. 3 explores the motivations of men's involvement in CD. The chapter illuminates some of the precursors that predispose men into CD. Chapter 4 highlights why men prefer CD in the midst of various traditional forms of commercial sex and non-commercial intimacies. It argues that the unique features of CD create an appearance that disguises the commercial nature of CD. The chapter explains how men have developed ideologies to justify their CD behavior and to differentiate CD from prostitution, *CCs* from sex workers, and themselves from clients of prostitution. Following on from men's rationales to engage in CD, Chap. 5 spells out men's process of becoming a *Brother* and describes the major stages that men might go through during their CD journey. Some men believe they have other roles and responsibilities in CD other than being a client. Such conception has a substantive implication on their moral integrity and hegemonic masculinity.

After discussing men's perspectives, Chap. 6 switches the focus onto *CCs*. It attempts to understand the lived experiences of *CCs* and their reasons for involving in CD. Instead of focusing on personal and psychological aspects, it focuses on social factors such as the transformation of intimacy, technological advancement, individualization, and the fragmentation of modern societies that have predisposed young women in an environment that is favorable to their development of CD behavior. The chapter also discusses the impacts of CD on the *CCs* physically and emotionally.

Chapter 7 discusses the relationships between CD participants. Building on Hochschild's (1983) notion of emotion work and Bernstein's (2010) concept of bounded authenticity, it stresses that CD requires emotional work not only on the part of *CCs*, but also on the part of the *Brothers*. Both parties need to put emotional effort to actualize an ideal CD encounter and relationship. This chapter argues that some *Brothers* desire more than just bounded authenticity and by transforming the supposedly bounded CD relationship into an unbounded relationship, they assert their masculinities.

The concluding chapter discusses whether CD should be considered as a form of prostitution or a variant of intimacy in late modernity. The chapter pulls together the major questions about the characteristics and structure of CD, the reasons that CD has emerged in the period of late modernity, the cultural specificity of CD in Hong Kong, CD participants' subjective notions of CD and their roles, the impact of cyberspace on sexuality, and how *CC–Brother* relationships reflect the wider gender pattern.

BIBLIOGRAPHY

Anonymous. (2009, September 5). Addicted to Materialism! Teenage Girls Engaged in CD for the Sake of Gucci Phone Accessories (in Chinese). *Now News*.

Anonymous. (2010a). 61 Years Old Accountant Had CD with over 100 Teenage Girls, Sent to Prison for 56 Months (in Chinese) *Wen Wei Po*. Hong Kong.

Anonymous. (2010b, August 15). Adolescent Girl Engaged in Compensated Dating for the Sake of Playing Online Game (in Chinese). *The Sun*. Retrieved from http://the-sun.on.cc/cnt/news/20100815/00410_096.html

Anonymous. (2011a, September 25). IT Technician Engaged in Compensated Dating with a Twelve-year-old Girl. *Appledaily*.

Anonymous. (2011b). A Nine-year-old Girl Engaged in Compensated Dating Online. Men Welcomed It and No One Stopped It. The Police Force Exclaimed: The Society is Getting Sick! (in Chinese). *Ta Kung Po*, p. A15.

Anonymous. (2012a, March 10). A 14 Years Old Girl Controlled Her 13 Years Old Classmate to Engage in CD (in Chinese). *Sing Pao Daily*, p. A06.

Anonymous. (2012b, March 10). A 14 Years Old Girl Forced Her 13 Years Old Classmates to Engage in CD. *Sing Pao Daily*.

Anonymous. (2012c, December 17). The Trend of Compensated Dating is Growing in the Cantone Province Because of Luxury Goods (in Chinese). *The China Press*.

Bandura, A. (1982). Self-efficacy Mechanism in Human Agency. *American Psychologist, 37*(2), 122–147.

Beck, U. (1992). *Risk Society: Towards a New Modernity*. Thousand Oaks, CA: SAGE Publications.

Bernstein, E. (2010). *Temporarily Yours: Intimacy, Authenticity, and the Commerce of Sex*. Chicago: University of Chicago Press.

Chan, M.-S. (2012, March 3). A Married Engineer Engaged in CD with a Girl under 13 (in Chinese). *Apple Daily*, p. A17.

Cheung, Y.-W. (2011, August 29). When a Compensated Dating Girl Meets a Social Worker (in Chinese). *Sing Tao Daily*, p. A22.

Chung, Y. (2009, July 30). About 15% of Sexual Victims in Hong Kong Met the Suspects on The Internet (in Chinese). *Sina*. Retrieved from http://finance-news.sina.com/sinacn/304-000-106-109/2009-07-30/20581125528.html

Cooper, A., David, L. D., Griffin-Shelley, E., & Robin, M. M. (2004). Online Sexual Activity: An Examination of Potentially Problematic Behaviors. *Sexual Addiction & Compulsivity, 11*(3), 129–143.

Department of State, U. S. A. (2014). Trafficking in Persons Report. U.S.A.

Giddens, A. (1990). *The Consequences of Modernity*. Cambridge: Polity Press.

Giddens, A. (1992a). Romantic Love and Other Attachments. In *The Transformation of Intimacy: Sexuality, Love and Eroticism in Modern Societies*. Standford, CA: Standford University Press.

Giddens, A. (1992b). *The Transformation of Intimacy: Sexuality, Love and Eroticism in Modern Societies*. Standford, CA: Stanford University Press.

Ho, J. (2003). From Spice Girls to Enjo Kosai: Formations of Teenage Girls' Sexualities in Taiwan. *Inter-Asia Cultural Studies, 4*(2), 325–336.

Hochschild, A. R. (1983). *The Managed Heart*. Berkeley: University of California Press.

Joshua, B. (2009). Police Saddened as Young Girls Lured into 'Compensated Dating'. *South China Morning Post*, p. 3. Retrieved from http://proquest.umi.com/pqdweb?did=1853572941&Fmt=7&clientId=17557&RQT=309&VName=PQD

Kong, T. S. K. (2002). The Seduction of the Golden Boy: The Body Politics of Hong Kong Gay Men. *Body & Society, 8*(1), 29.

Lai, Y.-k. (2007). Schoolgirls Fail to See Paid 'Dating' as Prostitution: Group. *South China Morning Post*, p. 4. Retrieved from http://proquest.umi.com/pqdweb?did=1364734281&Fmt=7&clientId=17557&RQT=309&VName=PQD

Lam, O.-W. (2003). Why Did Enjo Kosai Anchor in Taiwan but Not in Hong Kong? Or the Convergence of "Enjo" and "Kosai" in Teenage Sex Work. *Inter-Asia Cultural Studies, 4*(2), 353–363.

Lam, Y.-W. (2012). Mediators Take Advantage of Valentine's Day as a Business Opportunity. "Lovers for Rent" to Attract Clients (in Chinese). *Wen Wei Po*, p. A03. Retrieved from http://paper.wenweipo.com/2012/02/12/YO1202120003.htm

Lee, T. Y., & Shek, D. T. (2013). Compensated Dating in Hong Kong: Prevalence, Psychosocial Correlates, and Relationships with Other Risky Behaviors. *Journal of Pediatric and Adolescent Gynecology, 26*(3 Suppl), S42–S48.

Mok, D. (2017, April 3). Compensated Dating Ring that Earned HK$20 Million in Hong Kong Over Last Five Years Busted. *South China Morning Post*. Retrieved from http://www.scmp.com/news/hong-kong/law-crime/article/2084221/compensated-dating-ring-earned-hk20-million-hong-kong-over

Rubin, S. B. (2002). *Jon Inc.: The Making of Japan's Salaried Men into Clients of High School Prostitutes*. (M.A. MQ69653), University of Alberta (Canada), Canada. Retrieved from http://proquest.umi.com/pqdweb?did=766177711&Fmt=7&clientId=17557&RQT=309&VName=PQD

Sanders, T. (2008). *Paying for Pleasure: Men who Buy Sex*. Portland: Willan Publishing.

Smalley, S., Contreras, J., Childress, S., Bailey, H., & Sinderbrand, R. (2003). This Could Be Your Kid. *Newsweek, 142*(7), 44–47.

Tse, M.-M., & Mak, C.-W. (2011, April 2). A 11 Years Old Boy Enaged in Same-Sex CD Due to Sexual Curiosity (in Chinese). *The Sun*. Retrieved from http://orientaldaily.on.cc/cnt/news/20110402/00176_019.html

Udagawa, Y. (2007). *Compensated Dating in Japan: An Exploration of Anomie and Social Change in Japan*. Missouri: University of Central Missouri.

Ueno, C. (2003). Self-determination on Sexuality? Commercialization of Sex among Teenage Girls in Japan. *Inter-Asia Cultural Studies, 4*(2), 317–324.

Wong, Y.-Y., & Cheung, P.-K. (2012, March 5). The Police Force Considers to Define Online Discussion Forums as Publice Places; Online Compensated dating = Public Solicitation (in Chinese). *Apple Daily*, p. A12.

Yuen, Y. (2009). The Murder Case of a Teenage Girl Involved in Compensated Dating in Hong Kong was Brought to the Court: The Murdering Process was Revealed (in Chinese). Retrieved Oct 17, 2017, from Society Eastday. http://big5.eastday.com:82/gate/big5/news.eastday.com/eastday/06news/society/s/20090721/u1a4520555.html

Zhang, C.-M. (2011). Online Advertisement Duped Teenagers into CD (in Chinese). *Wen Wei Po*.

CHAPTER 2

Theoretical and Methodological Issues in Researching Compensated Dating

This study relies on three macroscopic sociological considerations to analyze the data obtained from in-depth interviews with 30 male clients and 12 female CD providers, cyber- and offline ethnography, and informal conversations with numerous CD participants to provide a dynamic and contextualized insiders' perspective on the phenomenon of CD. When I began this research I had no personal connection with the CD field. Apart from the news, media reports, and the very scant empirical research on CD, CD was an area of complete mystery to me. In the hope of getting a more comprehensive and undistorted picture of CD, I initially reached out to some non-profit social organizations concerned with the CD phenomenon and some social workers who worked with CD participants. Nevertheless, I found that their access to the CD field remained relatively superficial as the majority of their knowledge about CD was gathered from 'victims' who were either forced into CD or 'problematic schoolgirls' who were being referred by teachers or parents; thus, their information and perspectives tended to be limited and one-sided. Accordingly, I decided to develop my own theoretical framework to analyze the phenomenon of CD in a more objective light, collecting my own data from girls who participate voluntarily in CD and male clients who had been largely omitted in the CD scenario by positing myself within the CD field through ethnographic research. This chapter lays out the major theoretical concerns in conceptualizing CD, CD participants, and CD relations, as well as my process of accessing into the CD world.

© The Author(s) 2018   19
C. S. K. Chu, *Compensated Dating*, Gender, Sexualities
and Culture in Asia, https://doi.org/10.1007/978-981-10-6974-1_2

THEORETICAL FRAMEWORK

Instead of conceptualizing CD as an obnoxious form of men's sexual exploitation against women and an abhorrent site of men's oppression, victimization, and degradation of women in a patriarchal system, I conceptualize CD as a site of cultural subversion and a platform of agency where girls can make active use of their sexual autonomy and contemporary sexual order to resist patriarchal control over their sexuality and/or parents' control. The framework presumes a fluidity of power relationships between *CCs* and clients rather than an absolute domination of clients over *CCs*. Clients' greater economic power does not automatically lead to their exploitation of *CCs* where *CCs* are powerless and treated as if they were slaves (Ho, 2000). On the contrary, in many instances, *CCs* are the ones who decide and direct the intensity and authenticity of the emotions and thus the formation of *CC–Brother* relationships. The longer the *CCs* have been in the CD field, the more resourceful and competent they seem to become in challenging and subverting the myth of male supremacy. It is in this sense that *CCs* are viewed as active agents of power, not passive objects of exploitation.

The female target group of this study was girls who chose to engage in CD voluntarily and asserted sovereignty over their sexuality and their bodies. Inspired by Barry's (1995) and Ueno's (2003) perspectives on women's entry into commercial sex, young women's involvement in CD is regarded as a rational decision to obtain economic independence, assert their sexuality and resist their limited resources in a patriarchal system in the modern post-industrial society of Hong Kong. In conditions of modernity, women are now encouraged to reclaim their sexualities, which had been historically and culturally suppressed and denied in the past, for individual pleasures and self-realization. In other words, sexuality is no longer a male-oriented domain. Female sexuality that used to evolve around reproduction and male pleasures is now evolving around women's own sexual desires and fulfillment. Accordingly, the *CCs* in this study are considered to be autonomous agents who self-determined to engage in CD, which is perceived as a place that can possibly empower women, both economically and socially, and not a site that only dehumanizes women as if they were merely sex tools being used by men to satisfy their desires. Although the female body might be perceived as an objectified instrument, the human nature of woman is not. In other words, there is a separation of the body from the human nature such that the objectification of body does not necessarily follow by the objectification of the human nature (Chapkis, 1997). Moreover, the objectification of female bodies does not automatically imply the subjectification of men (Kappeler, 1996). All *CCs* in this study self-selected to objectify and commodify their body parts and sell them temporarily to exchange what they needed and wanted. They were the ones who were in charge of the use of their bodies to achieve their ends, not the clients. Hence, although the female bodies might be objectified, it was the women, not men, who transformed their bodies to become detached instruments momentarily. In some cases, the *CCs* objectified not only their bodies, but also the *Brothers'* in the sense that the *CCs* envisaged the *Brothers* as money or things that they wanted to own (Kong, 2003). For example, Rose, a 19-year-old *CC*, mentioned that every *Brother* to her was the same as she visualized the *Brothers* as the commodities that she would like to purchase after their encounters. As such, *CCs* are not conceptualized as passive exploited objects but autonomous individuals.

Another central theoretical consideration that makes up the conceptual framework of this study is the transformation of sex and intimacy, which is useful in the analysis of the nature of *CC–Brother* relationships. In late modernity, new forms of intimate relationships and love such as pure relationships, cyber-relationships, and confluent love have developed (Giddens, 1992). Love and sex have taken on different social significances and spaces from those in pre-industrial society. One obvious transformation is that in the present day, people fall in and out of love frequently and easily due to the great availability of alternatives and the fragmentations of traditional bonds. The commitment that was traditionally attached to love and sex has vanished as we enter into a modern 'risky' society which is full of uncertainties and personal insecurities (Bauman, 2000; Beck, 1992; Giddens, 1992). Non-commercial relationships can be as volatile, precarious, fragile, transient, and recreational as commercial ones. Moreover, conventional relationships are incorporating and relying on an increasing use of economic element in the establishment, maintenance, and negotiations in modern times such that romantic practices have progressively interlocked with, and became translated into, economic practices (Illouz, 1997; Zelizer, 2005). Because commitment, which is the defining characteristic of non-commercial relationships, is decreasing in modern intimacies, and the economic element, which is the chief component in commercial relationships, is increasing in modern intimacies, modern relationships share more similarities than differences with CD relationships, at least from the vantage point of CD participants. While CD relationships are fleeting, non-monogamous, recreational, and economic-centered in nature, so too are many non-commercial intimacies in modern times. CD participants therefore conceive CD as a derivative of modern relationships rather than a form of prostitution. Accordingly, the present framework theorizes CD relationships and non-commercial relationships as mutually non-exclusive events that are both embedded in the larger abstract social system such that the relational nature in CD is being understood together with the meanings and practices of love, sex, and intimacy in the overarching sociocultural milieu. The private concerns of romance and sexuality are intertwined with the broader patterns of social transformations that have occurred in recent decades.

The last building block of the present framework concerns the notions of emotional labor and the authenticity of emotions in commercial settings, which are helpful to analyze the emotional burdens and impacts of CD on CD participants, as well as the nature of emotions and reciprocity of intimacies in *CC–Brother* relations. The phenomenon of CD has been controversial because it involves the commodification of the erotic, which represents the deepest, strongest, and richest feeling that lies within each of us; the selling of the erotic, therefore, is 'an abuse of feeling' which not only destroys the innermost feelings associated with the erotic, but also attacks one's entire emotional life (Hoigard & Finstad, 1992; Lorde, 1991). Under this construct, I explore how CD participants are able to manage or even separate their emotions from the self so that their involvement in CD does not necessarily lead to the destruction of their ordinary emotional life (Hochschild, 1983). Emotion is perceived as a social skill that has to be learned, performed, created, and objectified, and thus as an external entity that can be controlled and exchanged without affecting the integrity of the authentic self (Chapkis, 1997). It is in this light that the authenticity of emotions in CD is being investigated. While most *CC–Brother* relations are initially founded by counterfeit intimacy, which is characterized by emotions manufactured by CD participants in order to make the commercial interaction appears to be more genuine, and bounded authenticity, which denotes the fact that the purchased intimacy is limited by time and economic constraints, I argue that the specific nature and context of CD facilitate *CC–Brother* relations being developed into authentic and unbounded relationships (Elizabeth Bernstein, 2007; Ronai & Ellis, 1989). Rather than polarizing the nature of emotion and intimacy around two diametrically opposing positions of authentic/counterfeit, commercial/non-commercial, and bounded/unbounded, which seem to be overly simplistic and monolithic,

I propose to conceptualize the nature of emotion and intimacy along a continuum that is flexible and changeable. *Brothers* and *CCs* constantly negotiate and construct their relation that is reflexive and flexible to different situations. The distinction between CD relationships and non-commercial relationships is therefore hazy not only because non-commercial relationships are highly commercialized and volatile in late modernity, but also because CD relationships are infused with the different intensity of authentic emotions and non-commercial elements. Moreover, since CD relationships are not delimited by moral, cultural, social, religious, and traditional expectations or long-term commitments, they are less rigid than the highly institutionalized marriage. The 'love' found in CD relations is more reflexive than that in legitimate relations, which are often associated with mundane obligations and constraints, which although are decreasing in modern relationships. Therefore, a pure relationship may be more likely to be achieved in *CC–Brother* relationships than in conventional couple relationships (Sanders, 2008b).

According to these three major theoretical considerations—the pro-sex feminist notion of prostitution, the transformation of sex and intimacy, and the authenticity of emotions in commercial setting—a conceptual framework is mapped out to comprehend the phenomenon of CD (Fig. 2.1). All the data in this book are organized and interpreted according to this conceptual model to reveal how CD can be seen as a reflection of sexual liberation and a site of cultural and economic subversion for girls to resist their limited resources in Hong Kong's patriarchal society. It also shows how CD is both a reflection and a consequence of modernity, and how CD emerges and stands out from the mists of existing forms of commercial sex. These analyses not only reveal the sexual culture in contemporary Hong Kong society, but also have important implications for the overarching gender relationships in late modernity.

METHODOLOGY

This study employed a qualitative design that was flexible rather than rigid. The research process was a reflexive one rather than a predetermined sequence restricted by an initial decision (Hammersley & Atkinson, 2007; Robson, 2011). This chapter explains my research approach, which includes four phrases: cyber-ethnography; in-depth interviews; informal conversations; and offline participant observation. These four phases did not follow a chronological order; rather, they were interwoven together.

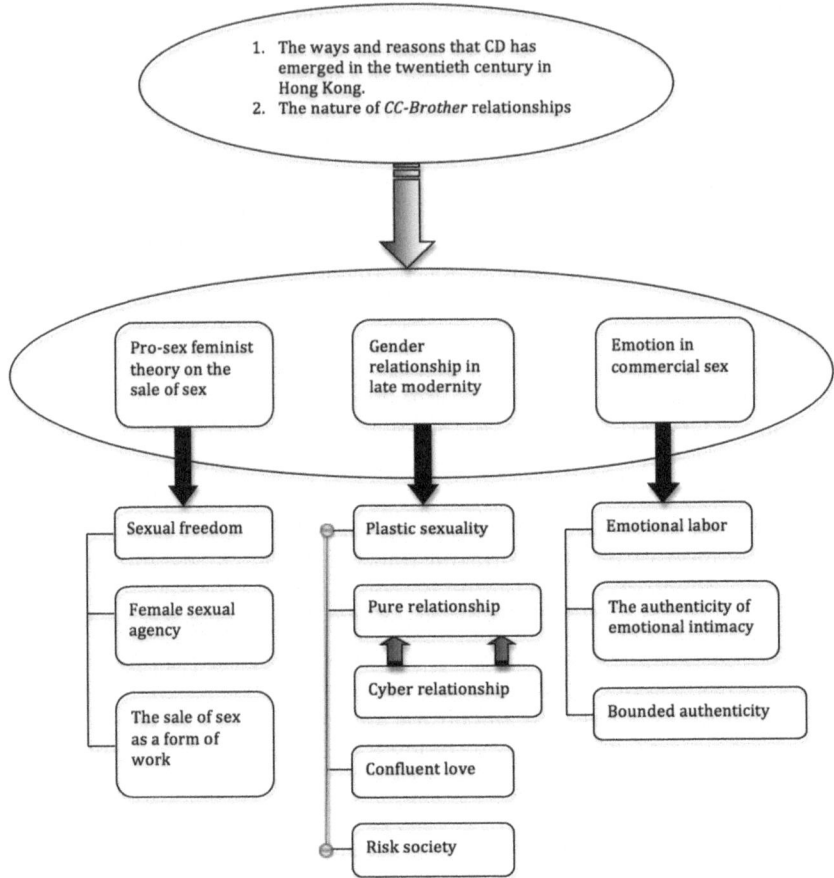

Fig. 2.1 Conceptual framework

The resulting qualitative data provided an in-depth description of individuals' personal experiences in their own meanings and their context, which could not be obtained in a relatively general quantitative survey that is constructed according to the researcher's categories (Greene & Caracelli, 1997). Finally, this chapter elucidates the reliability and validity of the data, the method of data analysis, as well as the difficulties, ethical issues, and practical problems in accessing and conducting research on CD participants.

As mentioned earlier, prior to this study, there was little empirical research on CD, meaning that a well-defined research scheme could not be anticipated in advance (Hine, 2015). Under this circumstance, I decided to employ a flexible qualitative interactive research paradigm, in which the research process did not have to follow a linear model and the various research phrases did not have to be arranged in an unvarying order (Maxwell, 2005). The four research methods were, therefore, dynamic and intertwined rather than adhering to a fixed sequence of procedures. In an underexplored CD field, it was unlikely that I would know in advance what interviews might be needed, what questions should be asked, what form of presence is appropriate, or whether a particular line of enquiry would be 'enough' to understand what was going on (Hine, 2015). As such, I had to be aware of, and responsive to, the way in which the research context was altering the actual design of the study, instead of simply attempted to implement a previously designed research plan rigidly (Maxwell, 2012, p. 75).

The interactive model allowed the design components, such as research questions, conceptual framework, and research methodology, to be responsive and interrelated. Under such a paradigm, the constructs and domains of this study could be constructed and reconstructed in response to new developments, emerging elements, and changing design components during every stage of the research process. This interactive approach worked out well as it allowed the actual design to be adaptable to reflect the real nature, setting, my social roles, and my relationships with that setting in practice, which I could not fully anticipate before I immersed myself in the CD field.

Due to the highly sensitive nature of the subject of CD, this study might raise ethical issues. After a thorough review of ethical concerns, the Non-Clinical Faculties Human Research Ethics Committee at the University of Hong Kong approved a detailed ethics application on August 26, 2010. This research strictly complied with all ethical standards and was conducted in an ethical manner, as stated in the ethics application. The quality of the data and the reliability of this research were also ensured by adhering to the standards and review procedures relating to academic research throughout the entire research process.

RESEARCH PROCESS

Phase I: Cyber-ethnography

In spite of the upsurge of smartphone applications as the newest method to negotiate CD, online CD forums remained to be a fundamental platform for CD participants to communicate, form interpersonal ties, make CD negotiations, and share their experiences. These forums, like the majority of blogs, contained a range of reflective, descriptive, interpretive, explanatory, and exploratory contents which provided important qualitative data (*The Sage Handbook of Qualitative Research*, 2011; Wilson, Kenny, & Dickson-Swift, 2015). Given the significance of the online CD forums to potential and existing CD participants, it was necessary to observe and analyze the virtual CD community; thus cyber-ethnography was conducted throughout the entire research process, in which I engaged in the online field, gathered data, and interpreted results in a way just like a traditional ethnographer would document a community or other cultural form (Fox & Roberts, 1999; Hine, 2015). However, in the method of cyber-ethnography, instead of observing people's actions in a traditional setting of a particular physical locale, I observed textual materials and images on a computer monitor by following a qualitative ethnographic research protocol that I had designed to address the major aspects of CD in Hong Kong. This aimed to discern the patterns, social rules, and sanctions in the CD community. Special attention was given to CD participants' construction of their identities, attitudes, and beliefs toward their CD behaviors, inter-group relationships, intra-group relationships, and the discussion of their CD experiences, as well as the interactive discourse amongst CD participants.

While cyberspace has become an increasing common and valuable venue for conducting research on its users, it has raised new ethical concerns and conundrums that contest methodologies and the application of 'rules' to researchers and researched, including the issues of 'consent, access, privacy, anonymity and identification, researcher integrity, misuse of data by researchers, representation, limits of 'public' and 'private' data, and ownership of data' (Buchanan, 2011, p. 89). The CD virtual communities that I studied were public forums. Neither registration nor subscription was needed to access the public postings on the forums. The participants in these forums are assumed to be aware of the fact that their public postings are fundamentally mechanisms for storage, transmission, and retrieval such that their communication is available for viewing by the public. If participants deemed their conversations as private and therefore did not wish their contents to be viewed publicly, they could always choose to converse in a private chatroom rather than through public postings on the forums. Since I only collected data from public postings, the ethical issue of informed consent for use of publicly available private materials was minimized in this research (Lunnay, Borlagdan, McNaughton, & Ward, 2015). In fact, according to the American Sociological Association code of ethics (1999/2008), researchers can conduct research in public places or use publicly available information about individuals without obtaining consent. Buchanan (2011) also pointed out that, according to US regulations, if a researcher is getting data from a public blog, approval or review is not necessary. Since the materials that I collected and analyzed on the CD forum were publicly available and did not contain personally identifiable information, informed consent was not sought during the course of cyber-ethnography (Salmons, 2016).

One obvious advantage of conducting cyber-ethnography was its anonymous nature, which could help with the collection of data from this disreputable and invisible CD group, which was involved in morally controversial or possibly criminal activities (Coomber, 1997; Liamputtong, 2009). The free-floating nature of cyberspace had profoundly facilitated my access to the socially marginalized CD group in the sense that I was able to communicate with a large and diverse pool of CD members which otherwise could not be made possible. Cyber-ethnography allowed me not only to peep into the present lived experience of CD members, but also to travel to the past to view older conversations, to follow the development of a theme through the discourses surrounding it, and to observe a social process over time with archived asynchronous communication (Hookway, 2008; Wilson et al., 2015). Cyber-ethnography was the key to open my door into the CD field and proved tremendously useful throughout my entire research process.

Despite the anonymous nature of the cyberspace, my respondents' privacy, anonymity, and confidentiality were still of grave concern to me when collecting online data on CD that might be related to socially undesirable or illegal behaviors. In order to protect participants' individual privacy, I never directly quoted the exact words of the authors of the public postings on the CD forums although I did observe, collect, and analyze them. Moreover, CD participants' personal identifiers were not collected and were not the concerns of the present study. I recorded only the pseudonyms created by the respondents, which were not even used in reporting my data because online pseudonyms were possibly traceable (Roberts, Smith, & Pollock, 2004). To further disguise and protect my participants, I created an additional set of pseudonyms on top of their actual pseudonyms. In fact, it was not uncommon for CD members to change their pseudonyms or use different pseudonyms at different times or for different purposes because in CD 'where secrecy is paramount, switching names takes on extra significance' (Sanders, 2005b, p. 124). Given these precautions carried out by my respondents and myself, it would be virtually impossible to trace their identities.

In the initial stage of my cyber-ethnography, I adopted an unobtrusive method of participant observation under which online CD users did not know that their normal discourse, which might possibly be considered as socially undesirable, was being observed and interpreted (Gosling & Johnson, 2010). This method was particularly useful to my research that attempted to understand a new phenomenon about which a comprehensive empirical investigation had yet to be done (Fox & Roberts, 1999). Another major reason for taking an unobtrusive or non-participatory role in the initial research process stemmed from my concern that CD members might reject me because I was not only an outsider and a stranger, but also a researcher who wanted to peep into their world and then reveal it to the general public. Based on the premise that CD participants were reluctant to illuminate their socially deviant CD activities and discourses, uneasiness or even hostility might arise amongst CD members upon a public disclosure of my identity and my purpose of entering into their community. Moreover, each virtual community has its own netiquette – specific standards of conduct that have to be followed in a particular virtual community (Fox & Roberts, 1999). Infringement of this netiquette might arouse reproofs from CD members, or even worse, the forum administrators, who were the gatekeepers of the virtual CD community, might deny my access to the forums. Therefore, I decided to keep my non-participatory role until I familiarized myself with the netiquette of the CD community. For six months, I studied three public online CD forums. I analyzed the patterns of the *CC's* 'advertisements,' *Brothers*' responses to the 'advertisements,' *Brothers*' reports on the *CCs* after their CD encounters, CD members' instant communications in the instant chatrooms, and other posts that contain CD members' complaints and personal feelings toward their CD experience. During this exploratory phase, I did not participate in any group discussion or interact with members in the virtual community. This early exploratory cyber-ethnography stage provided some basic knowledge about CD in context and informed decisions about methods, suggesting alternative approaches and identifying potential methodological problems or solutions; thus, it was a critical stage to decide the scope of the present study and test the research methods (Maxwell, 2005, p. 65). Without this preliminary stage, many features of the research design could not be determined. For example, I noticed that one particular forum had the largest pool of CD members, its members were more active, its server was more stable, and, more importantly, this forum included many active members of the other two smaller-scale forums but not vice versa. So, I decided to concentrate on investigating this one specific CD forum for the rest of the research process.

Reoccurring themes were also identified during the initial cyber-ethnography stage, according to which I had developed five broad dimensions to understand the phenomenon of CD and its participants. These dimensions are the *personal construct*, which includes marital status, private relationships, demographic data, sexual desires, and psychological state; the *social construct*, which includes socio-economic status and interpersonal relationships with friends inside and outside the CD circle; *behavioral construct*, which includes sexual practice, condom use behavior, and sexual history; *familial construct*, which includes relationships with parents and conventional romantic partners as well as family burden/support (emotional and financial); and, finally, the *CD construct*, which includes the reasons for engaging in CD, the perception of risks (emotional, physical, and economical), and the strategies that participants adopted to manage their CD relationships and social stigma. These five constructs would be used to develop an interview guide for the in-depth interviews.

Trustworthiness of the Qualitative Cyber-ethnographic Data
There have been debates concerning the validity and reliability of online data. One of the major controversies regarding virtual ethnography is whether cyberspace interactions and the virtual community are to be perceived as real and crucial or as mere imaginative constructions (Fox & Roberts, 1999). I believed that virtual community is as real as the offline community as they both construct social relations and use symbolic processes to maintain individual identity and group culture through interactive negotiation; thus, the Internet should be perceived as a cultural site that is as meaningful as other social contexts in the physical world (Hine 2015). Moreover, in modernity, the physical and virtual worlds are

mutually entangled. We are now embodied in a world that exists a social space that involves a complex interplay between traditional and technologically innovative modes of interactions and venues for social exchange; accordingly, the distinctions between the physical and the virtual world and between 'being online' and 'being offline' are anachronistic and even problematic (Buchanan, 2011; Elliott & Urry, 2010). We have to move beyond the simplistic dyadic imageries of the online world versus the offline world and embrace them into a more connected and fluid sphere. In the context of CD, the virtual domain is an indispensable part that cannot be removed from the experiences of CD participants. Online and offline spheres bind together to construct the realities of CD participants.

Other people might doubt the authenticity of online data because the anonymous nature of the online environments allows participants an increased ability to control their self-presentation, and therefore gives them greater opportunity to engage in misrepresentation (Cornwell & Lundgren, 2001). The virtual world offers individuals more freedom to explore playful, fantastical online personae that differ from their real life identities and experiences; thus, concerns about the prospect of online deception and narratives about deliberate identity manipulation and deception are not uncommon in both academic and popular outlets (Ackland, 2013; Joinson & Dietz-Uhler, 2002; Stone, 1996; Van Gelder, 1996[1985]). However, the issues of deception and manipulation of the truth are not exclusive to Internet research as these circumstances can happen in offline research settings such as survey, face-to-face interviews, and focus groups (Hookway, 2008). Most people present themselves differently in diverse social contexts even in the non-virtual world and conceal or misrepresent themselves in various degrees depending on the circumstance they are in (Goffman, 1959). As such, the problems of concealment and misrepresentation exist in both online and offline settings. The mere possibility that online data may not fully and authentically represent the personality of the informants does not mean that the data are not useful and valuable for the analysis of their experience. Moreover, although the unbounded and anonymous nature of the cyberspace allows users to be playful with their self-representations by creating multiple identities or by presenting an image that is completely different from the offline self, the particular context of an online dating environment tends to discourage deceptive communication as participants are typically seeking intimate relationships and anticipating future face-to-face interactions (Ramirez,

Fleuriet, & Cole, 2015). Online dating participants, including *CCs* and *Brothers*, tend to create more honest (or close-to-offline) self-image and encourage genuine self-disclosure (Berger, 1979; Ellison, Heino, & Gibbs, 2006). In fact, most online dating participants reported that they are truthful when presenting themselves online (Ellison, Hancock, & Toma, 2012). Thus, the data collected from the CD forum were considered as authentic.

The global range of the Internet enables research to be conducted without geographical constraints such that a more heterogeneous sample can be yielded (Alvarez, Sherman, & Van Beselaere, 2003; Berson & Berson, 2002; Oseni, Dingley, & Hart, 2017). Even though the sample of this study was unlikely to be representative of the whole CD population, the sample was perhaps the broadest that could be achieved by any other sampling methods. To further enhance the rigor of the data of this research, the methodology of triangulation was used to validate data from online and offline sources (i.e., face-to-face interviews and offline participant observations). Thus, the online data collected in this study were indicative, reliable, and valuable.

Phase II: In-depth Interviews

A major data source of this study came from in-depth interviews which aimed to elicit rich information from insiders' perspective on CD, which is captured in the participants' own words, ideas, insights, feelings, and experiences (Liamputtong, 2009). Before the interview, I had constructed an interview guide which was based on the five constructs that I had developed from the recurring themes in the initial cyber-ethnography stage, the aim of this study and the related literature, including those having to do with CD, commercial sex, prostitutes' clients, and sex workers (Fukuda, 2003; Ho, 2003; Kong, 2003; Lee & Shek, 2013; Ng, Leung, & Yau, 2009; Rubin, 2002; Udagawa, 2007; Ueno, 2003; Belza et al., 2008; Bernstein, 2001; Campbell, 1998; Gemme, Payment, & Malenfant, 1989; McKeganey, 1994; McKeganey & Barnard, 1996; Monto, 2000, 2001; Coy, 2009; Lever & Dolnick, 2010; Sanders, 2005a; Bernstein, 2010; Milrod & Monto, 2012; Sanders, 2005b, 2008a, 2008b).

Gaining Access

Following the six months of the exploratory cyber-ethnography stage, I had already acquired a solid understanding of CD netiquette, which equipped me with the communicative skills necessary to converse with CD members. At this point, I changed my role from a non-participatory observer to a participatory one, yet the degree of my participation was kept to a minimum in the hope that my participation would not disturb the normal CD discourse or provoke rebuke from the CD members. Instead of creating a public message on the forum or sending private mass messages to numerous random online CD members to invite them to take part in my research, I used purposive sampling to identify potential informants. To test reactions, I sent private messages to a few members of the group, in which I revealed myself as a researcher and invited them to be my interviewees. These few members were not selected randomly, but were identified carefully based on their cyber-accounts and the degree of activeness in the CD virtual world. I decided to contact those who were mildly active and those who were neither too idle nor too active, because I believed that such a strategy could minimize the risk of encountering individuals who were more likely to be perturbed by my solicitation, or who were more likely to disclose my identity to other CD members, to forewarn other online members to ignore me, or, even worse, to ruin my reputation in the CD community. If that happened, the consequences would be disastrous as it would hamper my research and make my entry into the CD community even more difficult. As a result of these concerns, to begin with, I contacted only three mildly active clients and three mildly active girls. All of the clients I approached were willing to continue to talk to me and discuss the possibility of having an interview in other more direct channels such as MSN Instant Messenger or on the phone. Of the girls, only one response was received; unfortunately, she refused to participate in the research. The other two girls simply did not respond to my message.

In contrast to previous empirical studies on the sex industry, where gaining access to sex workers was often found to be easier than gaining access to male clients (Campbell, 1998; McKeganey, 1994), I found that in this instance, it was easier to get in touch with the clients who were more willing to be interviewed and share their CD experiences than the girls. Such divergence might be for three major reasons. First, sex workers are more visible in traditional settings (on the streets, massage parlors, or in one-woman brothels) and are more vulnerable to police arrests than their clients; thus, it is easier for researchers to identify sex workers. In fact, most individuals involved in selling sex do not want to openly admit their dealings because of the fear of police interference and/or the whore stigma that is attached to 'the oldest profession' (Sanders, 2005b). Sex workers are easier to be recruited in research not because they are more willing to do so, but because they are more vulnerable to be exposed. The context of CD is different, however, because in an anonymous cyberspace, girls are as difficult to be identified as the clients. The comparative easiness to access the girls involved in CD was not observed in this study.

Second, being female gave me an advantage in reaching out the *Brothers* because many *Brothers* engage in CD not only because of sex but because they yearn for a female company and listener. Derrick, 35 years old, summarized quite well other *Brothers'* perspective: 'If you were not a girl, I wouldn't come out for an interview.' Although my gender had a major factor in attracting male respondents, it also attracted some sensual, aggressive, and personal inquiries or requests from the *Brothers* during our online and offline interactions. A total of ten *Brothers* expressed desires to date me personally after the formal interviews, but I rejected all of them. No hard feeling was resulted as the rejection was within their expectations: 'I knew you would reject me, but it never hurts to ask,' said one of the *Brothers*. Amongst the ten *Brothers*, one tried to hold my hand. I successfully avoided his attempt and re-emphasized that my role was as a researcher, rather than a *CC* or his potential intimate partner. The *Brother* apologized and never again made a similar gestures.

From the initial stage of the cyber-ethnography, I was already aware that sexual content and sexual banter are often included in CD discourse. So, I was mentally prepared for that before I actually communicated with CD participants. If I felt uncomfortable, intimidated, or offended because of sexual banter, then I probably would have been unable to mingle in the CD world and conduct this research. As a researcher, I should set aside my own values and standards of judging when conducting interviews; thus, I did not judge the respondents' behaviors and attitudes using my own ethical codes when I was interacting with them. Although I would probably deem the same sexual banter as offensive if it happened in my own normative world, I did not feel offended when I was in the CD domain, where sexual banter and fantasies were considered as innocuous. For example, a respondent said on a number of occasions that he wanted to have sex with me, sometimes saying that he wanted to rape me. I was not threatened by these expressions mainly because they were always limited to a discursive level when we were exchanging messages in a virtual setting. Although I was aware that online speech and dialogue can result in emotional harm and can occasionally precede physical violence, it was not the case here. The respondent was assuming an online identity that was drastically different from his offline identity. While his online persona might associate with socially undesirable and deviant qualities, his offline persona did not. In our various face-to-face interactions, this respondent never verbally or physically harassed me. In fact, he acted very courteously on every occasion that we met. Thus, I regarded his online remarks about having sex and raping me as jokes or mere sexual fantasies that would not transform into real-world actions.

The final reason that gaining access to the clients was easier than gaining access to the girls who provide CD was the relatively lower level of social stigma on the clients. Historically and culturally, men have always been more sexually permissive and are condoned to have multiple sexual partners due to their *natural* and *uncontrollable* sexual drive that ought to be released (Prasad, 1999). For some *Brothers*, their CD experiences are proof of their sexual prowess, which strengthens their hegemonic masculinity. Due to the relatively easier access to the *Brothers*, who tended to show a greater willingness to take part in my research and seemed to be less distressed by my approach, I decided to reach out to the *Brothers* first and hoped they would lead me to the *CCs*. At the end, this strategy worked out nicely.

Despite the relatively easier access to the clients than the *CCs*, it was no easy task to recruit the clients as interviewees. The process was time-consuming and needed a lot of effort, patience, and skills. Most men were suspicious when I first reached out to them through the CD forum. Most of them requested to talk to me on the phone or in cyberspace for weeks or even months before they could finally trust me, meet me, and agree to be interviewed.

An efficient way to gain access into the larger CD world was to establish and maintained amicable relationships with members who had a sound reputation in the CD community. CD members attained high reputation either because they had been in the CD field for a long time or because they had engaged in CD frequently. Letting other members in the CD community know that I have a trustful relationship with reputable *Brothers* gave me a major advantage. It reduced the worries and concerns of potential informants and enhanced my credibility in the CD world. For example, Jack, a 28-year-old *Brother*, had been hesitant to have a face-to-face interview with me even after numerous phone and cyber conversations every day for two weeks, but suddenly one day he called me and said he agreed to be interviewed:

I was being cautious with you because I was not sure whether you are indeed a researcher or not. I worried that you might be an undercover police or a reporter. But after Sam (a reputable *Brother*) told me that he had met you and interviewed by you, my doubts were immediately gone. He had attested your identity. So, I finally believe it is safe to meet you.

It transpired that Jack and Sam were virtual friends in the CD community. Being a respectable *Brother*, Sam's words were much more powerful and convincing than mine. After this incident, I realized that displaying good relations with trustworthy *Brothers* like Sam could help me to win the trust of and connect with other CD participants, including the *CCs*.

Interviewees Demography

30 *Brothers* and 12 *CCs* were being interviewed in this study. The first interview was conducted on February 2011 with a *Brother* and the last interview was conducted on December 2012 with a *CC*. 20 *Brothers* were recruited through the CD forum, seven through snowballing technique, and three through my offline participation in the CD members' social gatherings. Table 2.1 describes the demographic information on the *Brothers*. Their ages ranged from 23 to 43, with a mean age of 33.4 years. Their education level ranged from partial completion of Form 1 (Grade 7) to the possession of two master's degrees. One *Brother* was a full-time college student; 28 were employed full-time and one was unemployed at the time of the interview.

Regarding the 12 *CCs* whom I have interviewed, only one was recruited through the CD forum and the rest were through snowballing. Table 2.2 describes the demographic information on the *CCs*. Their ages ranged from 16 to 28, with a mean age of 22.2 years. Their education level ranged from Form 3 (Grade 9) to the possession of a master's degree. Two *CCs* were in college and one was in Form 7 (Grade 13) at the time of the interview. One worked full-time, two worked part-time, and six were unemployed and were not actively looking for a job.

16 interviews with the *Brothers* and nine with the *CCs* were conducted on a face-to-face basis. These interviews were carried out in restaurants, cafés, the library at the University of Hong Kong, or at the participants' residence. 14 interviews with the *Brothers* and three with the *CCs* were conducted over the phone because these respondents desired to remain completely anonymous due to the sensitivity of the topic. These respondents felt more comfortable, relaxed, and forthright when they were protected by the physical distance, which gave them complete anonymity.

Table 2.1 Demographic characteristics of 30 male respondents

	The Brothers (n = 30)
Chinese ethnicity	30 (100.0%)
Mean age	33.4 years old (range 23–43)
Last yr. education completed	
Form 1 or less (7 yrs or less)	1 (3.3%)
Form 2 (8 yrs)	0 (0%)
Form 3 (9 yrs)	0 (0%)
Form 4 (10 yrs)	0 (0%)
Form 5 (11 yrs)	5 (16.7%)
Form 6 (12 yrs)	0 (0%)
Form 7 (13 yrs)	2 (6.7%)
Some university or above	23 (76.7%)
Full-time student	1 (3.3%)
Employed	28 (93.3%)
Unemployed	1 (3.3%)
Married	11 (36.7%)
Divorced	1 (3.3%)
In a relationship	4 (13.3%)
Single	14 (46.7%)
Prior commercial sex experience	11 (36.7%)
No prior sexual experience before CD involvement	2 (6.7%)

Table 2.2 Demographic characteristics of 12 female respondents

	The CCs (n = 12)
Chinese ethnicity	12 (100.0%)
Mean age	22.2 years old (range 16 – 28)
Last yr. education completed	
Form 3 (9 yrs)	5 (41.7%)
Form 4 (10 yrs)	0 (0%)
Form 5 (11 yrs)	3 (25%)
Form 6 (12 yrs)	1 (8.3%)
Form 7 (13 yrs)	0 (0%)
Some college	2 (16.7%)
Master	1 (8.3%)
Full-time student	3 (25%)
Employed (full-time)	1 (8.3%)
Employed (part-time)	2 (16.7%)
Unemployed	6 (50%)
Single	6 (50%)
In a relationship	6 (50%)

All the interviews were semi-structured. Before the interviews, I clearly explained the research purpose, procedures, values of the research, and its potential dissemination in detail. I also promised their confidentiality and that all data collected would be for research purposes only. I made sure that they understood their participation was entirely voluntary and they could terminate the interview at any time without any consequence. They were also encouraged to ask any questions that they had on the study or anything related to the research procedures before, during, and after the interview. The consent form was reviewed thoroughly before the participants agreed to participate in the research. Written consent and verbal consent were sought from informants who participated in the face-to-face and phone interviews respectively.

Flexibility and openness highlighted the structure of the interview. I encouraged the informants to narrate their CD experiences and anything that they believed was relevant to their CD practice in their own terms as they perceived it rather than limiting our conversation in my own categories and ways of thinking such that they had more control over the course of the interview. Taking a narrative approach and following the interview guide, I aimed to elicit participants' personal narratives with regard to particular topics, events, and concepts related to CD as they understood and practiced it. Their sexual histories, attitudes and behaviors that were manifested in their lives were also discussed. The length of each interview ranged from one to four hours. The interviews were conducted in Cantonese. With the consent of the participants, all interviews were audio recorded and they were then transcribed and translated into English.

After each interview session, I made fieldnotes regarding the respondents' attitudes, emotions, and behaviors, including their stance, body language, gestures, and some particular behaviors that express their personality. I also recorded my personal remarks and impressions towards the interview process and the interviewees. For example:

> In the middle of the interview, right after I sneezed, the informant (a *Brother*) suggested switching seats with me because my seat was directly under an air conditioner and his was not. He said he was worried that I would catch a cold. It seemed to me that he was trying to break the client stereotype by showing some gentleman etiquette and presenting himself as a protector who can take care of women.

Phase III: Informal Conversations

I communicated with my (potential) informants daily through online communication whenever they were online during the research process. One *Brother* and one *CC* also phoned me regularly to talk about their personal relationships and CD experiences. They wanted to talk to me partly because they trusted me and partly because there was no one else they could talk to regarding their CD activities. The online and offline informal conversations greatly enhanced my rapport, trust, and interaction with CD participants. They helped me to follow up our formal interviews, such as clarifying and reaffirming the ideas, issues, and incidents that they narrated during the formal interviews, and allowed me to update their situations, beliefs, and attitudes. As such, a more comprehensive understanding of the informants and their CD journey were achieved.

Since the commencement of the first interview, I started to communicate with my informants in the CD forum's public real-time chatroom, which was called *cbox*. As the research progressed, the number of interviewees increased. Thus, I was able to converse with more CD members in *cbox* in a regular basis. Initially, I just wanted to strengthen the relationship with my interviewees, but to my surprise, my participation in *cbox* helped me to get acceptance by the larger CD community, expanded my CD network, and attracted potential interviewees. The chit-chat with my informants in *cbox* served as a testimony to my personality and credibility. For instance, a *Brother*, whom I had never contacted before, initiated conversation with me through private message. He was curious and asked: 'Can we talk? I saw you chatting with other *Brothers* in *cbox*. You seem to be a friend to them.' I then revealed my identity and my purpose on the forum. At the end, I successfully recruited him as my interviewee. This particular *Brother* had never created any public post or participated in *cbox*. So, it was very unlikely that I would get in touch with him if he did not approach me in the first place. This incident showed how chatting in *cbox* was a useful way not only to maintain relationships with existing informants, but also to attract potential informants, especially those who usually took a non-participatory role in the CD forum.

Phase IV: Offline Participant Observations

As I became acquainted with more CD participants and gained their trust, they began to invite me to their non-commercial and non-sexual social gatherings such as lunch, dinner, birthday parties, mahjong games, and karaoke at their homes, karaoke clubs, bars, and restaurants. I did not plan to conduct offline participant observation in my original research design because at that time I did not know there were social gatherings amongst CD participants. Even if I had known of the existence of such social events, I would not presume that they would invite me to join. So, when I was invited to join their social gathering for the first time, I immediately decided to incorporate offline participant observation into my research design because it would provide an invaluable opportunity for me to learn how CD participants interact with each other, the nature and transformation of their relationships, and their lived experience in context. For example, in this research phase, I witnessed how a *Brother* and a *CC* met for the first time and formed a CD relationship, which then developed into a non-commercial romantic relationship and finally into marriage. I was also able to share the struggles and difficulties that a *CC* faced when she tried to withdraw from the CD field and found a clerical job. We had lunch immediately before her job interview because she needed some support and encouragement. Through these offline participations and observations, I walked through the CD journey and their emotional highs and lows.

In these social gatherings, the atmosphere was more relaxing and therefore the role and power differences between me as a researcher and the CD members were reduced. Such environments encouraged more free-flowing conversations, in which the respondents tended to reveal more about their sensitive personal particulars and struggles that were not being discussed in the formal interviews. For example, a *CC* revealed to me over dinner that she had used illegal drugs and patronized male sex workers to alleviate her emotional burden from CD. When I asked why she had not disclosed them to me during our prior formal interview in which I did ask her about drug use and sexual behaviors outside CD, she said: 'We were not that close back then.' This incident proved to me that meeting informants after the formal interview in a more casual atmosphere helped to develop a better rapport, with which they felt more comfortable to divulge sensitive personal history. Thus, I almost always meet and talk to my respondents after our interview and joined their social gatherings whenever possible.

These offline participant observations allowed me to understand the elusive CD culture from an 'insider' perspective as I could directly experience the social activities, friendship dynamics, and tensions in the CD community. Moreover, joining these social gatherings had expanded my CD network as it enabled me to meet and interact with CD members other than my interviewees, including those who seldom participate in the virtual CD community and those who had already left CD. During these participant observations, neither audio recording nor note-taking was feasible, so after each offline participant observation, I made fieldnotes about the setting of the social gatherings, what had happened, people with whom I had interacted, our major conversations, and my own feelings and thoughts about things that I had observed and heard.

DATA ANALYSIS

Thematic coding was adopted to examine, analyze, and compare the data from cyber-ethnography, formal interviews, informal conversations, and fieldnotes generated from participant observation. Figure 2.2 illustrates the constructs and content domains developed from the major themes derived from these data, a thorough review of the literature, and the major research aims in this study.

One limitation of this study was that it was unlikely to produce results that could be generalized to the whole CD population in Hong Kong. Although a noteworthy number of CD participants used online forums to negotiate CD, there remained a portion of individuals who used alternative pathways (i.e., referrals, online games, online chatrooms, and phone applications) to enter into CD; thus, a segment of CD participants were not represented in the sample of this study. Moreover, those who decided to participate in the interviews were unlikely to represent the experiences of all CD participants. However, simply because the results could not be generalized to the larger CD populations this did not mean that they were not useful (Fricker, 2008). The findings of this study still reflected a large and diverse pool of CD participants and marked an advancement of the understanding of a generally invisible CD community

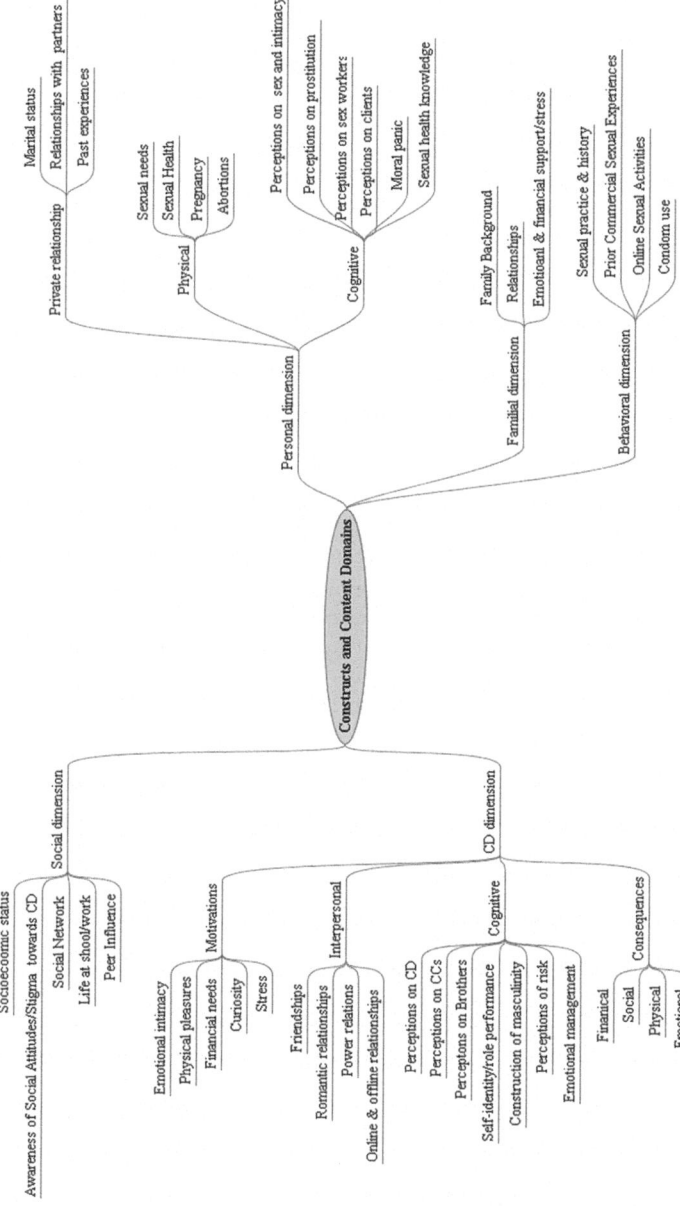

Fig. 2.2 Constructs and content domains

Bibliography

Ackland, R. (2013). *Web Social Science: Concepts, Data and Tools for Social Scientists in the Digital Age*. London: Sage.

Alvarez, M. R., Sherman, R. P., & VanBeselaere, C. (2003). Subject Acquisition for Web-Based Surveys. *Political Analysis, 11*(1), 23–43.

American Sociological Association. (1999/2008). *Code of Ethics and Policies and Procedures of the ASA Committee on Professional Ethics*. Washinton, DC: American Sociological Association.

Arendell, T. (1997). Reflections on the Researcher--Researched Relationship: A Woman Interviewing Men. *Qualitative Sociology, 20*(3), 341–368.

Barry, K. (1995). *The Prostitution of Sexuality: The Global Exploitation of Women*. New York: New York University Press.

Bauman, Z. (2000). *Liquid Modernity* (Vol. 9). Cambridge: Polity Press.

Beck, U. (1992). *Risk Society: Towards a New Modernity*. Thousand Oaks, CA: SAGE Publications.

Belza, M. J., Fuente, L. d. l., Suárez, M., Vallejo, F., García, M., López, M., . . . Bolea, Á. (2008). Men Who Pay for Sex in Spain and Condom Use: Prevalence and Correlates in a Representative Sample of the General Population. *Sexually Transmitted Infections, 84*(3), 207–211.

Berger, C. R. (1979). Beyond Initial Interaction: Uncertainty, Understanding, and the Development of Interpersonal Relationships. In H. Giles & R. N. S. Clair (Eds.), *Language and Social Psychology* (pp. 122–144). Oxford, UK: Basil Blackwell.

Bernstein, E. (2001). The Meaning of the Purchase: Desire, Demand and the Commerce of Sex. *Ethnography, 2*(3), 389–420.

Bernstein, E. (2007). Buying and Selling the Girlfriend Experience: The Social and Subjective Contours of Market Intimacy. In M. Padilla, J. Hirsch, M. Munoz-Labboy, R. Sember, & R. Parker (Eds.), *Love and Globalization: Transformers of Intimacy in the Contemporary World*. Nashville: Vanderbilt University Press.

Bernstein, E. (2010). *Temporarily Yours: Intimacy, Authenticity, and the Commerce of Sex*. Chicago: University of Chicago Press.

Berson, I. R., & Berson, M. J. (2002). Emerging Risks of Violence in the Digital Age. *Journal of School Violence, 1*(2), 51–71.

Buchanan, E. A. (2011). Internet Research Ethics: Past, Present, and Future. In M. Consalvo & C. Ess (Eds.), *The Handbook of Internet Studies* (pp. 83–108). New York: Wiley-Blackwell.

Campbell, R. (1998). Invisible Men: Making Visible Male Clients of Female Prostitutes in Merseyside. In J. E. Elias, R. N. Vern, L. Bullough, V. Elias, & G. Brewer (Eds.), *Prostitution: On Whores, Hustlers, and Johns* (pp. 155–171). New York: Prometheus Books.

Chapkis, W. (1997). *Live Sex Acts: Women Performing Erotic Labor.* New York: Routledge.

Coomber, Ross. 1997. "Using the Internet for Survey Research." 2(2).

Cornwell, B., & Lundgren, D. C. (2001). Love on the Internet: Involvement and Misrepresentation in Romantic Relationships in Cyberspace vs. Realspace. *Computers in Human Behavior, 17*(2), 197–211.

Coy, M. (2009). 'Moved Around Like Bags of Rubbish Nobody Wants': How Multiple Placement Moves Can Make Young Women Vulnerable to Sexual Exploitation. *Child Abuse Review, 18*(4), 254–266.

Elliott, A., & Urry, J. (2010). *Mobile Lives.* Oxford, UK: Routledge.

Ellison, N. B., Hancock, J. T., & Toma, C. L. (2012). Profile as Promise: A Framework for Conceptualizing Veracity in Online Dating Self-presentations. *New Media & Society, 14*(1), 45–62.

Ellison, N., Heino, R., & Gibbs, J. (2006). Managing Impressions Online: Self-presentation Processes in the Online Dating Environment. *Journal of Computer-Mediated Communication, 11*(2), 415–441.

Fox, N., & Roberts, C. (1999). GPs in Cyberspace: The Sociology of a 'Virtual Community'. *Sociological Review, 47*(4), 643–672.

Fricker, R. D. J. (2008). Sampling Methods for Web and E-mail Surveys. In N. Fielding, R. M. Lee, & G. Blank (Eds.), *The SAGE Handbook of Online Research Methods* (pp. 195–216). Los Angeles: SAGE.

Fukuda, A. (2003). *Feminism and Empowerment in Japan: Compensated Dating.* (M.A. MQ83578), Dalhousie University Canada. Retrieved from http://proquest.umi.com/pqdweb?did=766586401&Fmt=7&clientId=17557&RQT=309&VName=PQD

Gemme, R., Payment, N., & Malenfant, L. (1989). *Street Prostitution: Assessing the Impact of the Law.* Montreal, Ottawa: Department of Justice Canada.

Giddens, A. (1992). *The Transformation of Intimacy: Sexuality, Love and Eroticism in Modern Societies.* Standford, CA: Stanford University Press.

Goffman, E. (1959). *The Presentation of Self in Everyday Life.* New York: Anchor Press/Doubleday.

Gosling, S. D., & Johnson, J. A. (2010). *Advanced Methods for Conducting Online Behavioral Research.* Washington, DC: American Psychological Association.

Greene, J. C., & Caracelli, V. J. (1997). *Advances in Mixed-Method Evaluation: The Challenges and Benefits of Integrating Diverse Paradigms.* San Francisco, CA: Jossey-Bass Publishers.

Hammersley, M., & Atkinson, P. (2007). *Ethnography: Principles in Practice.* London\New York: Routledge.

Hine, C. (2015). *Ethnography for the Internet: Embedded, Emobodied and Everyday.* London: Bloomsbury Academic.

Ho, J. C.-J. (2000). Self-empowerment and 'Professionalism': Conversations with Taiwanese Sex Workers. *Inter-Asia Cultural Studies, 1*(2), 283–299.

Ho, J. (2003). From Spice Girls to Enjo Kosai: Formations of Teenage Girls' Sexualities in Taiwan. *Inter-Asia Cultural Studies, 4*(2), 325–336.

Hochschild, A. R. (1983). *The Managed Heart.* Berkeley: University of California Press.

Hoigard, C., & Finstad, L. (1992). *Backstreets: Prostitution, Money and Love.* University Park: The Pennsylvania State University Press.

Hookway, N. (2008). 'Entering the Blogosphere': Some Strategies for Using Blogs in Social Research. *Qualitative Research, 8*(1), 91–113.

Illouz, E. (1997). *Consuming the Romantic Utopia: Love and the Cultural Contradictions of Capitalism.* Berkeley, CA: University of California Press.

Joinson, A. N., & Dietz-Uhler, B. (2002). Explanations for the Perpetration of and Reactions to Deception in a Virtual Community. *Social Science Computer Review, 20*(3), 275–289.

Kappeler, S. (1996). Subjects, Objects and Equal Opportunities. In S. Jackson & S. Scott (Eds.), *Feminism and Sexuality: A Reader* (pp. 300–306). New York: Columbia University Press.

Kong, M.-H. (2003). Material Girls: Sexual Perceptions of Korean Teenage Girls Who Have Experienced 'Compensated Dates'. *Asian Journal of Women's Studies, 9*(2), 67–94.

Lee, T. Y., & Shek, D. T. (2013). Compensated Dating in Hong Kong: Prevalence, Psychosocial Correlates, and Relationships with Other Risky Behaviors. *Journal of Pediatric and Adolescent Gynecology, 26*(3 Suppl), S42–S48.

Lever, J., & Dolnick, D. (2010). Call Girls and Street Prostitutes: Selling Sex and Intimacy. In R. Weitzer (Ed.), *Sex for Sale: Prostitution, Pornography, and the Sex Industry* (2nd ed., pp. 187–204). New York\London: Routledge.

Liamputtong, P. (2009). *Qualitative Research Methods.* Australia and New Zealand: Oxford University Press.

Lorde, A. (1991). The Use of the Erotic; The Erotic as Power. In J. Barrington (Ed.), *Intimate Wilderness.* Portland, OR: Eighth Moutain Press.

Lunnay, B., Borlagdan, J., McNaughton, D., & Ward, P. (2015). Ethical Use of Social Media to Facilitate Qualitative Research. *Qualitative Health Research, 25*(1), 99–109.

Maxwell, J. A. (2005). *Qualitative Research Design: An Interactive Approach* (Vol. 41). Thousand Oaks, CA: Sage Publications.

Maxwell, J. A. (2012). *A Realist Approach for Qualitative Research.* Thousand Oaks, CA: Sage Publications.

McKeganey, N. (1994). Why Do Men Buy Sex and What are Their Assessments of the HIV-related Risks When They Do? *AIDS Care, 6*(3), 289–301.

McKeganey, N., & Barnard, M. (1996). *Sex Work on the Streets: Prostitutes and Their Clients.* Buckingham\Bristol: Open University Press.

Milrod, C., & Monto, M. A. (2012). The Hobbyist and the Girlfriend Experience: Behaviors and Preferences of Male Customers of Internet Sexual Service Providers. *Deviant Behavior, 33*(10), 792–810.

Monto, M. A. (2000). Why Men Seek Out Prostitutes. In R. Weitzer (Ed.), *Sex for Sale: Prostitution, Pornography, and the Sex Industry* (pp. 67–83). New York: Routledge.

Monto, M. A. (2001). Prostitution and Fellatio. *The Journal of Sex Research, 38*(2), 140–145.

Ng, W.-Y., Leung, P.-Y., & Yau, G.-S. (2009). 'Secondary School Students' Attitudes and Knowledge towards Compensated Dating': Findings. from Hong Kong Association of Sexuality Educators, Reserachers & Therapists Limited. http://www.hkasert.org.hk/Survey of compensated dating(Revised).pdf

Oseni, K., Dingley, K., & Hart, P. (2017). *Instant Messaging and Social Networks: The Advantages in Online Research Methodology.* Paper Presented at the The 6th International Conference of Educational and Information Technology Cambridge, UK.

Prasad, M. (1999). The Morality of Market Exchange: Love, Money, and Contractual Justice. *Sociological Perspectives, 42*(2), 181–213.

Ramirez, A., Fleuriet, C., & Cole, M. (2015). When Online Dating Partners Meet Offline: The Effect of Modality Switching on Relational Communication between Online Daters. *Journal of Computer-Mediated Communication, 20*(1), 99–114.

Roberts, L., Smith, L., & Pollock, C. (2004). Conducting Ethical Research Online: Respect for Individuals, Identities and the Ownership of Words. In E. A. Bunchanan (Ed.), *Readings in Virtual Research Ethics: Issues and Controversies* (pp. 156–173). Hershey, PA: Idea Group.

Robson, C. (2011). *Real World Research: A Resource for Users of Social Research Methods in Applied Settings.* Chichester: Wiley.

Ronai, C. R., & Ellis, C. (1989). TURN-ONS FOR MONEY Interactional Strategies of the Table Dancer. *Journal of Contemporary Ethnography, 18*(3), 271–298.

Rubin, S. B. (2002). *Jon Inc.: The Making of Japan's Salaried Men into Clients of High School Prostitutes.* (M.A. MQ69653), University of Alberta (Canada), Canada. Retrieved from http://proquest.umi.com/pqdweb?did=766177711&Fmt=7&clientId=17557&RQT=309&VName=PQD

Salmons, J. (2016). Using Social Media in Data Collection: Designing Studies with the Qualitative E-Research Framework. In L. Sloan & A. Quan-Haase (Eds.), *The SAGE Handbook of Social Media Research Methods* (p. 177). London: Sage Publications.

Sanders, T. (2005a). 'It's Just Acting': Sex Workers' Strategies for Capitalizing on Sexuality. *Gender, Work & Organization, 12*(4), 319–342.

Sanders, T. (2005b). *Sex Work: A Risky Business.* Cullompton: Willan Publishing.

Sanders, T. (2008a). Male Sexual Scripts: Intimacy, Sexuality and Pleasure in the Purchase of Commercial Sex. *Sociology, 42*(3), 400.

Sanders, T. (2008b). *Paying for Pleasure: Men who Buy Sex.* Portland: Willan Publishing.

Stone, A. R. (1996). *The War of Desire and Technology at the Close of the Mechanical Age.* Cambridge, MA: MIT Press.

The Sage Handbook of Qualitative Research. (2011). United States: Sage Publication.

Udagawa, Y. (2007). *Compensated Dating in Japan: An Exploration of Anomie and Social Change in Japan.* Missouri: University of Central Missouri.

Ueno, C. (2003). Self-determination on Sexuality? Commercialization of Sex among Teenage Girls in Japan. *Inter-Asia Cultural Studies, 4*(2), 317–324.

Van Gelder, L. (1996[1985]). The Strange Case of the Electronic Lover. In R. Kling (Ed.), *Computerization and Controversy: Value Conflicts and Social Changes* (2nd ed., pp. 533–546). San Diego, CA: Academic Press.

Wilson, E., Kenny, A., & Dickson-Swift, V. (2015). Using Blogs as a Qualitative Health Research Tool: A Scoping Review. *International Journal of Qualitative Methods, 14*(5), 1–12.

Zelizer, V. A. (2005). *The Purchase of Intimacy.* Princeton: Princeton University Press.

CHAPTER 3

The *Brothers*—Part I: Men Who Buy Compensated Dating

WHO ARE THE MEN WHO PAY FOR SEX?

In working towards an understanding of male clients of CD (the so-called *Brothers*), it would be useful to consider research concerning men who buy sex in general. With respect to the antecedents of why men purchase sex, several studies have suggested that men with certain personal and demographic characteristics are more likely to purchase sex. These studies attempted to distinguish between clients and non-clients. For example, Sullivan and Simon (1998) compared men who reported having paid a woman for sex with those who reported they had not through a survey of a random sample of 3432 adult men in 50 states of the United States. Their result showed that men who had patronized prostitution (17.7%) were more likely to have served in the military, older, more likely to be African American and Hispanic than white American, as well as more interested in sexual variety and exploration. Since Hong Kong's sociocultural and demographic conditions are different from those in the United States, some of the indicators identified in the United States may not be very helpful in the context of Hong Kong. For instance, unlike the United States, Hong Kong does not have a military force, and therefore a history of military service cannot be an indicator of patronization of commercial sex.

In terms of ethnicity, although the number of ethnic minorities in Hong Kong had significantly increased (by 31.2%) over the period between 2001 and 2011, they only represented 6.4% of the total population in

© The Author(s) 2018
C. S. K. Chu, *Compensated Dating*, Gender, Sexualities
and Culture in Asia, https://doi.org/10.1007/978-981-10-6974-1_3

Hong Kong in 2001.[1] In other words, Hong Kong remains very much a Chinese society, with ethnic Chinese composing more than 93% of the population. Moreover, unlike traditional forms of commercial sex such as one-woman brothels, massage parlors, and night clubs, which can be easily assessed by tourists even with language barriers, CD is a hidden and locally exclusive activity, which cannot be easily assessed by foreigners and ethnic minorities who do not speak Cantonese. Rather than being situated in a concrete physical world, CD is embedded in a virtual online world which is largely Cantonese-based. To get CD information and to negotiate a CD date, individuals must at least have the competence to communicate in Cantonese. The CD world is therefore very much a local community. In fact, all the *Brothers* with whom I had interacted were local people. Compared with the clients in the West and clients of other forms of commercial sex in Hong Kong, clients of CD are much more homogeneous in terms of ethnicity. Thus, in the specific context of CD, comparisons according to clients' ethnicity are irrelevant. Ethnicity is not a significant factor to differentiate men who patronize CD from men who do not.

In terms of age, Sullivan and Simon (1998) pointed out that men who patronized prostitution tend to be older, between 53 and 60; however, the clients of CD are generally young, in their 20s–40s according to the data in this study. This divergence is perhaps because CD is largely negotiated online and because individuals in the younger age cohorts tend to be more adapted to Internet usage and to advance information technology than individuals in the older age cohort. A survey of over 5000 respondents in the United States conducted by Assael (2005) showed that heavy Internet users (those browsing the Internet for at least 20 hours a week) were 40 percent more likely to be 18–34 and 20 percent more likely to be 35–44 than the older age cohort. Given that individuals generally have to spend quite a lot of time to explore and negotiate CD online, CD is more likely to attract younger generations, who tend to prefer to communicate through computer-mediated communication, than older generations.

In Hong Kong, the use of the Internet for sexual purpose is quite prevalent amongst young individuals. In their study of sexual media use by 964 Hong Kong young adults (18–27 years old), Janghorbani and Lam along

---

[1] Population Census. 2011 "Thematic Report: Ethic Minorities." *Hong Kong: Census and Statistics Department*. Retried September 8, 2012 (http://www.statistics.gov.hk/pub/B11200622012XXXXB0100.pdf).

with the Youth Sexuality Study Task Force (2003) reported that more than 80% had used and 58% had purchased or rented sexual media. They concluded that the prevalence was 'surprisingly high for young adults from a conservative and ethno-geographic region where the standards of sexual morality are supposedly high' (Janghorbani & Lam, 2003, p. 549). But to me, the result was not surprising at all. It is exactly because Hong Kong adolescents are still infused with conservative values regarding sexuality in both schools and at home that curious young adults are more likely to explore sexual materials on their own. Due to high level of institutional surveillance and social expectation of sexual morality for young adults in Hong Kong, the anonymity of cyberspace provides an ideal and safe social platform for adolescents to explore sexuality without scrutiny.

In spite of a lack of a reliable reference and statistic to estimate the demographic data of male CD clients in Hong Kong, I deduce that they are more likely to be aged between 18 and 44 and that the average age of the *Brothers* is probably younger than that of the clients in traditional forms of commercial sex. In fact, the age range of the *Brothers* in this study was between 23 and 43, with a mean age of 33.4, which echoes the demography in Japan where the most frequent customers of en*jo kosai* are found among men in their 30s. The young age of the *Brothers* contrasts with the stereotypical image of male clients who are presumed to be 'dirty old men with a mean desire toward an innocent, young girl' (Ueno, 2003, p. 322).

Instead of age, Gemme, Payment and Malenfant (1989) tried to draw a distinction between clients in terms of their socio-economic status. A majority of Canadian clients arrested under the communicating law came from the lower socio-economic class and were charged with attempting to purchase sex from street sex workers, who also happened to be in the lower socio-economic stratum of the sex worker hierarchy. When men in the upper-middle to upper socio-economic classes want to buy sex, they tend to patronize other kinds of commercial sex in the upper stratum in the sex work hierarchy, such as escort services and indoor commercial sex, which cost much more than streetworkers. Because escort services and indoor commercial sex are less exposed compared to street prostitution, higher-status clients are less likely to be captured under the communicating law and therefore are much harder to identify. Following the logic of Gemme et al. (1989), the socio-economic characteristic of the *Brothers* can be inferred: they are likely to be the members of the higher-status socio-economic group because CD costs much more than street prostitution and one-woman brothels for the same service (e.g., the price of vaginal intercourse in CD ranged from HKD 800 to HKD 10,000 whereas it costs as little as HKD 250 in a one-woman brothel). *Brothers* also tend to be well educated and have a white-collar job. Of the *Brothers* in this study, 22 (73.3%) of them work at a management to senior management level, indicating a middle to upper socio-economic status.

While some studies attempted to differentiate clients from non-clients by suggesting a difference in certain personal and demographic characteristics between the groups, other studies suggested that clients of prostitution do not differ from non-clients (Armstrong, 1978; Holzman & Pines, 1982). By comparing 66 brothel-visiting male clients with 60 non-clients in Australia, Xantidis and McCabe (2000) noted that the two groups did not differ demographically in terms of their age, education, marital status, or occupation. Similarly, Monto (2000), who compared men arrested for attempting to patronize prostitutes with nationally representative samples of men, stated that there was a significant overlap between the two groups; nevertheless, male clients of prostitution did differ from non-clients in several behavioral and attitudinal aspects. For instance, clients were more likely to be unmarried or separated, to have multiple sexual partners over the past year, and were more accepting of pre-marital sex, homosexual sex, extramarital sex, and adolescent sex. Similar to male clients in Monto's (2000) study, all *Brothers* in this research accept pre-marital sex, extramarital sex, and adolescent sex. A majority of them are also single or divorced (21 clients, 70%); however, unlike his sample, only six *Brothers* (20%) in this study hold a positive attitude toward homosexual sex.

WHY DO MEN BUY SEX?

Around the world, there are men who buy sex. Empirical studies have explored men's reasons for buying sex, some of which have attempted to developed typologies of the clients based on their motivations and attitudes. Historical analysis of why men pay for sex has suggested that a majority of them have more than a single motivation. Clients' motives vary with their social class, the sexual compatibility of their sexual partners, and their 'unique life-history into which, an infinite variety of strands, some economic and some not economic are woven' (Davis, 1937, p. 750).

There are eight broad motivations for men to buy sex: the ability and the desire to purchase certain sexual acts that are not normally accessible in their conventional relationship; the element of excitement and thrill involved in the illicit or risky nature of commercial sex; the capability to contact women with particular physical features; the inability to establish non-commercial sexual relationships; the fulfillment of sexual urge; the avoidance of emotional attachment or commitment in non-commercial sexual relationship; less pressure on sexual performance and achievement; and the great variety of women that can be contacted (Atchison, Fraser, & Lowman, 1998; Campbell, 1998; McKeganey & Barnard, 1996; Monto, 2000).

In the following sections, I will compare and contrast the most commonly identified male clients' motivations for frequenting sex workers with those discussed by the *Brothers*.

Desire for Particular Sexual Acts

A prevalent reason for men to buy sex is the desire for particular sexual acts that are not generally provided by their regular partners, either because their partners are unwilling or unable to perform (Campbell, 1998; McKeganey & Barnard, 1996; Monto, 2000). Through the study of 73 non-distressed and sexually functional married couples, Apt, Hurlbert, Sarmiento and Hurlbert (1996, p. 383) noted that fellatio was regarded as 'something one usually had to pay for and certainly did not do with a woman one respected'. I surmise such sentiment came from the historical, cultural and religious axiom of sex negativity – the idea that sex is a sinful, negative, destructive, and dangerous act that is tolerated only if it is performed for the purpose of procreation within marriage (Rubin, 1993). Fellatio is obviously not a reproductive form of sex, but a recreational act that is practiced merely for the sake of male sexual pleasure. Thus, fellatio is a non-legitimate sexual act that ought not to be performed even with legitimate partners. If fellatio is not practised in the legitimate sexual script, the only feasible way to experience fellatio and other 'bad sex' is in illegitimate settings such as prostitution.

Monto (2001) remarked that the desire for fellatio was a central theme for men to hire sex workers. In his study of men who were arrested for attempting to patronize female prostitution in three cities in the United States, clients were more likely than men in general to consider fellatio as highly appealing. Most clients reported that they had had fellatio experience with a sex worker. Fellatio was also cited as the most frequently practiced sexual act in commercial sexual encounters and in their most recent transaction with a sex worker.

Similar to the clients in the United States, clients in the United Kingdom also expressed that fellatio is a highly desirable sex act. In a survey involving telephone interviews of 70 men who had recently purchased sex, fellatio was reported to be the most commonly and frequently practiced sexual act during their commercial sexual encounters (McKeganey, 1994). While fellatio was the most frequently sought sexual practice, penetrative vaginal intercourse came second; anal sex and specialist sexual services, 'such as corporal punishment, whipping, bondage and various forms of physical degradation including being urinated or defecate upon' (McKeganey, 1994, p. 292), were cited only by a small number of men.

Similar to clients of prostitution in other parts of the world, *Brothers* in Hong Kong reported that fellatio and penetrative vaginal sex were the most practiced sex acts during their CD encounters, in which penetrative vaginal sex and fellatio always complimented each other as both sex acts are considered to be part of the normal sexual script in CD. Terry, 35 years old, said: 'I do not have to request for fellatio. The *CCs* will just do it. Fellatio is almost a guaranteed episode.' The data from my cyber-ethnography also confirms that fellatio (the so-called blowjob (BJ)) is indeed a sexual act that most *CCs* claimed to provide. For example, one *CC's* post indicated '$1300... including bath, wet kiss, BJ, ML'

Although fellatio is frequently performed in CD, it is not the major reason for *Brothers* to seek CD because all of the *Brothers* who received fellatio in CD were able to receive fellatio from their legitimate and regular partners. This might reflect that the sexual values based on a hierarchical valuation of sex acts have changed in late modernity. Fellatio is no longer regarded as 'bad/abnormal/unnatural sex', but is regarded as 'good/normal/natural' sex by all male and female respondents in this study, except for Jack, 28 years old, who found fellatio repulsive. He exclaimed:

> I am very conservative! I have no interest in fellatio. I usually reject it. I do not even want fellatio from my girlfriend. When a *CC* was about to perform fellatio on me, I would stop her and said: 'I do not like it. I do not need it.' I only have vaginal intercourse with the *CCs* and my girlfriends.

The rest of the informants' sexual values have showed otherwise. They categorized fellatio as a legitimate sex act and did not share the moral panic expressed by Jack and the respondents in the study done by Apt et al. (1996). Yet I am not arguing that the hierarchal valuation of sex acts has vanished entirely. In fact, the *Brothers* still dichotomize sex acts into 'good/normal/natural' and 'bad/abnormal/unnatural': 'I am not a pervert! I just do the normal and ordinary sex with the *CCs*,' said Ivan, 37 years old. What I am arguing here is that sexual ethics in late modernity have become increasingly pluralistic and less restricted than in the past. Some sexual behaviors, such as fellatio and other recreational forms of sex, which used to be viewed as illegitimate, are now viewed as legitimate.

Most *Brothers* have the same sexual acts with *CCs* as they normally have with their legitimate partners. Don, 40 years old, said: 'there is no difference between the sex with *CCs* and the sex with my wife in terms of sexual acts'. His narration echoed Sanders' (2008, p. 88) assertion that the 'sex worker—client relationship is not necessarily different in content from that of non-commercial sexual relationships where emotional and physical are produced and consumed'. In fact, the majority of clients in her (2008) study reported to have very similar sexual acts regardless of the commercial nature of the encounters. As such, *Brothers* engaged in CD was not because of the thrill or gratification in the aspect of sexual acts per se. The desire for fellatio did not constitute as a major motive for *Brothers'* to pay for CD as for clients of conventional prostitution, although fellatio was commonly and frequently practiced during the sexual encounters in CD.

Accordingly, unlike clients of prostitution who rationalize their patronization by contributing to the fact that their conventional partners refuse to engage in particular sex act that they long for, *Brothers* seldom use such rationalization to explain their CD behavior. This divergence can be contributed to the transformation of intimacies in two ways. First, marital sex is no longer confined in reproductive sex. Like commercial sex, marital sex can now be recreational. Recreational sex is no longer regarded as a vice, but a legitimate behavior. Second, the sexual valuations have changed. The stigma that is related to certain sexual behaviors such as fellatio has significantly reduced, if not disappeared. These transformations of the meanings and conceptions of sexuality and intimacies explain why the motives of *Brothers* are different from clients of prostitution in the past. The narratives of the *Brothers* show that fellatio is not a main incentive for them to pay for CD because fellatio is no longer condemned and can easily be sought in legitimate relationships if they desired.

The Great Variety of Women

The narratives of *Brothers* offer more support for Winick's (1962) argument that men patronize commercial sex because of the desire for a change in body type from their regular sex partners rather than because of the desire for any specific sex act or a variety of body types that they do not normally get in their conventional relationships. Peter, 36 years old, married, exemplified Winick's (1962) point: 'The feeling of receiving fellatio from a 18 years old girl with a youthful body is so different from that of receiving the exact same thing from my wife. The visual excitements and the gratifications are just incomparable.' But is it the case that all *CCs* are necessarily prettier and 'hotter' than their clients' girlfriends or wives? The answer is 'No.' Don, 40 years old, remarked that: 'my wife is actually much prettier and has a better body shape than all of the *CCs* with whom I have dated. She used to be a model.' I postulate that some men patronize sex workers because they desire a change of sex partner's mind and body, which present them with an entirely new experience and excitement, albeit that the involved sex acts may be the same as those in their conventional sex lives, or the physical attributes of the sex workers may be similar to, or even not as sexually appealing as, those of their regular partners. It seems that no matter how beautiful and sexy a man's regular partner and no matter how mundane the commercial sexual acts, these men still have the desire to have sex with other women, simply because of the thrill of trying something new and the idea of having sex with a different individual.

In the past, men who displayed such promiscuous desires might be subjected to a presumption of disreputability or mental illness such as a 'compulsive need for variety' (Vanwesenbeeck, 2001; Rubin, 1993). Today, promiscuity or, as Giddens (1992, p. 144) put it, 'episodic encounters' with a variety of women tend to be regarded as a feature of modern sexuality, namely 'plastic sexuality'. The capability of having sex with various women affirms men's hegemonic masculinity, which is partly defined by their sexual prowess. To illustrate this point, let me take the cases of Eric, 39 years old, and Peter, 36 years old, as examples. Eric revealed that after his divorce, his major life goal as a man has been to be able to have sex with 100 girls before his erectile dysfunction kicks in. When asked why he chose CD but not conventional prostitution that would likely to make the pathway to his life goal easier, quicker, and more economical, he contributed to the seemingly authenticity of CD and the desire for *girl-friend experience*. The sex that he desired was passionate sex with emotions rather than work sex, which would be devoid of emotions. For Eric, having mechanical sex with 100 women would not be enough to prove his masculinity. It is only if young girls being sexually attracted to him and thereby willing to have sex with him, can his sexual prowess and masculinity be constructed. CD provides an ideal platform to satisfy this kind of desires as Eric said:

> Anyone can obtain sex from prostitution as long as you have money. It says nothing about your personal charm. But in CD, it's not only about money; you have to win the *CCs'* heart in order to have sex with them, which says something about your personality. It gives me a sense of achievement if I can gain sexual favors from *CCs*.

For some *Brothers*, engaging in CD meant more than just sexual and emotional gratifications. Through episodic encounters with a variety of women, men can promulgate their sexual powers, construct their masculinities, and explore and develop the potentials of their selves.

Meanwhile, for Peter, 36 years old, CD offers an unprecedented opportunity to experience plastic sexuality. Besides the apparent sexual pleasures, CD is a social space for self-realization. In his responses, he used a metaphor of a wolf dog to express his feelings: 'I was like a wild wolf dog that had been domesticated for years, returning back to a jungle where it was supposed to belong. I could find my true self only when I am playing around.' Peter narratives illustrated that 'even in the shape of impersonal and fleeting contacts, episodic sexuality may be a positive form of everyday experiment' (Giddens, 1992, p. 147). By communicating and interacting with different types of women in different contexts of social situations, men are not only practicing plastic sexuality, but are also searching and developing a potential self. For men like Peter, sexuality is supposed to be plastic. They felt trapped by the overarching monogamous regime, which limits their potential, development, and self-esteem. Yet they do not want to sacrifice their legitimate monogamous relationships which offer them moral credentials. In order to balance the tension between social obligations and personal aspirations, CD appears to be a perfect solution, since it allows them to experience plastic sexuality and love without jeopardizing their secular obligations and relations.

What exactly is the pleasure of having episodic sexual encounters with various women? Victor, 34 years old, explicated:

> Although my girlfriend can satisfy my sexual needs and the sex acts that I have with her is no different from that with the *CCs*, the encounters with the *CCs* offer me with new sexual experiences. Sex is interactive; my experience depends upon my partner. So, each encounter with a different *CC* creates a brand new experience and excitement for me. Regarding the sex with my girlfriend... at the first beginning, of course there was a thrill with it, but gradually, the thrill faded away because now I can predict what she will be doing, how she is going to react, and what and how the sex is going to be like.

For men like Victor, it is the intangible and abstract inner feelings of pleasure during the voyage of plastic sexuality that has induced them to engage in CD, from which a new sexual self is constructed and their masculinity is reasserted. Each CD encounter represents an adventure for the *Brothers* because they experience something new in it; in this case, the interaction with different *CCs*. The sentiment of anticipation and the adventurous quality of interacting intimately with a new person are already sufficient to create pleasures and thrill for men to begin and sustain their CD behaviors, regardless of the level of physical pleasures that they will actually receive from any tangible feature associated with the *CCs* or particular sexual acts. In fact, the concrete physical pleasures that they obtain are influenced and shaped by their abstract feelings of eroticization of the episode encounters. Jack, 28 years old, said: 'Freshness comes from having sex with a new girl. I believe a lot of men have the same feeling as I do – the feeling of "freshness".' Here, 'freshness' refers to an experience of breaking away from the normality of life rather than being intertwined with their daily routines. Indeed, many *Brothers* shared such feeling of 'freshness' and it was one of the major elements that drove them into CD. For example, Isaac, 30 years old, revealed: 'I have a sense of freshness and excitement when trading with the *CCs*. Even if I have been dating this pretty *CC* for more than a year, the freshness still remains because I only meet her at most four times a month.' Given the significance of the sense of thrill or freshness in CD encounters, it is naïve to presume that the availability of a regular sex partner will preclude the need for CD or for commercial sex in general. Indeed, paid sex will continue to thrive and appeal to men as long as it offers a new (sexual) experience and a sense of adventure for men. Kent, 41 years old, elucidated:

Cassini: Do you still have sex with your wife?

Kent: Yes, but rarely… probably once a month or even longer.

Cassini: Is the sex with your wife different from the sex with the *CCs*?

Kent: They are completely different. The sex with my wife has become homework. The process is boring because it's the same each time. Having sex with *CCs* is different. If she is a new *CC* (new sexual partner), I will definitely have the feeling of 'freshness' even the sex acts are the same. In fact, there are really not many variations in terms of sex acts; the only variation is the sex partner, which really makes the difference. Once the sex partner has changed, the whole feeling and experience would be different.

Cassini: Would the sex with your wife become less boring or would the 'freshness' come back because you have sex with her less frequently now?

Kent: No, because I see her 365 days a year. There can be no 'freshness'. On the other hand, no matter how frequent I date or how close I am with a particular *CC*, I wouldn't sleep next to her every night. So, the sexual encounter with her still gives me freshness if even I have already dated her for many times.

I call this kind of pleasure the 'eroticization of freshness', which is an example of an adventure and is also a unique form of human experience (Waskul, 2003). Although monogamous sex can be non-reproductive and recreational in modern times, it lacks the experimental and explorative factors provided by the episodic encounters with a variety of women. The 'freshness' that plastic sexuality offers in CD allows *Brothers* to move clandestinely outside their everyday context of life and taken-for-granted sex. Such form of experience provides new meaning to their everyday life and identity, which becomes part of the reflexive project of the self.

Eroticization of Risk

Earle and Sharp (2007) suggested that the appeal of prostitution lies in the adventure and excitement that is associated with its risky nature, including health risks, the risk of discovery by partners, peers or police, and the risk of the exposure of social identity or self-identity. One male client in Campbell's study (1998, p. 145) divulged: 'the risk and danger is part of the thrill. It is a high, very real and exciting, as is the possibility of getting caught.' Campbell described this feeling as the 'eroticization of risk'. Note that not every individual eroticizes and enjoys risks. The perceptions of risk and thus the levels of pleasures and excitements gained from different kinds of risk-taking behaviors vary from individual to individual. In this study, no *Brother* reported such an 'eroticization of risk'. Some *Brothers* simply did not consider CD as a risky activity while for others, the risky nature of CD serves as deterrence rather than an encouragement to participate in CD. Johnny, 40 years old, explained why he did not consider CD as a risky activity:

> I believe the *CCs* have more risks than I do. I don't think I have anything to worry about. As a man, I don't think engaging in CD involves any risk. The *CCs* cannot take any advantage from me. The only risk that I may encounter is financial risk... I heard from others *Brothers* and *CCs* that some *CCs* do steal or cheat *Brothers* of their money but I don't have such experience. In terms of health risk, I always use condoms and I perform body check regularly. I don't think the *CCs* are strong enough to hurt me physically. So, I genuinely don't think CD presents any risk to me.

Meanwhile, *Johnny* eschewed the legal risks related to CD rather than indulging in them. He would ask the *CCs* to show their IDs before any sexual encounter took place in order to avoid the legal risk of having sex with minors:

> I only dated *CCs* who are 18 or above. The age was usually mentioned on the *CCs* post. However, if a *CC* looked too young, I would definitely ask her to show her ID card. If she refused to show her ID card, I would just call the date off.

Derrick, 35 years old, also indicated how the risky nature of CD acted as a deterrence rather than an impetus for *Brothers* to engage in such activities:

> A major reason why I have quitted CD is the health risk of being exposed to STDs. Another reason comes from my fear that my friends, colleagues, and girlfriend will discover my CD behavior. I always felt guilty for my girlfriend right before I arranged a CD date and right after the date was over. After all, engaging in CD is an act of betrayal to my girlfriend. I always struggled for a long period of time every time before I dated a *CC*. Even now, I do have an urge to date a *CC*, but because of all the mentioned considerations, I have been hesitant to put my thoughts into action.

Other than the risky nature of prostitution, McKeganey and Barnard (1996) suggested that the illicit and surreptitious nature of prostitution had attracted men to engage in it. Some men would achieve a sense of pleasure and satisfaction by misbehaving, by committing something that is in violation of the moral principles, or by disrupting the social order and then successfully escaping from it and returning to their everyday lives with their normal relationships safe and sound as if nothing had happened. Since prostitution is generally regarded as a morally deviant behavior, prostituting satisfies men's desire to challenge the entrenched social/moral codes and provides a unique risk-taking pleasure that they cannot obtain if they conform subserviently to the traditional sexual script: 'It's so exciting partly because I shouldn't do it,' said a respondent in Campbell's study (1998, p. 168). By doing something that his wife, his girlfriend, or his mother told him not to do, he obtained a feeling of power, mastery, and a triumph over his past. O'Connell Davidson (2003) argued that this type of excitement of paying a prostitute for sex comes from its representation 'as an act of vengeance against "good"' women's demands for monogamy and sexual restraint' (p. 209). Only one respondent in this study showed signs of any rebellious intent, yet his act of vengeance was directed in a different way from that of the male clients in prostitution:

> I didn't understand why my girlfriend broke up with me as I am such a decent guy. I was so mad that I decided to date a *CC* in order to show her that I can be a 'bad' guy too. Do not take my loyalty as granted. (Rooney, 28 years old)

Perceptions that their girlfriends are unfaithful drive some men, such as Rooney, to avenge their girlfriends by taking reciprocal unfaithful actions through CD. Since Rooney did not receive the mutual faithfulness that he expected from his girlfriend, he ceased to be monogamous. His CD encounters were acts of vengeance not against his girlfriend's demand for monogamy, but, on the contrary, against her violation of monogamy, his previous monogamous sexual identity, and 'good/normal' sense of self. The purpose of Rooney to engage in CD was to rebel the traditional monogamous regime that he had always believed in and complied with.

Other men find commercial sex exciting and erotic because by accepting the money, the sex worker turns herself into a commodity, and so 'legitimately' becomes nothing more than the embodiment of his masturbatory fantasy. O'Connell Davidson (2003, p. 195) contended that 'some men derive excitement from the idea of a woman (seemingly) consenting to her own sexual objectification, rather than (or perhaps as well as) from the idea of physically forcing a woman to submit to a rape'. Following this perspective, men want the sex worker's consent 'because, by voluntarily accepting money in exchange for her sexual use, she demonstrates herself to be a "dirty whore" and so a dehumanized and debased object' (O'Connell Davidson, 2003, p. 194). Yet no *Brother* in this study reported to have experienced this kind of masturbatory fantasy. None of the *Brothers* perceived *CCs* as sex workers, let alone dehumanized commodities. As Chap. 7 will show, *CC–Brother* relations are relatively democratic. The narratives of the *Brothers* show little support to the sexual objectification of *CCs*.

Avoidance of Intimacy

The fear of emotional involvement, commitment, and responsibilities inherent in conventional relationships had been identified as another common rationalization for men to engage in commercial relationships (McKeganey, 1994; Monto, 2000). Likewise, 12 *Brothers* in this study reported that they patronized CD because they wanted to have sexual encounters without any emotional and moral burdens. For these men, sex and love represent two different arenas that can be demarcated both in theory and in practice. Jack, 28 years old, explained how he compartmentalized sexual and emotional intimacy such that sexual promiscuous does not equate and lead to emotional infidelity:

> Love and sex are two isolated entities. I do not have the feeling of "love" for most CCs, but I do enjoy having sex with them. Moreover, patronizing CD is much better than developing an affair. An affair involves emotional attachment, but CD doesn't. I consider myself as emotionally monogamous even though I am not sexually monogamous.

Since Jack was not emotionally involved with any *CC*, he did not perceive his CD behaviors as a betrayal to his girlfriend. For him, CD is simply a way to experience plastic sexuality, which does not affect the integrity of the love for his girlfriend.

The sentiments expressed by the *Brothers* echoed that of the clients of prostitution, especially those who are married or in a conventional relationship. Both groups value the detached emotional aspect in commercial sex (McKeganey & Barnard, 1996; Peng, 2007). Kent, 41 years old, said:

I engage in CD rather than picking up a woman because the latter could be emotionally demanding and might jeopardize my marriage. In CD, however, I do not have to worry about such things. Engaging in CD has no strings attached, so it would not interrupt my normal life in a way that an affair or a one-night stand would have.

In some cases, the encounters with *CCs* are merely business or contractual transactions in which the *CCs* are 'socially dead' for men (O'Connell Davidson, 2003). *Brothers* do not care about the true identity, life history, or feelings of the *CC*. In the same sense, *Brothers* prefer themselves to be 'socially dead' to *CCs* because they want to remain anonymous and maintain a personal distance from the *CCs*. *Brothers* and *CCs* address one another only by pseudonyms that they adopted in the CD world and have no interest in the nature of each other's normative lives outside the CD niche. Once the *Brothers'* sexual urges were fulfilled and the *CCs* had been compensated, their relationship would immediately be over. The exchange of personal history, identity, or emotional intimacy is unnecessary and therefore absent in such a context. CD allows men to have relatively passionate sex with various women anonymously and absent any emotional responsibility.

Another reason that men avoid developing intimacy, even in conventional relationships, is that it requires tremendous mental, physical, and financial efforts. According to Giddens (1992) and Bauman (2003), modern intimacy is a difficult task that both involved parties have to work on it. Unfortunately, living in a tumultuous and vibrant place characterized by a fast pace of change and increasingly individualized society like Hong Kong, people are more hesitant to sacrifice their time and their private pleasures for the cultivation of a relationship, which is precarious and may not be worthwhile for personal growth (Beck & Beck-Gernsheim, 1995). Even non-commercial casual relationships, for some individuals, are considered to be too emotionally, financially, and time consuming. So, they would seek paid sex instead of seeking non-commercial casual sex: 'Why go through all the hassle of buying drinks for a woman, taking her out for a meal when you don't even know if you'll get anywhere? You might as well just pay a prostitute,' said a client in Campbell's study (1998, p. 168). Similarly, Sam, 32 years old, said:

When I went to a bar, I had to order two bottles of wine to invite women to be my company. Although I didn't actually pay cash to them, I was spending money to buy something in exchange of their companionships, which might not necessarily lead to sex.

In other words, what some men seek in non-commercial relationships, especially casual relationships, is very similar to what they seek in commercial relationships – sex. However, since sex is not guaranteed in non-commercial settings, even after a series of conventional rituals of courtship has been undertaken and considerable time, money, and energy have been forfeited by men, some of these men have lost their incentives to develop a plausibly unrequited non-commercial relationship. There are also some men who simply do not enjoy the traditional script of intimacy, which typically includes a romantic dinner, conversations, speculations of each other minds, and the giving of flowers or gifts. To make things worse, these men may not even get what they want after all these hassles. By contrast, in the context of CD and other commercial relationships, men can skip the courtship rituals if they want to, and at the same time they can also enjoy sex, which is almost always promised. As such, some men prefer to purchase sex directly from sex workers rather than sacrificing their individual freedom and investing financial, emotional, and temporal efforts to cultivate a conventional relationship, which does not assure the fulfillment of their personal desire. For those men who take pleasure in and would like to go through the conventional script of romantic relationship while at the same time have sex by the end of a date, CD offers the perfect option. The double pleasure embedded in CD is one of the factors that makes CD preferable to traditional forms of prostitution.

Giddens (1992, p. 147) pointed out that 'episodic sexuality may usually be a way of avoiding intimacy, but it also offers a means of furthering or elaborating upon it'. Most *Brothers*, including those who avoided the burden and commitment inherent in non-commercial intimate relationships, tended to seek an everyday experience that simulates a non-commercial intimate relationship, which highlights emotional exchange, deep conversation, self-disclosure, romantic elements, care, understanding, and support, all of which increases men's pleasures. Similarly, many Taiwanese clients indicated that they 'desire sex with mutual affection, if not love' (Peng, 2007, p. 326). CD was designed to perfect this desire. *CCs* are supposed to and expected to provide a feeling to their clients that they are experiencing a non-commercial romantic encounter, even though it is in fact a commercial encounter. The frequent communication, active interactions, and intense emotional exchange between *CCs* and the *Brothers* all help to create such an illusion.

Most *Brothers* in this study reported that emotional comfort was a more important factor than physical pleasure to sustain their continuation of CD. Jerry, 30 years old explained: 'CD is not only about sex. It involves love such as talking sweetly, caring for each other, flirting, etc.… as if a date in a conventional relationship.' All *Brothers* still maintain the myth that sex workers only provide sexual needs whereas *CCs* offers both physical and emotional comforts. From the *Brothers'* perspective, to focus solely on the sexual aspects of CD is to miss its essence – romance. Sex is simply a derivative of the romance. Leon, 43 years old, aptly expressed:

> If I just want sex, I can go to one-woman brothel which costs around HKD350, or even a call girl who charges around HKD800. I don't have to find a *CC* (it costs an average of HKD1200 for the services, and at least HKD250–400 for a love motel)

Clearly, besides sexual enjoyment, there was something else that triggered *Brother's* desire for CD – emotional intimacy.

At times when the *Brothers* simply want to seek emotional intimacy but not sex from a female, they will seek part-time girlfriend (*PTGF*) services from a *CC* or date a *PTGF* who does not provide sex but provides companionate services, such as watching movies, dining, singing karaokes, etc. (Theoretically, *PTGF* services do not include sexual favors, but practically, many *PTGFs* offer a limited degree of physical intimacy, such as holding hands, kissing, and caressing. Some *PTGFs* would even perform oral sex, masturbation, and sexual intercourse upon clients' requests and persuasions.) *PTGF* services constitute a niche market for men who seek primarily emotional intimacy:

Cassini: Have you ever dated a *PTGF*?
Cyrus: Not yet. But this is what I am trying to do right now. I have been looking for a *PTGF*, but I haven't found the right one yet. So, I am still searching for one. I just want to go to karaoke, have dinner, and watch a movie with her.
Cassini: Why can't you do all these things with your own friends?
Cyrus: I can, but *PTGFs* are different… I can talk with the *PTGFs*. I mean I do not usually disclose personal matters and feelings to my friends. Guys seldom talk about their innermost feelings. We just drink, banter with each other and have fun. Although I am aware that I can hug, kiss or even do some more intimate physical contacts with some *PTGFs*, I do not want that. I think this is

> unnecessary and misses the point of dating a *PTGF*. If I want to
> have physical/sexual interactions as well, then I would just date a
> *CC*, not a *PTGF*.

Even if the involved female party is a *CC* but not a *PTGF*, sex does not necessarily have to take place in CD. Ten respondents reported that they had dated a *CC* without having sex with her although they had made the full payment for sexual services. David, 30 years old recalled:

> I didn't have sex with the *CCs* in my first four CD encounters. We just
> talked and watched TV naked. I just wanted a girl to be next to me. It eased
> my pressures and made me feel relaxed.

Emotional intimacy has a strong exchange value in the context of CD. 'Girlfriend feel' is widely marketed and emphasized by the *CCs* on their posts on the CD forums. For example, a *CC* highlighted on her post: 'Services: Shower, BJ (with condom), wet kiss, 69... girlfriend feel (100% no trade feel!)' (written and posted by a *CC* in May 2010). *Brothers* often appraised the *CCs* if they received a girlfriend experience:

> Although she was shy, she was willing to follow my requests. When we took
> a break in the middle of our session, we had some romantic chats. It really
> gave me 100% girlfriend feel! (written and posted by a *Brother* online in
> January 2010)

Even in traditional forms of prostitution, Peng (2007) found that an affectionate and emotional encounter is always appreciated and desired. Indeed, West, Koken and her colleagues (2010) indicated that *girlfriend/boyfriend experience* was the primary marketing strategy adopted by male and female escorts and call girls/boys in their advertisements to attract potential clients. Undoubtedly, there is a group of clients who desire not merely sex, but also an experience of a conventional sexual script that accentuates emotional intimacy. 'This is why many club girls and some higher-end prostitutions sometimes try to seduce clients romantically,' remarked Peng (2007, p. 327). CD takes the commodification of emotional intimacy into the next level. The online communication, the chat on phone, the stroll in a park, the giving of presents, the watching of a movie, the shopping, dining and meeting of each other friends and even family, all mimic the atmosphere and formula of a non-commercial romantic relationship. *Brothers* value such *girlfriend experience*, which is the reason why they engage in CD rather than conventional prostitution.

At first glance, the desire for *girlfriend experience* may seem contradictory to the desire of avoiding intimacy in a conventional relationship; however, they are not inherently mutually exclusive if we debunk the seeming paradoxical desires. Some men shun the idea of developing intimacy in conventional setting due to the responsibilities, commitments, and constraints that are associated with it, but it does not mean that they do not desire emotional intimacy per se. Men, especially those who are single or in an unhappy conventional relationship, still yearn to experience emotional connection and intimacy with a romantic partner because, as Beck and Beck-Gernsheim (1995) argued, it is the only place where individuals can get emotional dependence, support, and security in this chaotic and difficult modern society that is uncertain and infused with all kinds of risks. Emotional intimacy is vital for individuals' physical and psychological well-being because it is a site from which men can obtain emotional comfort and thus become a refuge for them. It is therefore not a coincidence that Kent, 41 years old, regarded CD as a shelter such that he can maintain a mental balance amongst himself, his work, and family:

> *Kent*:   I was searching for something that can assure me that I would have a place to go and something to do for spiritual support. If I knew something/someone was waiting for me after work, then I could survive from the eight working hours easily. If not, I would not have a purpose after work and the eight hours of work would become very hard for me. I wanted to escape from the pressures at work and the isolated working environment. Thus, I usually pre-arrange CD dates a week in advance. I feel relieved when I knew I have somewhere to go in the following days between Monday and Friday after work.
>
> *Cassini*: Can't home be your escape?
>
> *Kent*:   No. If the relationship with my wife was good, then I did not have to engage in CD. If I could tell everything to my wife, then I would not have to talk to *CCs*. CD is an escape for me from home as well as from work.

In Kent's case, his marital relationship and home failed to provide a source of emotional support. CD thus offered a safe emotional refuge for him. Yet Kent stressed: 'I wouldn't sacrifice my family for another woman. I have the responsibility to take care of my wife and daughters.' This was the reason why he had never had an affair, which could easily jeopardize his marriage due to the higher level of emotional demand compared to CD. For men like Kent, they are reluctant to develop a non-commercial relationship simply because they do not want to shoulder the associated responsibilities; it does not mean that they do not yearn for emotional intimacy. In other words, they desire the fruits of a conventional romantic relationship but do not want to put any efforts into cultivating it in a legitimate way because it is too difficult; therefore, they turn to a less demanding but deviant means – CD, which sells 'an experience of seemingly genuine affection, mutual affection, and stimulating companionship' (Koken et al., 2010, p. 215) and presents to men as an innovative alternative to obtain emotional intimacy that provides ontological security and psychological comfort without having them to make any emotional commitment.

Inability to Form a Conventional Relationship

Some male clients patronize prostitutes because they have difficulties in establishing a non-commercial relationship, either because of their physical unattractiveness or disability or psychological factors (Campbell, 1998; Monto, 2000). Frequenting prostitution allow these men to explore and enact their sexualities. It also provides an opportunity for them to create an intimate connection with women that they otherwise are not able to form in regular social setting (Monto, 2000).

Meanwhile, Sanders (2007) suggested that men with physical and sensory impairments form a core group of clients that visit commercial female sex workers because these men usually have struggles, anxieties, and frustration with establishing a conventional intimate sexual relationship. Similarly, Brown (1994) pointed out historically, people living with impairments were being 'de-sexualized' or being regarded as asexual, oversexed, innocents, or perverts, thus their rights of sexual expressions, sexual opportunities, and relationship building are being constantly denied or reduced. Barnes (1991, p. 182) also indicated that 'disabled people's ability to participate in mainstream recreational pursuits and establish "normal" social contacts and relationships is severely restricted as a result of the economic, environment and asocial barriers'. Therefore, forming an ordinary emotional tie that is sexually fulfilling is fraught with barriers for men with impairments and the easiest solution for men living in a disable world to experience romantic and sexual intimacy is most probably through paid sex (Sanders, 2007). When I said paid sex is the easiest option, it is in a relative sense; it is not easy at all. Although none of the *Brothers* in this study have any apparent physical or mental disability that prohibit them from forming a non-commercial relationship or finding a sexual partner, one female respondent, Gloria, 28 years old, reported that she had encountered a *Brother* with physical impairment and she had rejected to have CD with him because of his physical disability:

> One time, as usual, I dated a *Brother* to wait in front of the main gate of a hotel. He was a new customer and I had never seen him before. I was shocked when I met him. He had vitiligo. I was so scared. I really couldn't accept the idea of having sexual intercourse with him. So, I apologized to him and said I cannot trade with him. He should have told me that he had vitiligo in advance. If I knew his condition, I would not have agreed to trade with him in the first place! It was a waste of both of our time, but I felt pity for him.

Even in a commercial setting, this man with vitiligo had difficulties in forming an intimate liaison. It is logical, therefore, to presume that he probably struggled more to establish an intimate relationship in a conventional context. However, since none of the respondents in this study had a disability, the desire and experience of disabled men who seek CD cannot be elaborated in this book.

Despite a healthy state of mind and body, five *Brothers* reported having difficulties in forming conventional relationships because of various personal factors and thus started their pathway into CD. Ryan, 33 years old, explained how his upbringing and social circle had restricted his opportunities in forming conventional romantic liaisons:

> (Sigh…) Since my high school years until now, I have had very few opportunities to get in touch with females. I went to an International junior high school in Hong Kong in which most students have an open-minded attitude towards casual relationships. However, many girls were "bad" ones who always went to bars and flirted with different guys… Then, I went to a very small town in Toronto for high school. There were only few people from Hong Kong and since I didn't like to develop intimate relations with

foreigners and girls from Mainland China, I didn't date any girls. After grad-
uating from high school, I returned to Hong Kong and worked in a manu-
facturing company where all my colleagues were either men or married
women. For all these reasons, it has always been hard for me to meet and get
to know a single female around my age, not to mention developing an intimate relationship.

Ryan started CD because potential female romantic partners were absent
in his ordinary social network. CD provided an outlet for him to interact
with women intimately. He continued to say: 'I dated a part-time girlfriend (*PTGF*) once before. I will date a *PTGF* again if I suddenly desire to
have a female companion and experience the tenderness of a woman and
her femininity.' Similar to Ryan, Harvey's working environment had pre-
cluded him from meeting and associating with women in his everyday life,
not to mention a romantic partner. Harvey, 33 years old, revealed: 'I have
never been in a relationship because as a fisherman, my social circle is very
small. I always stay on the boat and thus it is very difficult for me to find a
girlfriend.'

While the isolated working environment had inhibited some *Brothers*
from forming non-commercial relationships and drove them to seek intimate partners through CD, fear of the insecure and precarious nature of
modern intimate relationships had inhibited some *Brothers* from cultivating non-commercial relationships and thus propelled them to seek intimacy through CD. Alex, 32 years old, said:

> I have never been in a relationship. I am reluctant to start one because I have
> witnessed too many unsuccessful marriages around me, including my
> friends' and parents'. I have and will never take an initiative to start a rela-
> tionship. There were girls who expressed affections to me, but I always
> rejected them. CD is a good way to satisfy my emotional as well as sexual
> needs. In CD, I can experience the good and romantic side of a relationship
> and without going through the fragile and ugly side of it.

The notions of 'one and only one', 'happily ever after', 'love till death do
us part' of couple relationships have become a myth in modern times.
Even marriage cannot provide the assurance and stability of the bond and
commitment that they used to have. In Hong Kong, according to the
Census and Statistics Department (*Women and Men in Hong Kong Key
Statistics*, 2016), the number of divorces had risen substantially from
2062 in 1981 to 22,271 in 2013 and then dropped slightly to 20,075 in

2015. Plastic sexuality and the concomitant lack of security in modern intimacy have prevented some individuals from establishing a conventional relationship. In such a context, CD becomes a convenient way and a new site where men can have more control to experience physical and emotional intimacies when they are unable or unwilling to form a conventional relationship.

Under the overarching influence of hegemonic masculinity in a patriarchal society, men who are unable to establish successful non-commercial romantic and/or sexual relationships with women are likely to be devalued, leading to them being stereotyped as 'losers' (Weatherall & Priestley, 2001). Some people, including sex workers, subscribe to a myth about men who pay sex that they are inadequate and desperate men who fail to attract sexual partners for free. By paying money in exchange for sex, men violate the concept of sexual 'naturalness' (Sanders, 2007) and thus jeopardize their masculinity, ability, and social desirability.

Despite the 'loser image' of men who buy sex is not uncommon, I agree with Armstrong (1978) and Earle and Sharp (2007) that this stereotypical representation can hardly reflect all men who engage in commercial sex. Although some who frequent commercial sex are indeed due to their inability to form non-commercial romantic and/or sexual relationships such that commercial sex is their only platform to associate with women emotionally and sexually, it does not inherently mean that these men are socially, physically, or mentally inadequate. Some men seek commercial sex not because they cannot but because they do not want to invest time and energy to cultivate a conventional relationship. Moreover, many men who buy sex do have regular sex partners, girlfriends, or wives, which prove that they are not unable to get sex for free. Indeed, more than half (62.5%) of the *Brothers* in this study do have sex partners in non-commercial settings.

While some *Brothers* are unable to or do not want to establish a conventional relationship, some *Brothers* are frustrated by their existing conventional relationships. A relationship break-up, or being in an unhappy and unsatisfying relationship were often cited by the *Brothers* as one of the incentives to take part in CD.

Five *Brothers* in this study initiated CD because of a relationship break-up. 'My girlfriend's betrayal of me was the root cause of my involvement in CD,' said David, 30 years old. Similarly, Edward, 33 years old, revealed: 'I broke up with my long-term girlfriend last year. It was very hard to take. I wanted someone to talk to but I seldom disclose my feelings to my friends. So, I thought *CC* might be a convenient company.' Given the precarious nature of modern intimate relationships, CD serves an emotional therapy for the breakup. It was *Brothers'* hope that the company of *CCs* could provide some comforts and helped them to get out from their breakups.

Despite the risky nature of modern relationships, 12 men in this study still expressed a desire to form a conventional romantic relationship or a marriage. They claimed that they would quit engaging in CD if they entered into a legitimate relationship. Sam, 32 years old, said:

> I had never dated a *CC* or other girls when I was in a relationship. Once I broke up, I would play around... like a mess. But once I found a new girlfriend, I would become good again. It was like an infinite cycle. When I got out of a relationship, I felt that I had lost something, which I didn't know where to find. So, I tried to search for it in CD.

For men like Sam, CD serves as an emotional refuge that offers temporary gratification of their emotional needs. *CCs* are short-term companions and *CC–Brother* relationships are a transitory substitution for a potentially long-term conventional relationship.

For some men, however, instead of perceiving CD as a replacement for conventional relationships, they perceive CD as an addendum to their stable relationships. Nine respondents in this study sought CD to complement their unsatisfying sexual and/or emotional relationships with their regular partners:

> Everything is fine with my wife, except sex. It's about the frequency and quality. My wife cannot satisfy me in both aspects. (Terry, 35 years old)
>
> My sex life with my wife is very bad. We haven't had sex for three months. (Jeremy, 28 years old)
>
> Let's put the sexual relationship with my wife in this way: I love to eat raw meat; nonetheless, my wife serves well-cooked meat to me every day. She never understands what I want sexually and emotionally. So, I decided to find comforts in CD. (Peter, 36 years old)
>
> My relationship with my wife has turned bad since two years ago. She said she has no feeling for me anymore, so she cannot have sex with me. That's why I started CD. I am a very conservative man. If it were not because of my wife refusal to have sex with me, I wouldn't find *CCs*. (Cyrus, 42 years old)

Kent, 41 years old, attempted to ignite the sexual sparkle with his wife again, but in vain:

> Besides my wife and I, there are two other people in my house: my daughter and the domestic helper. If we have sex in our room, they can certainly hear us. My wife does not want them to hear us. Moreover, there is no excitement between us anymore. So, I proposed to go to one of the several very nice love motels in Kowloon Tong, in the belief that a new environment may bring new excitement to our sex life, but my wife rejected immediately and adamantly: 'No. I don't want it.' That's it. So, we can only have sex when everybody is not home... probably once a month if I am lucky.

Two respondents reported that their girlfriends were too shy and passive to explore sex. For example, Derrick, 35 years old, said: 'my girlfriend is very pure and innocent. I feel embarrassed to tell her what I want sexually. But in CD, the *CCs* ask me what I want and what makes me feel comfortable.' These men sought CD for sexual pleasures that they could not achieve in their normative relationships and this tendency echoed Peng's (2007) findings that some Taiwanese men sought prostitution for sexual enjoyment to supplement their frustrated sex lives with their regular partners.

While five *Brothers* who were married or in a committed relationship reported that they still took pleasure in having sex with their wives or girlfriends, four reported that they had completely lost interest in having sex with their regular partners. Nonetheless, all of them still continued to have sex with their wives or girlfriends, either because they believed it was their duty to do so or because they wanted to avoid their partners suspecting that their sexual needs had already been gratified by other means. Kent, 41 years old, said: 'the wives would feel weird if their husbands didn't have sex with them for a considerable length of time'. Leon, 43 years old, expressed a similar sentiment: 'if a husband doesn't have sex with his wife for a long time, she will suspect and wonder: "Why don't you have sexual needs?" So, a husband must have sex with his wife regularly.' All four respondents who no longer enjoyed sex with their long-term partners shared the feelings that having sex with them was just like 'doing or submitting homework'. They perceive sex with their regular partners as a chore or responsibility rather than an expression of emotional intimacy or a desire for sexual pleasures. In their cases, it was the conventional sex, rather than commercial sex, that is regarded as mechanical sex. Two *Brothers* even reported to have the feeling of sexually abused during the sexual intercourse with their legitimate partners: 'I felt like I was being raped while having sex with my wife,' said Don, 40 years old. For men who no longer enjoy sex with their partners, CD offers an opportunity to retrieve their pleasures in sex.

DISCUSSION

This chapter reviews existing literatures and data that have bearings on the demographic characteristics of men who buy sex and reasons for men to frequent prostitution, which can shed light on the demography and motivations of men who take part in CD.

Regarding the major demographic characteristics of *Brothers* in Hong Kong, I project that they tend to be middle to upper socio-economic class local men aged between 18 and 44. The findings of this study support those given by other studies of clients (Atchison et al., 1998; McKeganey & Barnard, 1996; Monto, 2001) that men have not one but multiple motivations to seek commercial sex.

While the desire to purchase particular sexual acts, predominantly fellatio, was commonly reported by men as a major motive for frequenting traditional forms of prostitution, it was apparently not the main motive for men to seek CD. I suggest that this difference was partly due to the transformation of sexual values: While fellatio was regarded as a degrading and deviant act that had to be paid for and ought not to be enacted with a legitimate partner in the past, fellatio is largely being regarded as a 'good and normal' sexual act that is commonly practiced in conventional relationships in modern times. *Brothers'* narratives show that although the concept of the dichotomization of 'good/normal/natural' sex and 'bad/abnormal/ unnatural' sex still exists, the contents in the categorizations have changed. Recreational sex and non-productive sex have shifted from 'bad and abnormal sex' to 'good and normal sex'. Since *Brothers* can access fellatio in a normative setting, the desire for fellatio, despite often being practised in CD sexual encounters, is not a major motive for *Brothers* to seek CD.

Rather than desiring a particular sexual act, *Brothers* are more attracted to the idea of having sex with a variety of women. Episodic encounters with various young women provide pleasures to men through the 'eroticization of freshness'. CD exposes men to new sexual experiences and helps them to realize their self-identities, including their sexual selves, through which they assert and strengthen their masculinity by sexual conquest (Giddens, 1992). Accordingly, CD is conceptualized as a site to experience plastic sexuality and has become part of *Brothers'* reflexive project of the self.

Another discrepancy between *Brothers* and clients of conventional prostitution is that the former group did not share the 'eroticization of risk' that the latter had when engaging in CD. This is mainly because *Brothers* do not consider CD as a form of prostitution; rather, they see it as an avenue into the world of plastic sexuality. They therefore did not experience the risky nature related to prostitution frequenting.

A common 'pull' casual factor that is shared by both *Brothers* and clients of conventional prostitution to enter into commercial relationships is that they either do not want to, or are unable to, establish an intimate relationship in non-commercial settings. I argue that this is partly due to the transformation of love and intimacy in late modernity, which is increasingly democratic, precarious, and fragile such that increasing efforts are required to develop and maintain an intimate relationship, especially on the part of men, due to the rising women's status and role in both the private and public spheres. Some *Brothers* reported experiencing struggles, tensions, and frustration in the course of their 'normal' relationships. Some had even given up hope on love and forming trustful relationships altogether. They simply did not want to shoulder the emotional responsibilities, efforts, burdens, and risks that are associated with modern intimate relationships and thus, chose to pay for sex and intimacy. In other words, refusing to form an intimate relationship is not the same as rejecting emotional intimacy. Apparently, there was an emotional lack and a sense of 'inner homelessness' in these men's lives (Beck & Beck-Gernsheim, 1995). They still wanted to experience the emotional intimacy that is inherent in an intimate relationship. Yet the uncertainties and risks in modern relationships had prompted them to seek and reconstruct psychological comfort and ontological security through commercial relationships. CD, which offers *girlfriend experience* – a combination of romantic love, passionate love, and aspects of the courtship rituals, but devoid of all the responsibilities associated with non-commercial relationships, thus became a wonderland for men who found the increasingly democratic modern intimate relationship too demanding and difficult. CD serves not only as an attempt to engage in heterosexual sexual relationships, but also as a platform to develop emotional intimacy, whether authentic or inauthentic, with a woman, which cannot otherwise be achieved in their conventional settings.

BIBLIOGRAPHY

Apt, C., Hurlbert, D. F., Sarmiento, G. R., & Hurlbert, M. K. (1996). The Role of Fellatio in Marital Sexuality: An Examination of Sexual Compatibility and Sexual Desire. *Sexual & Marital Therapy, 11*(4), 383–392.

Armstrong, E. G. (1978). Massage Parlors and Their Customers. *Archives of Sexual Behavior, 7*(2), 117–125.

Assael, H. (2005). A Demographic and Psychographic Profile of Heavy Internet Users and Users by Type of Internet Usage. *Journal of Advertising Research, 45*(01), 93–123.

Atchison, C., Fraser, L., & Lowman, J. (1998). Men Who Buy Sex: Preliminary Findings of an Exploratory Study. In J. E. Elias, V. L. Bullough, V. Elias, & G. Brewer (Eds.), *Prostitution: On Whores, Hustlers and Johns* (pp. 172–203). New York: Prometheus Books.

Barnes, C. (1991). *Disabled People in Britain and Discrimination: A Case for Anti-discrimination Legislation*. London: Hurst & Company.

Bauman, Z. (2003). *Liquid Love: On the Frailty of Human Bonds*. Cambridge: Polity Press.

Beck, U., & Beck-Gernsheim, E. (1995). *The Normal Chaos of Love*. Cambridge: Polity Press.

Brown, H. (1994). 'An Ordinary Sexual Life?': A Review of the Normalisation Principle as It Applies to the Sexual Options of People with Learning Disabilities. *Disability and Society, 9*(2), 123–144.

Campbell, R. (1998). Invisible Men: Making Visible Male Clients of Female Prostitutes in Merseyside. In J. E. Elias, R. N. Vern, L. Bullough, V. Elias, & G. Brewer (Eds.), *Prostitution: On Whores, Hustlers, and Johns* (pp. 155–171). New York: Prometheus Books.

Davis, K. (1937). The Sociology of Prostitution. *American Sociological Review, 2*, 744–755.

Earle, S., & Sharp, K. (2007). *Sex in Cyberspace: Men Who Pay for Sex*. Hampshire: Ashgate Publishing Limited.

Gemme, R., Payment, N., & Malenfant, L. (1989). *Street Prostitution: Assessing the Impact of the Law*. Montreal, Ottawa: Department of Justice Canada.

Giddens, A. (1992). *The Transformation of Intimacy: Sexuality, Love and Eroticism in Modern Societies*. Standford, CA: Stanford University Press.

Holzman, H. R., & Pines, S. (1982). Buying Sex: The Phenomenology of Being a John. *Deviant Behavior, 4*(1), 89–116.

Janghorbani, M., & Lam, T.-H. (2003). Sexual Media Use by Young Adults in Hong Kong: Prevalence and Associated Factors. *Archives of Sexual Behavior, 32*(6), 545–553.

Koken, J., Bimbi, D. S., & Parsons, J. T. (2010). Male and Female Escorts: A Comparative Analysis. In R. Weitzer (Ed.), *Sex for Sale: Prostitution, Pornography, and the Sex Industry* (2nd ed.). New York: Routledge.

McKeganey, N. (1994). Why Do Men Buy Sex and What are Their Assessments of the HIV-related Risks When They Do? *AIDS Care, 6*(3), 289–301.

McKeganey, N., & Barnard, M. (1996). *Sex Work on the Streets: Prostitutes and Their Clients.* Buckingham\Bristol: Open University Press.

Monto, M. A. (2000). Why Men Seek Out Prostitutes. In R. Weitzer (Ed.), *Sex for Sale: Prostitution, Pornography, and the Sex Industry* (pp. 67–83). New York: Routledge.

Monto, M. A. (2001). Prostitution and Fellatio. *The Journal of Sex Research, 38*(2), 140–145.

O'Connell Davidson, J. (2003). Eroticizing Prostitute Use. In R. Matthews & M. O'Neill (Eds.), *Prostitution* (pp. 189–224). Aldershot, Hants, UK; Burlington, VT: Ashgate/Dartmouth.

Peng, Y.-W. (2007). Buying Sex: Domination and Difference in the Discourses of Taiwanese Piao-ke. *Men and Masculinities, 9*(3), 315–336.

Rubin, G. (1993). Thinking Sex: Notes for a Radical Theory of the Politics of Sexuality. In H. Abelove, M. A. Barale, & D. M. Halperin (Eds.), *The Lesbian and Gay Studies Reader* (pp. 3–44). London: Routledge.

Sanders, T. (2007). The Politics of Sexual Citizenship: Commercial Sex and Disability. *Disability & Society, 22*(5), 439–455.

Sanders, T. (2008). *Paying for Pleasure: Men who Buy Sex.* Portland: Willan Publishing.

Sullivan, E., & Simon, W. (1998). The Client: A Social, Psychological, and Behavioral Look at the Unseen Patron of Prostitution. In J. E. Elias, V. L. Bullough, V. Elias, & G. Brewer (Eds.), *Prostitution: On Whores, Hustlers, and Johns* (pp. 134–155). Amherst, NY: Prometheus Books.

Ueno, C. (2003). Self-determination on Sexuality? Commercialization of Sex among Teenage Girls in Japan. *Inter-Asia Cultural Studies, 4*(2), 317–324.

Vanwesenbeeck, I. (2001). Another Decade of Social Scientific Work on Sex Work: A Review of Research 1990–2000. *Annual Review of Sex Research, 12,* 242–289.

Waskul, D. D. (2003). *Self-games and Body-Play: Personhood in Online Chat and Cybersex.* New York: Peter Lang.

Weatherall, A., & Priestley, A. (2001). A Feminist Discourse Analysis of Sex Work. *Feminism & Psychology, 11*(3), 323.

Winick, C. (1962). Prostitutes 'Clients' Perception of the Prostitutes and of Themselves. *International Journal of Social Psychiatry, 8*(4), 289–297.

Women and Men in Hong Kong Key Statistics. (2016). Hong Kong: Census and Statistics Dpeartment.

Xantidis, L., & McCabe, M. P. (2000). Personality Characteristics of Male Clients of Female Commercial Sex Workers in Australia. *Archives of Sexual Behavior, 29*(2), 165–176.

CHAPTER 4

The *Brothers*—Part II:
Why Compensated Dating?

After comparing the major reasons for men to pay for compensated dating (CD) and commercial sex in general, let us now turn the focus on the unique features of CD, *Brothers'* personal and behavioral patterns, and the sociocultural factors that are related to the transformations of intimacy, sexuality, and gender relationships in contemporary Hong Kong society that have induced *Brothers* to choose CD over other forms of commercial sex even though they were usually less costly and conveniently available in Hong Kong. Examining these interrelated features is useful in understanding why CD has become rampant in recent years. I will first elaborate on the highlighted *girlfriend experience (GFE)* in CD and how *GFE* shapes *Brothers'* conceptualization of their CD behaviors and themselves. Then, I will discuss how a new female biography and the modern notion of the pure relationship, which underscores sexual and emotional equality, have gradually eroded traditional gender patterns and have threatened men's hegemonic masculinity, which lead men to seek a refuge—CD—to polish their male identity and anchor their emotional life. The *Brothers'* narratives will illuminate how the traditional ideology of 'men are the protectors and women are the protected' is restored and men's masculinity is reconstructed through the enactment of *GFE* provided in CD. Finally, I will discuss how technological advancement has allowed the phenomenon of CD to blossom. Before discussing the social milieus that lead men to partake in CD, let us consider their personal perceptions on commercial sex, which predispose them to CD.

© The Author(s) 2018
C. S. K. Chu, *Compensated Dating*, Gender, Sexualities
and Culture in Asia, https://doi.org/10.1007/978-981-10-6974-1_4

EXPERIENCE OF PURCHASING SEX

Men in this study can be categorized into two extreme groups in terms of their sexual behaviors prior to their involvement in CD: One had no experience of purchasing sex, the other had extensive experience in patronizing prostitution or casual sex. 19 *Brothers* (63.3%) had never purchased sex before they took part in CD. Amongst them, all except one had never engaged in sexual activities outside the context of a committed relationship. Two of them did not even have any sexual experience before they involved in CD. What happened in these men's lives that had broken their traditional moral code, prompted them to step into a taboo sexual world, and practised 'abnormal' and 'condemned' sexuality? For these men, their initial CD encounter signifies their first time to be located outside the privileged charmed circle and to be situated in the 'abnormal' or 'pathologized' outer limits of Rubin's (1993) sex hierarchy. It represents a decision to explore something that is new, uncertain, unfamiliar, or unknown, and, more significantly, it marks the milestone for adventuring into a sensitive social taboo and enacting a socially deviant behavior. The initiation of CD is therefore significant not only in a practical sense, but also in a symbolic sense that marks their experimentation with a deviant sexual identity. Don, 40, years old said:

> Engaging in CD for the first time is like opening a door. Some men may never open this door. However, once it is opened, you are being exposed to a whole new world, a world of taboo sex.

The contexts of engaging in CD are crucial in the sense that they function as a key that opens the 'door of taboo sex', which unleashes men to break the regulative monogamous regime to experiment different sexual practices and to enjoy the fluidity of sexuality while preserving their mores through CD. Peter, 36 years old, explained how CD emerged as a new opportunity for sexual adventure that was previously unavailable to him:

> When I was young, I wasted all my time on studying and missed out on the chance to experience 'girls hunting'. My wife was my first and only sexual partner at the time of marriage. CD gives me a chance to experience what I should have experienced when I was young.

According to traditional codes of sexuality, sex should only occur within the context of a marital relationship. That was probably why Peter did not engage in sexual intercourse prior to his marriage. Today, there has been a transformation in the meaning of sexuality. The traditional restraints have become relaxed such that recreational sex and non-marital sex are more tolerated, if not accepted. Such a change in the cultural atmosphere has encouraged Peter to forge his individual sexual pleasures through CD, which represents a new avenue for him to explore the possibility of sexuality freely without or with fewer moral burdens, stigma and social restraints.

While 19 *Brothers* had not engaged in recreational sex or paid sex before they partook in CD, 11 *Brothers* (36.7%) had numerous experiences in casual sex or in patronizing different forms of prostitution, including one-woman brothels, call girls, and massage parlors in Hong Kong, Mainland China, Macau, and other places in East Asia before they engaged in CD. These men consider CD as a contemporary way to seek young sexual partners or as a new commercial sex model that has emerged from a constantly evolving sexual culture:

> I played around a lot when I was young. I was a tour guide in Asia. I patronized prostitutes everywhere. (Leon, 43 years old)

> I have been engaging in commercial sex since I was sixteen. I just enjoy having sex with different girls. CD is a popular way to find casual sex partners nowadays. (Jeremy, 28 years old)

> For me, CD is just a contemporary model of commercial sex. The old mechanism, whatever it was, had practically gone. Sooner or later, CD will be obsolete and another new sexual model will replace CD. I am just going with the trend. (Ben, 32 years old)

Regardless of their experience in purchasing sex, all *Brothers* reported curiosity as a major motivational factor for them to engage in CD for the first time. Many of them reported that they had heard a lot about CD from the news and the media, which provoked their desire to find out what CD is and to 'try it':

> Initially, it was because of curiosity. The media had widely reported CD after a girl was being killed by her male client, so I was like… 'What is CD?' 'Who are these girls engaging in CD?' (Jack, 28 years old)

> All of a sudden, there were a lot of reports on CD. Although I had been patronizing prostitution for a long time, the reporters portrayed CD as if it is something very exciting and mysterious. So, I was curious about it, and I was tempted to try it. (Ben, 32 years old)

The media often reported incidents about adolescent girls engaging in CD. I had always wondered whether or not the reports were true and if it was true that there were so many young girls selling sex. (Sam, 32 years old)

While 25 *Brothers* purposefully searched CD information online after their curiosity was ignited by widespread media reports, five men accidentally came across online CD forums or online CD discourse that had aroused their curiosity:

At first, I thought the online forum was simply a 'normal' social networking site, but I realized that it was about CD very soon. After reading several girls' posts and clients' reports, I became curious and wanted to try it. My first CD encounter happened just two days after I had discovered the forum. (Harvey, 33 years old)

I was browsing an (non-CD) online discussion forum one day and there were people talking about CD, which had aroused my curiosity. One of them posted a link to the CD forum. So, I clicked the link and browsed the CD forum. That was how I got started in CD. (Edward, 33 years old)

Curiosity was a crucial factor which incited men's interest in CD, yet curiosity alone was not sufficient to actualize and sustain men's CD behavior. It must be considered with the nature of CD. All the *Brothers* who had purchased sex in traditional forms of prostitution found that their prostituting experiences were unpleasant or unsatisfying, and therefore they favored CD: 'I have patronized all forms of commercial sex that are available in Hong Kong. I prefer CD to any other paid sex,' commented Sam, 32 years old. Nick, 23 years old, explained why CD is not only the latest, but also the best, model of commercial sex:

I would not remember the face of the sex workers in one-woman brothels or the process of our sexual encounters, but I would remember the face of every *CC* and experience in CD. Moreover, I could perhaps start a friendship or a romantic relationship with the *CC* after our CD date.

This relatively dynamic and intense emotional experience is produced by *girlfriend experience* (*GFE*).

GFE is a very important feature of CD. It is a seemingly authentic emotional and physical connection that simulates and produces some genuine desire, pleasure, and erotic aspects in a conventional, non-commercial romantic relationship. *GFE* is not a unique feature of CD; it is also sold in traditional forms of sex work (Elizabeth Bernstein, 2007; Huff, 2011). Prostitution, especially indoor-based prostitution, is not merely the supply and purchase of physical intimacy, but also emotional intimacy (Elizabeth. Bernstein, 2010; Campbell, 1998; Lever & Dolnick, 2010; Sanders, 2008a). However, most *Brothers* drew a clear line to separate the experiences and services that they received in CD from that in conventional prostitution. In the specific context of Hong Kong, although Kong's (2006) study of 13 female sex workers have already shattered the myth that prostitutes sell only sex and have indicated that 'providing care, concern and offering a sympathetic ear to clients seem to be essential skills in their work' (p. 420), *Brothers* still perceived that traditional sex workers offer merely 'fast food sex'; namely, fast, cheap, convenient, standardized, and impersonal sex that renders efficient, predictable, calculable female bodies to consume (Hausbeck & Brents, 2002). A client in Blanchard's (in Monto, 2000, p. 80) study said prostituting is 'like going to McDonald's; most people are looking for a good quick cheap meal. It's satisfying it's greasy, and then you get the hell of there.' Many *Brothers* in this study shared such sentiment and all *Brothers* who had patronized conventional forms of prostitution reported that the services that they received were merely a series of standard procedures that was being performed mechanically and repeatedly without 'heart' or passion by the sex workers. Their sexual performance was strictly physical and unemotional. Sam, 32 years old, explained:

> Traditional sex workers are too used to sex. It's a mundane task for them. They are too professional. Although they put a lot of efforts to serve me, I could clearly feel that they treated me like a statue. There was a lack of emotional connection. At first, I thought I could simply be satisfied by having sex with a variety of women but, as it turned out, I could not.

Sam's narration answered Giddens' (1992, p. 202) rhetorical question: 'Who can live without passion...?' Sam desired the type of sexual experience that is infused with passion and that is marked by 'a generic connection between love and sexual attachment' (Giddens, 1992, p. 37). *GFE* in CD draws upon and accentuates such ideal such that *Brothers* found their CD experiences emotionally satisfying. When asked why they engaged in CD but not other forms of commercial sex, Ali, 30 years old, explicated:

I am seeking the feeling of courtship rather than pure sex. My reason of not patronizing one-woman brothels in Hong Kong and prostitution in China is that the women there are professional who mechanically provide standard sexual services indiscriminately to all clients. They never ask or care about my feelings and preferences. In other words, I would receive services that they choose to provide, not the services that I want. Moreover, sex is something that is expected to happen. There is no surprise to it. However, in CD, there is a kind of anticipation as if I was pursuing a girl. The journey started from gaining her attention to finally winning her sexual favors. For example, there was a CC who declined to have sex and only agreed to dine out with me at the beginning. It was not until our third date that she finally agreed to have sex with me. Although the progress was still a few steps quicker than that in conventional courtships, it had already given me a sense of anticipation. Sometimes, the CC would adjust her schedule in order to accommodate mine. I feel like there is someone who would make changes in her life just for me.

It could be deduced from Ali's account that an important element that differentiates CD from prostitution is that the former is embodied in conventional heterosexual scripts, which offer less mechanical and more sensual and personalized experience. Although CD is theoretically a commercial encounter, it is practically enacted to be experienced as a noncommercial romantic encounter and *GFEs* are the props that turn CD relationships into what some *Brothers* consider to be an egalitarian, conventional, private relationship (Sanders, 2008b). From the *Brothers'* perspectives, the less business-like nature of CD and the custom-made *GFEs* make CD a model that is preferable to the other commercial sex models. Harvey, 33 years old, said:

I want to find a girl who can provide genuine emotions and fulfill my sexual needs at the same time. I guess the sex workers from one-woman brothels cannot give me girlfriend feel. Although I have not been to a one-woman-brothel before, I am sure that the ladies there would not hang out with me outside the brothel. For *CCs*, I can at least meet them up on a street, dine with her, and have conversations with her before having sex with them.

For the *Brothers*, GFE in CD is more attractive because it draws upon not only the sexual and erotic compulsion in passionate love, but also elements of conventional courting rituals. Even if traditional forms of sex work provide more than physical sex and offer emotional intimacy, they seldom incorporate conventional courting rituals. That is the reason why, despite both CD and traditional forms of sex work offer *GFE*, the *GFE* in CD is unique and more intense. Ben, 36 years old, further explained how *GFE* in CD is different from that in prostitution. While the former integrates the psychic communicative elements in romantic love, the latter does not:

> The problem of one-woman brothel is that it merely resolves your physical needs, and nothing else. After half an hour, she kicked me out. I felt like something was missing. There was really no room for communication and emotional interaction. In contrast, each of my CD encounter normally lasted for two hours, which allowed us to know more about each other. The *CCs* were willing to spend time with me. For many *Brothers*, like me who feel empty and lonely, it is really a great feeling that the *CCs* are willing to listen, to talk, and to care about us.

GFE is about a joining together of the bodies and souls (whether authentic or inauthentic is another issue that will be discussed in the next chapter). CD allows *Brothers* to cultivate plastic sexuality alongside passionate love and romantic love. This complex experience constitutes the major part of their pleasures and primary motivations to engage in CD: 'I did not mind paying more if I can experience *GFE*,' said Johnny, 40 years old, because '*GFE* is a surreal experience!' echoed Peter, 36 years old.

GFE is 'surreal' because romantic love, which is something desired by *Brothers*, is gradually fragmented and replaced by confluent love in conventional modern intimacy (Giddens, 1992). Men tend to prefer romantic love because of their privileged position in relation to women. The relationship of romantic love has always been imbalanced in gender terms as it is embedded in the division of social spheres and the differentiation of power relations in which women are subordinate and men are dominant. The fostering of romantic love is predominantly the task of women, who unilaterally service men. In confluent love, however, men no longer enjoy their privileged position because this form presumes equality between the two genders such that both men and women should put equal efforts to work at the heterosexual intimate relationship. Some men find confluent love too demanding. Peter, 36 years old, complained:

> I can't take care of the children and do housework during weekdays because I have to go to work. So, during weekends, my wife expects me to stay at home to do the household chores and spend time with her and the children. I have to 'apply for leave' from her if I want to play football with my

friends during weekends. Home becomes a battlefield in which I have to fight after the battle at work... CD provides an emotional comfort for me. It is a place where I can relax and be myself.

The nature of love in Peter's marriage was more like a companionate love and less like a romantic love. The erotic compulsion between him and his wife had also vanished. It was only through CD that he could experience romantic love with other women while still maintaining a companionate and marital relationship with his wife.

Since unconditional and romantic love is becoming more difficult and demanding to achieve in an increasingly fragmented and individualized society, some *Brothers* rely on *GFE*, which embraces plastic sexuality, romantic love, and passionate love, but without the efforts and responsibilities required in contemporary non-commercial intimate relationship, as a source of emotional support, even though *GFE* might be transient, episodic, and inauthentic.

Destigmatization: CD vs. Prostitution, *CCs* vs. Sex Workers, and *Brothers* vs. Clients

One consequence of *GFE* is the destigmatization of CD behaviors, *CCs*, and *Brothers*. The dynamic interactions between *CCs* and *Brothers*, as well as the simulations of conventional courtship rituals, create an illusion for CD participants that CD is a non-commercial romantic encounter rather than a form of prostitution. Wilton (1999) pointed out that within society's normative moral framework, one is not expected to pay for sex or to charge for sex, those who engage in commercial sex are thereby condemned. The element of romance and the sense of mutual sexual compulsion provided in *GFE* serve to suspend the commercial nature of CD such that all *Brothers* in this study conceptualize CD differently from prostitution, which is still considered as a stigmatized institution in late modernity (Holzman & Pines, 1982; Pitts, Smith, Grierson, O'Brien, & Misson, 2004). When asked whether they perceive *CCs* as sex workers, the answers of all *Brothers* were negative. Interstingly, some *Brothers* were unable to rationalize and articulate the nature of CD, the role of *CCs*, and the identity of themselves, if they are not prostitution, sex workers, and clients, respectively. Ivan, 34 years old, illustrated this perplexity:

Cassini:	Do you regard *CCs* as sex workers?
Ivan:	This thought has never come across my mind.
Cassini:	Then, how do you see them?
Ivan:	I do not know how to answer this question.
Cassini:	Do you feel like you are frequenting prostitution when you are engaging in CD?
Ivan:	I have never had such feeling. I do not know why but I just do not classify *CCs* as sex workers and CD as prostitution.

Harvey, 33 years old, attempted to clarify the role of *CCs*:

> I think *CCs* are just normal girls. There is no need to categorize/label them. I mean some people think that they are prostitutes, but I just don't see them in that way. They are different from prostitutes.

CCs are considered to be 'normal girls', who enacted plastic sexuality, rather than sex workers whilst CD is conceptualized as a means to endorse plastic sexuality rather than prostitution.

The separation of CD from prostitution, a socially deviant behavior, is particularly important because such segregation has attracted a group of men, especially those who are affected by the negative connotations of prostitution and therefore have never purchased sex before CD, to initiate CD. As mentioned earlier, more than half (19) of the *Brothers* had no history of buying sex before they engaged in CD because these men perceive the idea of patronizing prostitution as morally repugnant. Even after they have engaged in CD, they still despise prostitution and discriminate clients and workers of prostitution.

It is worthwhile to re-emphasize that all *Brothers* in this study believe *CCs* are intrinsically different from sex workers. Sam, Victor, and Patrick offered quite good illustrations of how most *Brothers'* differentiate *CCs* from sex workers:

> Subjectively, I don't perceive *CCs* as sex workers. I feel like they are my friends whom I can pay for sex. (Sam, 32 years old)

> Girls involved in CD are not sex workers. They are just normal young girls and schoolgirls. They are purer and much more innocent than sex workers. (Victor, 34 years old)

> Sex workers are dirty; girls involved in CD are not. (Patrick, 33 years old)

Here, the notion of 'dirty' comes from the presumption that sex workers are being prostituted for numerous times by many different men every day. They regard sex workers as 'vulgar' women who are willing to have sex with whoever pays. They believe that sex workers enter into frequent sex trades every day and thus are 'used' by too many different men. Similarly, in Peng's study of prostitution in Taiwan, some clients 'felt that prostitutes are "dirty" in the sense that they run a higher risk of contracting sexually transmitted diseases, a view that is shared by the public and that explains why some men never buy sex' (Peng, 2007, p. 328).

In addition to being prostituted for numerous times, the negative stereotypes of clients who patronize prostitution, which is then transferred to the sex workers, are another cause of the sentiment of 'dirtiness' that *Brothers* have imposed on sex workers:

> *Terry:*   Sex workers in one-woman brothels are dirty. They might have more chances of having STDs. Who knows what kinds of people with whom they have had sex? They could be construction workers or other blue-collar men from lower socio-economic classes.
>
> *Cassini:*   You do not know what kinds of people have had sex with the *CCs* too. So, what is the difference?
>
> *Terry:*   I DO know the *Brothers*. Most of us are well educated and from the middle class. We are not perverted. I know it because I have talked to them and interacted with them on the CD forum. I have even met some of them! We are different!

All *Brothers* in this study share Terry's sentiment, which indicates not only that *Brothers* make a distinction between *CCs* and sex workers, but also that *Brothers* see themselves as being different from prostitutes' clients. *Brothers* believe that they are more respectable than other clients because they tend to be more educated, have a more decent job, and have a higher disposable income (CD costs triple or more than one-woman brothel). *Brothers* assert that they have more morally upright personal characteristics than conventional clients in the world of commercial sex. Hence, in order to safeguard their moral identity, it is important for *Brothers* to draw a distinction between themselves and clients of prostitution. These perceptions about sex workers and clients certainly do not have empirical credentials; however, such stereotypical conceptions are prevalent among *Brothers* and explain why some men buy sex at the moment in the history when CD emerges but not previously.

It should be clear by now that, the 'whore stigma' is vividly present in *Brothers'* discourse surrounding prostitution and because of this entrenched 'whore stigma' in *Brothers'* mind, the distinction between *CCs* and sex workers is particularly critical to explain their engagement in CD, but not other forms of commercial sex. All *Brothers* perceive *CCs* as normal, ordinary, innocent, and pure teenage girls or young women who do not have sex with just any man who pays, but only with men whom the girls feel comfortable and connected with. Instead of conceptualizing the *CCs* as 'dirty', *Brothers* commonly endorse the idea of 'clean' to describe *CCs*. Leon, 43 years old, said:

> Sex workers engage in commercial sex in a full-time basis. They have sex with numerous clients each day! *CCs* are different. Most of them do not engage in CD every day. Some of them engage in CD only once or twice a month. So, *CCs* are cleaner and cannot be considered as sex workers.

This sentiment is echoed by Taiwanese clients in Peng's (2007) study, who often mentioned that CD girls are 'cleaner' than full-time sex workers. Both groups of *Brothers* in Taiwan and Hong Kong believed that *CCs* engage in commercial sexual encounters less frequently than conventional sex workers. The frequency of being prostituted is crucial in men's differentiation between *CCs* and sex workers. The fewer the number of times of being prostituted, the better. Therefore, *CCs* are preferable to sex workers and attract men who have never buy sex before to engage in CD.

From *Brothers'* perspectives, *CCs* are much more selective with regard to whom they have sex with. *CCs* have the power to choose and reject their clients, whereas sex workers usually do not; accordingly, *CCs* are fundamentally different and more morally respectable than sex workers. *Brothers* believe that *CCs* agree to go on a CD date and have sex with a *Brother* not only because of money, but also because of emotional attractions and romantic feelings that are developed through virtual communications and offline non-sexual interactions. While romantic feelings between clients and sex workers might also be found in conventional settings of commercial sex, these feelings have usually developed after the clients become regulars and unlikely to embark before their first physical encounter (Sanders, 2005). In other words, while the romantic attraction that arises in prostitution is a consequence and seldom the

cause of sexual encounters, in CD, it is both the cause and a consequence. There is a widespread assumption among the *Brothers* that
romantic attraction is a not a decisive factor for sex workers to receive a
client, but it is a determining factor for *CCs* to decide to go on a CD
date with a *Brother*. Although one may say that it is simply a myth that
Brothers created, it is vital in formulating *Brothers'* subjective experiences
and meanings of their CD behaviors and identities. *Brothers* feel that if
they are being "chosen" by a *CC*, there must be something special about
them. Such belief gives them sentiments of excitement, pride, and privilege. Don, 40 years old, noted:

> Many *Brothers* said it's very hard to date Apple (a *CC*) because she is very
> selective about her clients. She only goes out with guys who are tall and
> good-looking. But somehow, she was willing to go out with me. I was
> thrilled.

Such senses of thrill and privilege are unlikely to emerge when patronizing
prostitution because *Brothers* assume that sex workers are always available
for sex indiscriminately at a price. *Brothers* tend to take the sexual availability and obligation of sex workers for granted and do not expect sexual
rejections from sex workers. Hence, the thrill of being accepted as clients
is generally not present in the context of traditional forms of commercial
sex. The context of CD is different, however, since *CCs* are not always
available and willing to provide sexual favors and companionships to any
men, some *Brothers* feel excited simply by being able to date a *CC* successfully, which marks the kickoff of their CD experience.

In addition to the 'power' and 'selectiveness' of *CCs* in the aspect of
choosing their clients, a related factor that leads *Brothers* to deny *CCs* as
sex workers and CD as a form of prostitution is the transitory availability
of *CCs*. Many *Brothers* believe that although most girls voluntarily involve
in CD, they do so only because of emergent situations such that they
would end selling their bodies and companionships once they have earned
enough quick cash to overcome their financial hardships. Ben, 36 years
old, said:

> I don't see *CCs* as sex workers because they engage in CD for a very short
> period of time. CD is not their job. Many *CCs* engage in CD because they
> have a debt or need a certain amount of money for some reasons. Once they
> got that money, they would leave. But sex workers generally wouldn't leave
> the commercial sex field easily because they sell sex for daily subsistence.

The ephemeral and sporadic availability of *CCs* in the commercial sex market separates them from conventional sex workers and makes *CCs* more exotic. *Brothers* perceive a *CC* as if she was a limited edition product—if they missed out on the rare opportunity to purchase it when it is on the market, the opportunity would be lost forever. In the same sense, if *Brothers* do not grasp the fleeting chance to date a particular *CC* when she is still on the CD market, the chance of dating her will be gone forever. Such sentiment makes *CCs* unique among sex workers and CD unique among other forms of commercial sex.

Another rationalization that the *Brothers* frequently used to deny that their CD behavior is a form of prostituting is that they believe CD does not necessarily entail sex whereas prostitution always involves sex. During our interviews and communications, *Brothers* often emphasized their non-sexual CD experiences as if they wanted to persuade me that CD is not the same as prostitution:

> The girl said she was having her period. So, I didn't have sex with her. I was fine with that. We had dinner together instead. (Edward, 33 years old)

> We cuddled each other and watched TV in a hotel room. We did not have sex, but we had a nice time. (Derrick, 35 years old)

> On one occasion, I did not want to have sex with the girl because I missed my ex-girlfriend so much. So, we just talked and cuddled each other. (Rooney, 28 years old)

In these CD encounters, even though sexual intercourse did not take place as agreed and expected, all *Brothers* paid the *CCs* the agreed amount of payment in full. *Brothers* reasoned that sex is the essence and is almost an obligation in prostitution whereas sex is not a requisite or the primary focus in CD. As such, *Brothers* think that CD and prostitution are essentially different activities, and thus they deny that they were buying sex or prostituting in CD. Such sentiment predisposed men, particularly those who have high level of prejudice about prostitution, to initiate CD. Accordingly, their CD behaviors are detached from the stigma associated with purchasing sex. By disassociating CD from the model of prostitution, *Brothers* also disassociate themselves from men who buy sex, whose behaviors are regarded as morally inappropriate in the normative world (Wilton, 1999).

Ueno (2003) contended that the term *enjo kosai*, or *compensated dating*, helps to normalize men's purchase of sex, which entails male deviant sexual practices and desires according to the social standard of morality.

Enjo kosai or CD reduces the negative connotation of prostitution because the terms trivialize the financial aspect of the sexual transaction whilst emphasizing the emotional aspect of interpersonal relationships, social networking, as well as assistance and support. *Brothers'* moral burden is mitigated by locating CD in the category of charity and generosity to help the poor rather than in a discreditable and stigmatized category, which is how it would usally be categorized by the general public. Moreover, while the word 'prostitution' is sometimes understood as something men do to women or a form of male exploitation, victimization, oppression, subordination, and degradation of women (Barry, 1988; Dworkin, 1989; Jeffreys, 2008), the term *enjo kosai* or CD implies a sense of reciprocity, which does not upset the power balance between the *CCs* and the *Brothers*. This notion is illustrated by Ben, 36 years old, who said: 'I consider *CCs* as people who need my help and at the same time, I also need their help. I help them financially and spiritually while they help me sexually and spiritually.' As such, the gender relations implied by the term *enjo kosai* or CD is more interactive and more equalitarian.

In practice, in addition to direct monetary payment in exchange for (sexual) services, CD can emerge as a form of barter. Barter, particularly a gift barter, does not involve exact calculations of value, and therefore, dilute the commercial sense as opposed to a straightforward cash payment (Swader et al., 2013). The business nature of CD is, in many senses, hidden, especially when there is no direct exchange of cash. As such, there are discrepancies between men's subjective perceptions of CD and conventional forms of prostitution, as well as of *CCs* and sex workers. Kent, 41 years old said:

> I helped one *CC* to pay for her tuition. I transferred the tuition to her school bank account and she showed me the tuition statement. She didn't take a dime!!! She didn't want money. She just wanted to continue her education. Moreover, she seldom asked me for cash. If she wanted to buy something, she would tell me and then I would buy it for her. For instance, before we went to a vacation, she wanted to buy a new luggage. So, we went shopping for luggage together, and I paid for it. She had never asked me for cash. Again, cash was not what she wanted; it was a particular commodity or experience that she desired. She even rejected me when I suggested giving her some cash so that she could buy whatever she wanted during our trip in Japan!

Since the intention to purchase sex can be disguised by the intention to help young women in the context of CD, all *Brothers* consider themselves different from conventional male clients. They have constructed a hierarchy of male clients, with themselves, the *Brothers*, at the top. At the bottom of the hierarchy are all other male clients of commercial sex exchanges. The *Brothers* perceive themselves as more respectable than other types of clients because they are not merely looking for physical pleasure generated from *work sex* or impassionate sex, but also looking for emotional connection and intimacy. Moreover, engaging in CD reduces the typical 'loser image' of men who buy sex because as Eric, 39 years old, mentioned: '*Brothers* need to win the *CCs* for sexual favors, not just buy them.' From *Brothers'* perspectives, receiving sexual favors from *CCs* reflects not only the financial power of the *Brothers*, but also their personal charisma, which polishes their masculinity.

MASCULINITY

The online and offline spaces of CD allow men to create multiple masculinities that might not be plausible in conventional setting because of various personal and social constraints. Connell (1995, p. 71) suggested that 'rather than attempting to define masculinity as an object (a natural character type, a behavioral average, a norm), we need to focus on the process and relationships through which men and women conduct gendered lives'. Since masculinity is a configuration of practice organized in relation to the structure of gender relations, it is important to look at the relationships and power differentiation between the two sexes, which has undergone radical changes in response to the direct challenge of women's emancipation in late modernity (Connell & Messerschmidt, 2005).

Although contemporary Hong Kong society is still being influenced by Confucian and Taoist values and structures, it is also reshaped by the changes and circumstances of more recent socio-economic developments, as well as by the forces of Westernization, modernization, industrialization, and the women's rights movement in the West and modern China (Koo, 1985; Westwood, Ngo, & Leung, 1997). Under these influences, Hong Kong women have made dramatic changes in their roles in the past few decades, which have in turn led to concomitant changes in cultural expectations for men and women and for the wider sociocultural conditions, such as the labor market, family structures, and gender relationships.

Even though there is still some gap before gender equality can be fully attained and that it is far too optimistic to say that women have transcended the role of domestic labor, which remains as the drudgery for many women even at the beginning of the twenty-first century (Dunphy, 2000), many traditional restrictions on women have been alleviated and the material, existential, relational, and attitudinal statuses of women have improved (Westwood, 1997). While men dominated in the public arena in the past, women have gradually come into play in the public sphere in Hong Kong society. Although women's share is not as big as men's, women have at least been working toward the progress of equality. Men may still enjoy some privileges in some social domains, but they no longer have as much power and control that they used to have over the means of production and in most cases, over the labor of women (Westwood et al., 1997). Since women today have better educational access and economic resources, they can become a provider on their own. The ideologies that women's 'proper' place is at home and that women are dependent on the male 'breadwinner' have turned around. Women do not necessarily have to rely on men anymore; or at the very least, women are not as dependent on men as before financially and socially. Thus men's traditional hegemonic masculinity is being threatened.

Men experience crisis in their masculinity not only in the public sphere, but also in the private sphere. Today, marriage is no longer the only destiny for women. In Hong Kong, women have been getting married later, having children later and having fewer children (refer to Fig. 4.1). According to the report created by Census and Statistic Department (*Women and Men in Hong Kong Key Statistics*, 2016), the number of never married women aged 15 and over had drastically increased by 62.4% during 1986 to 2015. As increasingly more individuals received more education and entered into the labor force, the median age at first marriage for women had steadily increased for both women and men between the period of 1981 and 2015. The median age at first marriage for women had risen from 23.9 in 1981 to 29.3 in 2015 while that for men had shifted from 27.0 in 1981 to 31.2 in 2015. These figures reflect that more women and men decided to be single and married at a later age. Giddens (1992) suggested that young women do not speak much about marriage 'because they are participants in, and contributors to, a major reorganization in

在個別年齡組別內每千名女性的活產嬰兒數目
Number of live births per 1 000 women in respective age group

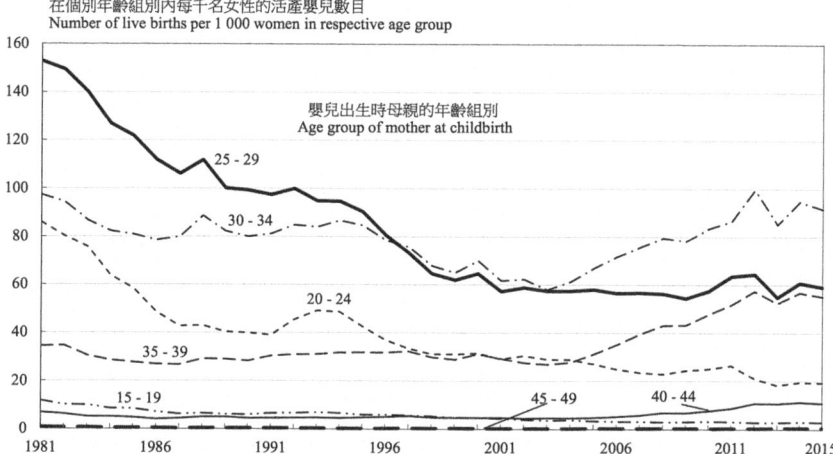

Fig. 4.1 Fertility rates at specific ages, 1981–2015 (From Women and Men in Hong Kong Key Statistics (2015: 48) by Census and Statistics Department)

what marriage, and other forms of close personal tie, actually are. They talk of relationships rather than marriage' (p. 57–58). The increasing trends of later age of marriage for women and women being single are also likely to be associated with the progress towards better educational access for women (refer to Fig. 4.2) and the trend that more women enter into the work force. In Hong Kong, the proportion of women in the labor force had increased from 42.8% in 1971 (S.-C. Ho, 1984) to 54.5% in 2013 (*Thematic Household Survey Report No. 52*, 2013), which may reflect a transforming social trend as well as women's desire to continue their independence, freed from child-rearing responsibilities, and for women to pursue full-time employment longer (Westwood et al., 1997). As Beck and Beck-Gernsheim (1995) pointed out, the new individual female biography, which is inclined against the tradition gender roles and male-centered social reality, has created threats to male masculinity and insecurities of their own social position for men.

The changes in women's social role and position inevitably change the cultural expectations of being a man and heterosexual intimate relationships. Because of the increased individuality and financial dependence of women, more and more women are unwilling to take the subordinate role in interpersonal relationships. They require a more democratic and

千人
Thousands

性別／教育程度 Sex/Educational attainment	1986	1991	1996	2001	2006	2010	2011	2012
女 Female								
未受教育／學前教育 No schooling/ Pre-primary	430.9 (21.4%)	404.5 (18.5%)	371.9 (14.4%)	310.6 (10.8%)	264.6 (8.6%)	245.3 (7.5%)	235.9 (7.1%)	216.1 (6.4%)
小學 Primary	576.6 (28.6%)	547.8 (25.0%)	587.5 (22.7%)	620.9 (21.5%)	597.4 (19.4%)	579.0 (17.7%)	569.8 (17.1%)	579.5 (17.1%)
初中[2] Lower secondary[2]	274.2 (13.6%)	281.2 (12.9%)	353.1 (13.7%)	409.1 (14.2%)	449.9 (14.6%)	466.2 (14.2%)	466.5 (14.0%)	469.0 (13.9%)
高中[3] Upper secondary[3]	572.8 (28.4%)	735.5 (33.6%)	904.2 (35.0%)	1 027.5 (35.6%)	1 092.6 (35.4%)	1 208.0 (36.9%)	1 240.3 (37.3%)	1 266.8 (37.4%)
專上教育（非學位課程）[4] Post-secondary (non-degree)[4]	111.4 (5.5%)	132.6 (6.1%)	179.3 (6.9%)	199.8 (6.9%)	237.4 (7.7%)	225.1 (6.9%)	226.8 (6.8%)	232.6 (6.9%)
專上教育（學位課程） Post-secondary (degree)	50.4 (2.5%)	85.9 (3.9%)	190.6 (7.4%)	315.4 (10.9%)	440.7 (14.3%)	551.3 (16.8%)	585.3 (17.6%)	620.6 (18.3%)
總計 Total	2 016.4 (100.0%)	2 187.5 (100.0%)	2 586.6 (100.0%)	2 883.4 (100.0%)	3 082.6 (100.0%)	3 274.9 (100.0%)	3 324.6 (100.0%)	3 384.7 (100.0%)

Fig. 4.2 Women Aged 15 and Above by Educational Attainment (From Women and Men in Hong Kong Key Statistics (2012: 60) by Census and Statistics Department)

egalitarian intimate relationship in which men share practical and emotional responsibilities in the maintenance of the well-being of intimate relationships, as well as the demands of marriage-related, child-rearing, and nurturing roles (F. M. Cheung, Lai, Au, & Ngai, 1997).

This new demand from women, along with their resistance to the traditional role of an obedient wife (Confucian ideology demands women to obey their husband after marriage), and/or to be a good wife, a good mother and a good daughter-in-law exclusively, have challenged male supremacy as men no longer have absolute power and control over women in the social and interpersonal spheres. Moreover, while men's 'rights' over women have gradually decreased, their 'obligations' have increased. Maintaining the traditional hegemonic paradigm of manhood in light of the changing gender structure in late modern Hong Kong society is thus difficult.

The transformation in women's social status and the power relation in gender relationships, along with the uncertainty and changeability in Hong Kong political, social, and economic environments, have made men insecure about their masculine role, self-identity, as well as social positions. To help them ward off anxiety and avoid the feeling of powerlessness, men need to reclaim the absolute power and control in certain domains. One important constituents of hegemonic masculinity is sexual prowess; CD helps *Brothers* to strengthen this sexual prowess and thus polish their masculinity. Through 'clienting', *Brothers* are able to select from abundance of young women choices, which is a privilege that is usually not available in *Brothers'* everyday conventional contexts. CD is therefore a plausible site for men to re-enact hegemonic masculinity, which allows men's dominance over women to continue (Connell & Messerschmidt, 2005). Moreover, *CCs*, are easier to control such that it is easeier for *Brothers* to display their male dominance from men's perspective, partly because the *CCs* are generally young, innocent, and sexually inexperienced, and partly because they are paid to play the obedient role. Some *Brothers* prefer CD over non-commercial relationships and traditional forms of sex work because modern women and professional sex workers seem to exercise too much control over themselves and the sex, which might threaten men's masculinity. *CCs* on the other hand, do not usually present such threat. Sam, 32 years old, said:

> *CCs* are generally sexually inexperienced and therefore, they can still have fun with sex. Some *CCs* know very little about sex, probably because they have just engaged in CD for a very short while or they seldom engage in CD. They sort of know the rules, sort of know what to do, but they are still very innocent about lots of things. So, I have to teach them.

Sam's desire for *CCs* is similar to some men's desire for child prostitutes over adult prostitutes. A male client in O'Connell Davidson's (2003, p. 197) study revealed:

> They (child prostitutes) are not innocent, but they are fresh. They don't have the attitude of the older whores. Little girls, they are not experienced. They want to please you, they don't know what to expect, you get a better service from them.

The advantage of *CCs* and child prostitutes, from clients' perspectives, lies in their innocuous and inferior social status. Because of their youth and their ignorance of sexual matters, *CCs* or child prostitutes do not present threats to men in the same way as adult prostitutes and adult women in a non-commercial setting. Thus, men would have fewer pressures in sexual performance and achievement, which explains why some men engage in CD or other forms of commercial sex. They pay sex to enjoy, not to please. Men did not need to perform or to be as 'considerate' of the sex workers as they would have to be in non-commercial settings (Peng, 2007). This sentiment is further exacerbated in commercial encounters with sexually naïve *CCs* and child prostitutes because men do not have to confront the presumably sexually experienced adult sex workers such that they can take the dominated role again and re-establish or strengthen their masculinity. Consequently, through CD, *Brothers* can reclaim their control and fortify hegemonic masculinity that they may not be able to achieve in contemporary society where women have increasingly become men's competitors rather than subordinates.

Technological Evolution

Technological advancement and the increasing prevalence of the Internet have facilitated the growth of the sex industry and have transformed the commercial sex model in late modernity. Some *Brothers* said that although they had heard a lot about prostitution, especially one-woman brothels in the past, they did not know how to actualize it or did not have the courage to visit the brothels, either because of the fear of being socially stigmatized or because of the 'filthiness' of the establishment of the brothels. The emergence of CD has greatly reduced men's fears and embarrassments because CD is largely mediated by the Internet, which allows them to be anonymous during their exploration of recreational sex. Men no longer have to visit the "filthy" establishments for paid sex.

Cooper (1998) identified three core characteristics of the Internet that make it so powerful in the domain of sexuality: anonymity, affordability, and accessibility. He named this triad as 'the triple A engine'. *Anonymity* refers to the hidden identity of Internet users, allowing individuals to explore sexuality without people knowing their 'true' identities. In the virtual CD community, all *Brothers* take on identities and names that are different from those in their normative world:

> My colleague told me not to register in CD forums with my real name. He created a nickname for me, which I have been using until now. (Don, 40 years old)

> My real name is Alvin. Please do not disclose it to Mary (a *CC* who introduced us). She only knows me by my online name. (Alvin, 23 years old)

The anonymous nature of the Internet provides an escape from surveillance such that men feel free and safe to explore, experiment, discuss, and share their sexual fantasies and CD information. Anonymity is a critical feature in the model of CD, which appeals to many *Brothers*, particularly to those who have never patronized prostitution previously due to its stigma. *Affordability* means the availability of low cost or free services and materials that are related to sexuality online. Men can get CD information or communicate with various *CCs* online at no cost. *Accessibility* pertains to the ease of access to the Internet at any time with few geographical constraints. The online CD forum is a milieu without time, space, physical, and structural limitations. It is an open enabling environment with lots of possibilities that are unlikely to be made possible in an offline setting. While many *Brothers* who work in an office use their personal computers to constantly stay connected with the virtual CD community during office hours, those who work outside an office manage to stay connected with the virtual community with their smart phones or other mobile communicative devices. The evolution of technology contributes to the dynamic and instant interactions amongst CD participants and makes CD negotiations easier and more convenient than ever before.

The effects of the 'triple A engine' also permits *CCs* and *Brothers* to interact both before and after the actual CD encounters take place, which is rarely observed in the contexts of conventional commercial sexual exchanges. Virtual communication embarks *CC–Brother* relationships before they physically meet and allows their relationship to foster after their CD encounter. It is through this virtual communication that many *Brothers* feel emotionally connected with the *CCs*, even in situations where they meet each other for the first time: 'Since the girl and I had talked through msn for a period of time before we actually met, I felt like we were very closed already, so there was no embarrassment,' said Victor, 34 years old. Edward, 33 years old, further explained how virtual communication is a unique and important feature of CD:

> I had talked with this girl on MSN for three weeks before I met her for the first time. The communication was really important as it made me feel more comfortable and made the whole encounter more natural. It's unlike other kinds of commercial sex exchange.

Accordingly, virtual communication can foster positive and warm interpersonal connections, including romantic feelings, which may indeed carry over into 'real life' (Alvin Cooper & Sportolari, 1997). The intense cybercommunications therefore gives a significant advantage to the model of CD compared to other forms of commercial sex.

The following example from Don, 40 years old, demonstrates how all three aspects—personal, socio-cultural changes and behavior patterns—of the casual structure effect simultaneously to induce men initiation in CD:

> When I first started CD, my wife was pregnant with our second child. During my wife's first pregnancy, we didn't have sex because we thought sexual intercourse might harm the fetus. But, of course, we were wrong, as we later found out that pregnant women can have sex as usual. In the third month of my wife's second pregnancy, my wife wished to resume our normal sex life. Rationally, I knew it was fine to have sex with her; however, emotionally, I did not want to do it while she was pregnant because our child was inside her womb! I couldn't overcome this idea. I just thought it was weird. In spite of my psychological discomfort, I unwillingly had sex with my wife upon her request. You know, pregnant women are especially prone to mood swings and depressions, so for my wife's emotional well-being, I did have sex with her although I did not want to. I mean I did have sexual needs and I still had sexual desires for my wife. I just didn't feel like having sex with her while she was pregnant. The feeling was just not good.
>
> My male colleague was aware that I was emotionally down during that period of time, so one day he showed me the CD forum and suggested me to browse through it. He said it might help. That was how I got started in CD. To date, I have never patronized prostitution, but CD is a different thing. Let's put it this way, if my colleague had never introduced CD to me, I wouldn't have paid sex even though I was frustrated about my sex life. However, if I had a satisfied sex live, I wouldn't have the incentive to initiate CD even if my colleague recommended CD to me. But at that moment, everything just occurred at the same time!

In Don's case, the fact that her wife was pregnant (personal), his despair (personal), his discomfort of having sex with his pregnant wife (personal), his desire for emotional sustenance (personal), the instance that his colleague recommended the CD website to him (external stimulus), the ease of contacting *CCs* and accessing CD information online (sociocultural), his rebuff and discrimination against prostitution (personal and behavioral pattern), his perceptions that CD is different from prostitution and that the girls involved in CD are different from sex workers (personal), as well as his sexual abstention during his wife's first pregnancy (behavioral pattern), all functioned as co-factors that caused his initiation into CD. Any co-factor alone would not be sufficient to instigate Don to step into the CD field and open the 'the door of taboo sex'.

Discussion

This chapter has examined how *Brothers'* individual perceptions on prostitution and various social transformations in contemporary Hong Kong society, including women's role and status, gender pattern, and technological evolution, have created a milieu that predisposes *Brothers* to engage in CD.

Apparently, curiosity is an important personal factor that induces men's initiation in CD. Yet it is not the only one. A necessary and unique attitude that is shared by many *Brothers* explains why men, especially those who condemn and therefore shun prostitution, to pay for CD but not other forms of prostitution, is the denial that CD is a form of prostitution. On the one hand, removing CD from the institution of prostitution helps to reduce the stigma that is culturally attached to men who buy sex. On the other hand, relegating CD to the institution of plastic sexuality assists participants to justify their CD behavior.

Despite the general public perception that CD is merely an euphemism of adolescent prostitution, none of the *Brothers* hold this opinion. For the *Brothers*, prostituting literally means the buying of sex, which is not the crux but merely a derivative of CD; therefore, paying for CD is not the same as prostitution. From *Brothers'* perspectives, CD is a contemporary avenue to form intimate relationships with the opposite sex and a new opportunity to experience emotional intimacy and plastic sexuality, rather than a channel to obtain impersonal physical and sexual gratification.

The segregations of CD from prostitution, and *CCs* from sex workers play an important role in men's initiation of CD because mainstream culture remains a zone where commercial sex is still considered as an immoral and stigmatized behavior on the part of men, even though the general public is more likely to accept non-marital sex than in the past as sexuality has become more plastic and recreational in late modernity (Giddens, 1992). By denying CD as a form of prostitution and denying *CCs* as sex works, men's moral burden is lessen and the "whore stigma" is removed; henceforth, they have justifications to step into the field of CD while still preserving their personal integrity.

The separation of CD from the institution of prostitution and *CCs* from sex workers concomitantly separates *Brothers* from men who patronize prostitution. All *Brothers* perceive themselves as being different to and classier than conventional clients because they feel that they belong to a higher socio-economic class due to the higher price of CD than conventional prostitution. They also claim to seek deep emotional intimacy rather than superficial physical gratification. More importantly, they believe the nature of relations between *Brothers* and *CCs* is different from that between clients and prostitutes. While *CC–Brother* relationships are generally more egalitarian, mirroring certain aspects of conventional intimate relationships or pure relationships (Giddens, 1992), sex worker–client relationships are generally unequal with the power lying on the hands of the clients, reflecting impersonal business contracts. Unlike conventional clients who buy (unilateral) sexual pleasures, *Brothers* believe that they are cultivating a genuine emotional intimacy in CD.

Technological evolution in late modernity has precipitated men to initiate CD and changed their behavior patterns. The easy access, anonymity, and affordability of the virtual CD community help individuals to escape from social surveillance and therefore have attracted a group of men who have never engaged in commercial sex before to enter into CD. The effects of the 'triple A engine' have also contributed to the dynamic relationships and emotional intensity between *CC* and *Brothers* because they allow *CC–Brother* interactions to take place outside the restricted physical and commercial boundary, which not only leads *Brothers* to believe that *CC* is different from prostitutes, it also generates a major source of *Brothers'* pleasure.

In modernity, where the gender patterns are currently undergoing tremendous changes, CD provides a space where men can retrieve and strengthen hegemonic masculinity, which is being jeopardized, in contemporary Hong Kong society. Hong Kong society is trammeled by traditional Chinese norms as well as Western values. Although the values, beliefs, and attitudes of Hong Kong people are premised on Confucian and Taoist value systems and Chinese traditions, they have also been heavily infused with Western influences, the forces of modernization, industrialization, and the women's movements. Women's socio-economic status has been steadily climbing up and the traditional gender role has been eroding. The cultural expectations for being a man have changed. On the one hand, they have to compete with not only men, but also women in the public sphere. On the other hand, they are expected to share the emotional responsibilities in the private sphere which have traditionally been regarded as women's obligations. Some men are therefore insecure about their masculine position in both the public and private realms. In CD, men's masculine and paternalistic roles can be restored because *CCs* are more easily controllable due to their youth, sexual inexperience, and unsophisticated minds, and, more importantly, they were paid to enact the traditional scripts of gender role and intimate relationships, where women are subordinate to men. Accordingly, men's desire to engage in CD not only stems from their sexual fantasies for young girls, but is also linked to the effects of an increasingly complex and chaotic nature of intimacy, the changing gender structure, social environments, and the cultural expectations of being a man in contemporary Hong Kong society. CD relationships serve as a compensation for men's disempowerment in conventional gender relationships and other aspects of life.

BIBLIOGRAPHY

Barry, K. (1988). Female Sexual Slavery: The Problem, Policies and Cause for Feminist Action. In E. Boneparth & E. Stoper (Eds.), *Women, Power and Policy: Towards the Year 2000* (pp. 282–306). London: Pergamon Press.

Beck, U., & Beck-Gernsheim, E. (1995). *The Normal Chaos of Love*. Cambridge: Polity Press.

Bernstein, E. (2007). Buying and Selling the Girlfriend Experience: The Social and Subjective Contours of Market Intimacy. In M. Padilla, J. Hirsch, M. Munoz-Labboy, R. Sember, & R. Parker (Eds.), *Love and Globalization: Transformers of Intimacy in the Contemporary World*. Nashville: Vanderbilt University Press.

Bernstein, E. (2010). *Temporarily Yours: Intimacy, Authenticity, and the Commerce of Sex*. Chicago: University of Chicago Press.

Campbell, R. (1998). Invisible Men: Making Visible Male Clients of Female Prostitutes in Merseyside. In J. E. Elias, R. N. Vern, L. Bullough, V. Elias, & G. Brewer (Eds.), *Prostitution: On Whores, Hustlers, and Johns* (pp. 155–171). New York: Prometheus Books.

Cheung, F. M., Lai, B. L. L., Au, K.-c., & Ngai, S. S. Y. (1997). Gender Role Identity, Stereotypes, and Attitudes in Hong Kong. In F. M. Cheung (Ed.), *Engendering Hong Kong Soceity: A Gender Perspective of Women's Status* (pp. 201–235). Hong Kong: Chinese University Press.

Connell, R. W. (1995). *Maculinities*. Cambridge: Polity Press.

Connell, R. W., & Messerschmidt, J. W. (2005). Hegemonic Masculinity: Rethinking the Concept. *Gender & Society, 19*(6), 829–859.

Cooper, A. (1998). Sexuality and the Internet: Surfing into the New Millennium. *CyberPsychology & Behavior, 1*(2), 187–193. https://doi.org/10.1089/cpb.1998.1.187.

Cooper, A., & Sportolari, L. (1997). Romance in Cyberspace: Understanding Online Attraction. *Journal of Sex Education and Therapy, 22*(1), 7–14.

Dunphy, R. (2000). *Sexual Politics: An Introduction*. Edinburgh: Edinburgh University Press.

Dworkin, A. (1989). *Pornography: Men Possessing Women*. New York: Plume New York.

Giddens, A. (1992). *The Transformation of Intimacy: Sexuality, Love and Eroticism in Modern Societies*. Standford, CA: Stanford University Press.

Hausbeck, K., & Brents, B. G. (2002). McDonaldiztion of the Sex Industries? The Business of Sex. In G. Ritzer (Ed.), *McDonaldization: The Reader* (pp. 91–106). Thousand Oaks, CA: Pine Forrest Press.

Ho, S.-C. (1984). Women's Labor Force Participation in Hong Kong, 1971–1981. *Journal of Marriage and the Family, 46*, 947–953.

Holzman, H. R., & Pines, S. (1982). Buying Sex: The Phenomenology of Being a John. *Deviant Behavior, 4*(1), 89–116.

Huff, A. D. (2011). Buying the Girlfriend Experience: An Exploration of the Consumption Experiences of Male Customers of Escorts. *Research in Consumer Behavior, 13*, 111–126.

Jeffreys, S. (2008). *The Idea of Prostitution*. North Melbourne, Australia: Spinifex.

Kong, T. S. K. (2006). What it Feels Like for a Whore: The Body Politics of Women Performing Erotic Labour in Hong Kong. *Gender, Work & Organization, 13*(5), 409–434.

Koo, L. C. (1985). The (non) Status of Women in Traditional Chinese Society. *Bullentin of the Hong Kong Psychological Society, 14*, 64–70.

Lever, J., & Dolnick, D. (2010). Call Girls and Street Prostitutes: Selling Sex and Intimacy. In R. Weitzer (Ed.), *Sex for Sale: Prostitution, Pornography, and the Sex Industry* (2nd ed., pp. 187–204). New York\London: Routledge.

Monto, M. A. (2000). Why Men Seek Out Prostitutes. In R. Weitzer (Ed.), *Sex for Sale: Prostitution, Pornography, and the Sex Industry* (pp. 67–83). New York: Routledge.

O'Connell Davidson, J. (2003). Eroticizing Prostitute Use. In R. Matthews & M. O'Neill (Eds.), *Prostitution* (pp. 189–224). Aldershot, Hants, UK; Burlington, VT: Ashgate/Dartmouth.

Peng, Y.-W. (2007). Buying Sex: Domination and Difference in the Discourses of Taiwanese Piao-ke. *Men and Masculinities, 9*(3), 315–336.

Pitts, M. K., Smith, A. M. A., Grierson, J., O'Brien, M., & Misson, S. (2004). Who Pays for Sex and Why? An Analysis of Social and Motivational Factors Associated With Male Clients of Sex Workers. *Archives of Sexual Behavior, 33*(4), 353–358.

Rubin, G. S. (1993). Thinking Sex: Notes for a Radical Theory of the Politics of Sexuality. In H. Abelove, M. A. Barale, & D.-M. Haplperin (Eds.), *The Lesbian and Gay Studies Reader* (pp. 3–44). London: Routledge.

Sanders, T. (2005). *Sex Work: A Risky Business*. Cullompton: Willan Publishing.

Sanders, T. (2008a). Male Sexual Scripts: Intimacy, Sexuality and Pleasure in the Purchase of Commercial Sex. *Sociology, 42*(3), 400.

Sanders, T. (2008b). *Paying for Pleasure: Men who Buy Sex.* Portland: Willan Publishing.

Swader, C. S., Strelkova, O., Sutormina, A., Syomina, V., Vysotskaya, V., & Fedorova, I. (2013). Love as a Fictitious Commodity: Gift-for-Sex Barters as Contractual Carriers of Intimacy. *Sexuality & Culture, 17*, 598–616.

Thematic Household Survey Report No. 52. (2013). Hong Kong: Census and Statistics Department.

Ueno, C. (2003). Self-determination on Sexuality? Commercialization of Sex among Teenage Girls in Japan. *Inter-Asia Cultural Studies, 4*(2), 317–324.

Westwood, R. I. (1997). The Vertical Dimension and Theoretical Accounts of the Sexual Division of Labour at Work. In F. M. Cheung (Ed.), *Engendering Hong Kong Society: A Gender Perspective of Women's Status* (pp. 101–156). Hong Kong: Chinese University Press.

Westwood, R. I., Ngo, H.-Y., & Leung, S.-M. (1997). The Gendered Segmentation of the Labour Market. In F. M. Cheung (Ed.), *Engendering Hong Kong Society: A Gender Perspective of Women's Status* (pp. 41–100). Hong Kong: Chinese University Press.

Wilton, T. (1999). Selling Sex, Giving Care: The Construction of AIDS as a Workplace Hazard'. In N. Daykin & L. Doyal (Eds.), *Health and Work: Critical Perspectives* (pp. 180–197). New York: St. Martin's Press.

Women and Men in Hong Kong Key Statistics. (2016). Hong Kong: Census and Statistics Dpeartment.

CHAPTER 5

The *Brothers*—Part III: Becoming and Being a *Brother*

Existing studies on men who buy sex have largely focused on men's personal and social characteristics. While some researchers developed client typologies, others examined men's reasons for purchasing sex, their condom use behavior, and their risk of the transmission of human immunodeficiency virus (HIV) or other sexually transmitted diseases (STDs) (Leonard, 1990; Faugier & Cranfield, 1995; Albert, Warner, & Hatcher, 1998; Belza et al., 2008; Lau, Siah, & Tsui, 2002). As mentioned in Chap. 3, there are still other studies that differentiated clients from non-clients, suggesting a difference in certain personal characteristics between the two groups of men (Pitts, Smith, Grierson, O'Brien, & Misson, 2004; Monto & Hotaling, 2001; Ward et al., 2005). For instance, Xantidis and McCabe (2000) indicated that compared to non-clients, male clients of brothels in Australia showed lower levels of social-sexual effectiveness, higher levels of sensation-seeking behavior, and a significantly less feminine sex-role orientation. However, even if clients do possess some *characteristics* that predispose them to prostituting, these *characteristics* cannot be imported indiscriminately to understand the *characteristics* of *Brothers* because of the specific cultural and social qualities of CD. Since clients' experiences vary depending on the particular social organization of the commercial sex in which they engage, the experiences of the *Brothers* in CD deserve separate

© The Author(s) 2018
C. S. K. Chu, *Compensated Dating*, Gender, Sexualities
and Culture in Asia, https://doi.org/10.1007/978-981-10-6974-1_5

attention from that of clients of other forms of commercial sex. Moreover, although existing studies on clients have provided important insights on the general *characteristics* of the client demography, their motivations, the external factors precipitating their commercial sexual behavior and its health consequences, the process of becoming a male client and the issues of how men come to understand their role in relation to the sex workers have received less attention.

Given the increasing trend of the phenomenon of CD in Hong Kong and other Asian cities, and the emergence of a group of newcomers, who had never purchased sex before the rise of CD, to the commercial sex market, men's pathway into CD, and their subjective meanings of their experiences and roles shall be investigated. *Brothers* represent the demand side and are therefore, the crucial actors in CD. At an immediate level, *Brothers'* personal meanings of various aspects related to CD are central to the understanding of the phenomenon of CD. On the broader level, *Brothers'* desire and experiences in CD have important implications on men's sexuality and the construction of their masculinity in late modern society.

Since *Brothers* are not simply passive agents who receive sexual and emotional services provided by the *CCs,* but are active agents, constantly involve in the process of CD to create their experiences, I conceptualize the *Brothers* as self-asserting individuals who continuously negotiate their desires and responses according to their subjective meanings and interpretations of the actions of other CD participants, particularly the *CCs.* The relationships that *Brothers* have with other CD participants are reflexive and negotiable because the personal meanings and interpretations that they give to their interactions are not homogeneous, but are dependent on each other's behaviors and various situational factors. Accordingly, CD is projected as a social process of complex web of interactions between the *Brothers* and *CCs,* amongst the *Brothers,* and amongst the *CCs.* Drawing on the narratives of both *Brothers* and *CCs,* this chapter continues to interpret the personal meanings that *Brothers* construct for their CD behaviors, the self, and *CCs,* and how these subjective interpretations affect their CD experiences, interactions, and relationships with the *CCs.*

THE PROCESS OF BECOMING

The many guises of becoming and being a *Brother* are intriguing as they reveal the complexities of the social organization of CD, *CC–Brother* relationships and how men's CD behaviors can be an enactment of hegemonic masculinity. Men go through various psychological and phenomenological phases during the process of becoming a *Brother*. Drawing from my interviews and ethnographic data, I have identified three major stages of how a man becomes a *Brother*. The first stage is *exploration*, during which newcomers learn the CD script, perspectives, and culture by observing existing CD posts, CD discourse, and interactions among CD participants in the virtual CD community and/or by consulting other CD participants, especially the more experienced *Brothers*. The second stage is *actualization*, a stage in which men take actions to negotiate and arrange a CD encounter with a *CC* and learn the practical skills and tactics necessary to proceed CD through direct interactions with a *CC*. The last stage is *protection*, a stage in which *Brothers* perform the role of guardians to protect *CCs* from potential risks in CD and to preserve the social order in the virtual and non-virtual CD community.

It should be noted that not every *Brother* goes through all three of these stages. Some never completely go through the first exploration stage (being unable to date a *CC* successfully despite a long period of online observation and/or online interactions with the *CCs*), and some stop at the actualization stage. The following sections discuss men's personal experiences in each stage of the process of becoming a *Brother*.

STAGE I: EXPLORATION

An online CD forum was the first place where most *Brothers* would learn about the operation of CD. While some *Brothers* encountered the CD forum inadvertently or through unsolicited links when they were surfing the Internet, others intentionally sought out the CD forum. Either way, after the initial encounter of the CD forum, all except one *Brother* spent a period of time, ranging from a few weeks to a few months, exploring the CD forum before they actualized their first CD date. Victor, a 34-year-old man, said: 'I kept reading *CCs'* posts and *Brothers'* reports prior to my first attempt to contact and date a *CC*.'

Online CD participants, whether *Brothers* or *CCs*, who only read the posts, reports, and CD discourse, but not 'talking' or 'contributing' to the

CD forum are known as *CD-Rom*. This type of online users is not unique in the virtual CD community as it can also be found on other commercial sex-related online sites. For example, in the context of the first UK-based website to facilitate the exchange of information on prostitution in the UK, people who simply read and use the information without contributing are known as *lurkers* (Sanders, 2008).

While some men take a silent, hidden, and passive role, others take a more active role in the virtual CD community. Besides reading CD posts and information, they engage in CD discourse and communicate with other online CD participants. Sam, 32 years old, described:

> I simply typed, 'compensated dating' (in Chinese), in the Google search engine. At first, I thought there would be lots of related forums, but to my surprise, there were only two. I registered in both forums and started to spend a lot of time reading peoples' posts and chatting with the girls and other *Brothers* in *cbox* (the instant chartroom within the online forums).

Some newcomers also seek advice from more experienced CD participants. For example, Rooney, 28 years old, said:

> Before my first time dating a *CC*, I spent one and a half months to try to understand what CD is and how CD works by chatting with other *Brothers* and *CCs*. I also read a lot of posts on the forum. If I came across something that I did not understand, I asked. I asked all types of questions until I got a thorough understanding of the CD tactics.

However, their questions sometimes go unanswered. Cyrus, 42 years old, reported:

> After spending two weeks on reading the posts and reports, I finally had the courage to add a *CC's* MSN; however, since I had no experience in CD before, I sent a private message to an experienced *Brother* and asked if he knew whether or not this *CC* was a 'real' *CC* (non-agent *CC*) or undercover police, etc. However, the *Brother* didn't give me any response. Anyways, I just went ahead and dated this *CC*. I told her that it was my first time engaging in CD.

It is not uncommon for *Brothers* to become completely immersed in the CD forum, especially at the beginning of their exploration. Ben, 32 years old, said he was addicted to the virtual CD community; he dedicated a considerable amount of time and energy each day to read the posts and reports on the CD forum, to communicate with online CD participants, and to add newly joined *CCs* into his MSN accounts:

> I was addicted to the CD forum. I connected to the forum once I returned home from work. After I ate and showered quickly, I would chat with the CD participants again until I fell asleep.

From the perspective of men, one of the major appeals of CD is that they can chat with various *CCs* without any structural constraint and financial cost. The virtual CD community allows men to connect with *CCs* outside the temporally and commercially bounded physical context. This quality makes CD and *CC–Brother* relationships significantly different from traditional forms of commercial sex and conventional sex worker–client relationships, respectively.

After exploring the virtual CD community for a period of time by reading *CCs'* posts and *Brothers'* reports, and/or consulting and exchanging CD information with other online CD participants, men should have grasped a general idea of their roles as *Brothers* as well as the procedures, operations, culture, and tactics in CD, which include: the language, rules, and restrictions of the CD world; how to choose a *CC*; how to differentiate individually operated *CCs* from *Agent girls*; how to contact a *CC*; how to arrange a CD encounter; when to pay a *CC*; what to do and what not to do during the CD encounter; how a 'good' *Brother* should behave; how to treat a *CC*; how to win a *CC's* trust; how to avoid undercover police and reporters; the ideal *CC–Brother* relationship; the possible consequences of overattachment to a *CC*; and, finally, how to prevent CD relationships from interfering with *Brothers'* personal private life and relationships.

According to the *Brothers' narratives* and my cyber-ethnography, *Brothers* are keen to engage in chit-chat with the *CCs*. Yet a significant part of the CD discourse is constituted among *Brothers* rather than between the *Brothers* and the *CCs*. The *Brothers* explained that this is because the *CCs* are usually too busy negotiating CD with potential clients in MSN. Many *CCs* have neither the time nor the interest to entertain and engage in casual chats with men who do not appear to be potential clients.

Generally speaking, a *CC* receives numerous MSN messages from various *Brothers* every day. It is not uncommon for a *CC* to receive over a hundred MSN messages within the course of just a few days. After receiving the messsages, she has to spend a great deal of time sorting out the messages, replying to CD inquiries, as well as negotiating and setting up CD dates with potential clients. From the *Brothers'* perspectives, the major purpose for the *CCs* in being online in MSN is to look for potential trades. When a *CC* is online in MSN, she is probably communicating with multiple *Brothers* simultaneously. As such, a *CC* seldom engages in casual chat in MSN with *Brothers* who do not intend to trade because her time has already been taken up by *Brothers* who intend to trade. Nick, 23 years old, explained:

> If a *Brother* is not serious in trading but merely looking for casual chats, it annoys the *CCs* because it's a waste of their time. The reason for *CCs* to get online in MSN is to seek clients, not to make chitchat with *Brothers*. If *CCs* want to have chitchat, I suppose they would rather chat with their own friends, using their personal MSN account, not their CD MSN account(s).

CCs in this study have confirmed Nick's insight that *CCs* generally feel annoyed with non-CD-related solicitations. Crystal, 20 years old, complained:

> When the *Brothers* asked me some non-CD-related questions, I felt like they were wasting my time. What's the point of asking me 'what are you doing?' It's none of their business! Even when some men asked me the price or some basic personal information, I also felt very annoyed. These information were all stated in my post! So, I just told them to read my post first before talking to me. I am tired of answering their questions of which they could find all the answers in my post. I think *Brothers* who ask me such basic questions are not sincere about dating me because it implies that they have not read my post carefully.

Similarly, Doris, 26 years old, commented:

> I used to find clients' MSN messages annoying. It was really bothersome. I mean there were lots of messages. I didn't even know how to start. Then some *Brothers* would suddenly ask, 'oh, why are you not replying my message?' or sent '???' to me. I would become furious and replied, 'I am not talking with you only. Can't you wait?'
>
> Now, it's better, because my attitude has changed. It was much crazier in the past. I mean I had many more clients in the past. Now, I try my best to reply every client politely unless he is impolite or just trying to engage in casual chat with me without any intention to trade.

The CCs also confirm Nick's observation that it is common practice for *CCs* to have more than one MSN account: a personal one for non-CD socializing and at least one other for CD interactions. Katy, 28 years old, reported:

> I have several MSN accounts in order to denote the period of time and the website from which I know the clients. For instance, if a client is in my Account #1, then I instantly know that I met him from 'forum ABC' during the early stage of my CD career. I have taken on different personas and different online names in various forums. So, having different MSN accounts helps me manage the clients more effectively. And of course I have a private MSN account to communicate with my friends outside CD. I don't disclose this personal account to clients.

During the exploration stage, *Brothers* learnt that it is not appropriate to initiate casual conversations with the *CCs* in MSN, unless this is initiated by the *CCs*. However, it is acceptable to chat with *CCs* in *cbox*, an instant chatroom, a space for synchronous communication on the CD forum. Rooney, 28 years old, said:

> I seldom engage in casual chat with a *CC* in MSN because I believe that she is *talking* with probably 30 other *Brothers* at the same time. Even if I see her online, I would not want to bother her and stay in her way of negotiating CDs with other *Brothers*. If I want to date a *CC*, I would directly ask her if she wants to trade with me. If she is OK, then we would compromise over the date, time, and venue of the CD date. That's it. I never initiate to talk about other meaningless matters. Like, I wouldn't ask her, for example, 'have you had dinner yet?' I feel like it is very inappropriate. If I ask such non-CD-related question, I believe she will be very annoyed. If I want to chat with the *CCs*, I will go to *cbox*, not through MSN.

As illustrated, CD has its own communication etiquettes. The exploration stage helps men to understand the operational mode of CD and the dos and don'ts in the CD culture, which can greatly facilitate men's interaction with *CCs*, to become a member of the CD community, and most importantly, to actualize a CD date.

STAGE II. ACTUALIZATION

Once men familiarize themselves with the CD culture, they will normally begin the process of actualizing a CD date, after which they will officially be recognized in the CD arena as a *Brother*. It is at this stage that they enact the CD norms and tactics, and must now practise the CD script that they have learnt in the exploration phase.

Amongst all the 30 *Brothers* in this study, Kelvin, 24 years old, was the only one who had not yet actualized a CD date at the time of the interview despite his various attempts to interact with several *CCs*:

> I have added many *CCs* to my MSN account, but I have seen only a few of them online. I don't want to arrange a CD date so hastily because, you know, it's a lot of money. I want to chat with them for a while to make sure that we click and that she is the type of girl that I like before I actually date her. However, most *CCs* seemed like they didn't want to talk to me. Anyways, I will keep searching for one.

Kelvin had probably failed to actualize a CD date because he did not follow the CD etiquette and gave a wrong impression to the *CCs* that he just wanted to make chit-chat rather than trading with them. From the perspective of *CCs*, such attitude and behavior is a reflection of an 'insincere' *Brother*. Ben, 36 years old, explained:

> You have to understand that the major incentive for girls to engage in CD is money. You have to fulfill this need first before you want something from them. *Brothers* who are being rejected by *CCs* are those who do not show enough sincerity to express their intention to date them. No *CC* would bother dealing with insincere *Brothers*.

Actualizing an encounter in CD is not as quick and convenient as in conventional prostitution. While the conventional commercial sex model has conditioned clients to expect instant sexual gratification from sex workers, the CD model conditions men to anticipate for days or even months before they meet a *CC*, especially in the past when information technology was not as advanced and CD was not as common. According to the *Brothers* who have longer histories in the CD field, it was not unusual to take several weeks to communicate and negotiate with a *CC* for a CD date. Kent, 41 years old, recalled his early experience in CD:

Back in 2009, there was much less information about CD than there is today. Today, the CD forums make it so easy to find and date a *CC*. However, in the past, it was not that convenient. We didn't have an instant chatroom. There was no synchronous communication with the *CCs* and we could only rely on *CCs'* posts to know about them. My first *CC*, her name was Bernice. Her contact method was via email... yeah, I know, none of the *CCs* use email nowadays, but at that time, I would say approximately half of the *CCs* were using email as their method of contact. Anyhow, after I read Bernice's post, I emailed her. We had exchanged emails for more than a month before we actually met. The communication through email was not as interactive and quick as in MSN. So, it took a much longer time to date a *CC* back then. The interaction between *Brothers* and *CCs* was not as direct as it is today.

With the help of advanced information technology and the adoption of quicker communicative tools, interactions amongst CD participants have become increasingly dynamic and intense. The more direct and immediate communication has a profound impact on *CC–Brother* relationships and on the commercial sex market in general. It has facilitated the spread of CD information, has shortened the period of time needed to actualize a CD date, and has reduced, if not eliminated, the need for a pimp or middleman to arrange a CD date between *Brothers* and *CCs*. All these changes resulted from technological evolution have contributed to the blossom of the phenomenon of CD.

Today, *Brothers* and *CC* no longer depend on emails to communicate. Before the end of 2014 when MSN Messenger (later known as Windows Live Messenger) was discontinued, CD participants most commonly made use of this platform to initiate communication. During the exploration stage, potential *Brothers* would generally obtain and add numerous *CCs'* contacts into their MSN accounts. Sam, 32 years old, indicated:

> At the very beginning of my CD life, I added the *CCs'* into my MSN account indiscriminately. Once I saw a *CC* on *cbox* (the instant chatroom), I would add her; once I saw a new *CC* post, I would add her, even without actually reading her post. I had more than four hundreds *CCs'* contacts on my MSN list.

In contrast, some *Brothers* are more selective. Terry, 35 years old, said:

I opened a new MSN account specifically for contacting the *CCs*. I didn't just add every girl. I only added the girls whom I think they are my types after carefully reading their posts. I think I had added over a hundred girls.

After adding the *CCs* to their MSN accounts, men have to wait for the *CCs* to be online in MSN. Once the *CCs* are online, the *Brothers* will initiate conversations and/or negotiate a CD date with them. Michael, 32 years old, said: 'When I saw a *CC* online, the first thing I would do was to look at her MSN profile picture. If she was quite good looking, then I would ask her for a CD date.'

A *Brother* and a *CC* usually negotiated all the details of a CD date in MSN, which include price, date, time, venue, and services. After they had agreed upon everything, they would exchange telephone numbers to facilitate later communication. On the day before the actual CD date, the *Brother* had to contact the *CC* to reconfirm the date. Indeed, some *Brothers* would even confirm the date once again on the day of the encounter. This 'confirming' step was extremely important as the case of Derrick, 35 years old, illustrated:

> The first time when I dated a *CC*, I knew nothing. I mean I didn't aware of the unarticulated CD norms. Anyway, one day, I had set up a CD date with this *CC* and we arranged to meet up at a subway station on the following Friday 7pm. I think that was it. So, on Friday, I arrived at the subway station on time. I waited for half an hour, but no one showed up. I called her, but she did not answer the phone. I did not know what went wrong. I did not know what to do. So, I continued to wait. Another half an hour later, she called me and asked me if our date was today. I said yes and she exclaimed: 'you need to confirm it! It's not like a week ago you said our date is this Friday 7pm, and then the date is firmed. You have to reconfirm it before the prearranged CD date!' Then, she said she could arrive in half an hour and asked me if I could wait. I agreed and I continued to wait. So, on my first CD date, I had waited for the *CC* for one and a half hour in a subway station.

The 'confirming' procedure is not only necessary to actualize a CD date, but also useful to rekindle and establish the interaction and connection between the *Brother* and *CC*. The initial 'confirming' procedure enacted by the *Brother* and the following responds from the *CC* are highly appreciated by both *parties,* especially if it is the first time they meet each other, as these behaviors provide a sense of reassurance and sincerity for each other.

Unlike in one-woman brothels and with call girls, *Brothers* and *CCs* do not wait for each other in a brothel or in a hotel room. They often meet at a subway station, a mall, a café, or a location near the hotel that they will head to. Meeting outside a commercial boundary mirrors aspects of conventional social relationships. It is a quality that attracts *Brothers* and separates CD from conventional prostitution. Meeting in non-commercial setting not only provides emotional pleasures for men, but also mitigates the stigma of CD and normalizes CD. Andrew, 26 years old, said:

> The circumstance when I met a *CC* for the first time was just like the situation when I first met you (Cassini). Just when we were about to meet, we would talk on the phone, describe our looks, the colors of our outfits, etc. until we identify each other.

In contrast to conventional prostitution, the activities involved in CD are often more spontaneous and free-flowing. *Brothers* and *CCs* may engage in social activities that are not prearranged. *Brothers* often get a sense of thrill and satisfaction from these activities as these are not a part of the obligations of *CCs*. Since *Brothers* do not pay for these kinds of random non-sexual and non-commercial activities, they regard these activities as a bonus, making *Brothers* feel special about themselves and the CD date: 'After the sex, this *CC* said she was hungry. So, we went to eat. Then, she suggested going to a movie. I was so surprised. I had a great time with her!' said Isaac, 30 years old. Isaac's experience is a perfect example to showcase the difference between a CD date and a traditional form of paid sexual encounter which, as Peng (2007) pointed out, ends in the client's ejaculation.

In CD, many *Brothers* seek mutuality not only in terms of sex, but also in terms of an emotional bond with the *CCs*. Reciprocal sex constitutes only part of an ideal CD encounter; verbal communications and non-sexual interactions are equally important. Such non-sexual interactions are vital to the *Brothers'* conceptualization of their CD behaviors as they help *Brothers* to rationalize that CD is different from prostitution where (sexual) action is all that is required (Browne & Minichiello, 1995). As such, verbal and relational exchanges are something that ought to occur on a CD date.

It is worth noting again that for 19 *Brothers* in this study, their first CD encounter was their first time to purchase sex and, in the case of two *Brothers*, their first CD encounter also represented their first sexual encounter. For these *Brothers*, the whole CD process was a new life experience, which had developed a new sexual identity and self-identity for them. Harvey, 33 years old, stated:

> At the beginning, I knew nothing. I didn't know where I could find an hourly love hotel, as I had never been to one before. It was the *CC* who led me to one. So, everything was new to me! I was thrilled.

Unfortunately, there are two sides to this coin. While the initial CD experience can create thrills, excitement, and a positive experience, it can also create nervousness, anxiety, and a feeling of loss for first-timers. Michael, 32 years old, revealed:

> I felt like an idiot on my first CD date. Not only the waiting of the *CC*, but the whole process. I had no clue about the procedure, so I was a bit nervous. It was the *CC* who led me up to a hotel. When we were inside the room, she told me what I should do. Everything we did was her call. After the sex, she said she had to leave, so we left. I remembered that even after the sexual encounter when we were ready to leave the room, I still acted like an idiot because I was very naïve at that time. 'Happy' definitely could not be used to describe my first CD experience. I engaged in CD because I wanted to be relaxed and happy, unfortunately, I didn't have such feelings. All I had was the feeling of being an idiot.

Feeling 'like an idiot' is not a good experience, but it is certainly not the worst. Ryan, 33 years old, for example, described his initial CD encounter as miserable and greatly disappointing:

> This *CC* actually met all my requirements, the appearance, age, etc. But once she took off her clothes, I was immediately scared off. Her body was full of red spots. She said that was allergy caused by the food that she just had earlier. Yet I immediately wondered in my mind: 'does she have STDs?' Although I still tried to have sex with her, I just couldn't do it physically because I had been turned off already.

Interestingly, despite the unsatisfactory initial CD encounter, *Brothers* still continued to engage in CD. Ryan carried on and divulged:

My first CD experience did scare me. That's why it was not after a while until I dated a second *CC*. I thought the first terrible CD experience was just my bad luck, so I decided to give it another shot. Coincidently, I came across a new *CC* post. Once I added her MSN, she was already online and when I sent her a message, she responded immediately. You know, most girls are not willing to chat with *Brothers*, but this girl chatted with me. I felt that she was very genuine, so I dated her.

Given that even those *Brothers* who had a disappointing initial CD encounter continued to engage in CD, it should not be a surprise that satisfactory first-timers would continue their CD journey. Don, 40 years old, who had never purchased sex before he engaged in CD, said:

Once you have done it for the first time, it's like you have opened a door; you have broken a barrier. A whole new arena is waiting for you to explore... CD is like a drug addiction. It's actually worse than a drug addiction because there are new girls entering into the CD world every day. There is always someone new that drags you into CD again.

Despite sharing Don's feeling of 'addiction', five *Brothers* reported to have lost sight of the point of dating *CCs*. As a result of their encounters, they had experienced feelings of loss, depression, and emptiness and therefore, wanted to withdraw from the CD scene. Victor, 34 years old, said:

At the beginning, I dated *CCs* very frequently. I always went onto the CD forum and chatted with *CCs* online. If I found a *CC* whom I like, I would date her immediately. But now, even if a girl were right for me, I would not date her because I just don't see the point now. Yes, I had fun during the CD encounter with a *CC*, but what then afterwards? I took part in CD previously because of curiosity, sexual, and emotional needs. Although I still have sexual needs, I think it's not that important anymore. Simply put, my attitude has changed. I sometimes felt empty and loss rather than emotionally fulfilled after a CD encounter.

The ambivalence and emotional struggles that some *Brothers* experienced in CD had led them to consider withdrawing from the CD field; yet all of the *Brothers*, who had expressed intention to quit CD during our formal interviews, had admitted in our subsequent online or offline informal conversations that they had strong desires to date *CCs* again, and that they had still been searching for and dating *CCs*. Take the case of Derrick, 35 years old, as example. In our formal interview, he said: 'I do not want to engage in CD anymore because I feel guilty for my girlfriend.' However, four days later, he told me:

> I wanted to date *CCs* again. There are several *CCs* whom I want to date. I am in struggle now: to date or not to date? To be honest with you, I had already dated one *CC* and I am meeting her on the coming Thursday. I know it's bad... but it's the desire of freshness that drives me to date *CCs* again.

Accordingly, even though some *Brothers* expressed an intention to stop engaging in CD for reasons of guilt, loss, or confusion, most of them would ultimately resume their CD practice as they were not able to suppress their desires.

STAGE III. PROTECTION

16 of the *Brothers* in this study feel that, as *Brothers*, they have a responsibility to protect vulnerable *CCs*. These *Brothers* believe CD to be a risky business for *CCs*, but not so for men, and that's why they feel like they are in a superior position, in which they should keep an eye on the *CCs*. Eric, 39 years old, summed up these *Brothers'* perception of *CCs'* risk in CD:

> For me, the risk of taking part in CD is almost zero. I never brought my iPhone and credit cards to a CD date; I only took the amount of money that was just enough to pay for the trade with me. So, there was nothing that I can lose. But for the *CCs*, the risk could be very high. Obviously, we (*Brothers*) are physically stronger than the girls and they will be in a vulnerable position if a conflict occurs. There was a case in which the *Brother* fled after having sex with the *CC* without paying when the *CC* was still in a shower. She could not chase after him because she was naked! I don't know whether I should use the term 'stupid' or 'innocent' to describe some *CCs*. Some of them just don't know how to protect themselves. We (*Brothers*) have to teach the girls how to prevent themselves from getting hurt and being cheated.

One way for *Brothers* to protect *CCs* is to safeguard and regulate the CD culture. *Brothers* not only closely follow the expected lines of action defined in the CD world, but also single out *bad Brothers* who violate the CD rules. They would warn *CCs*, newcomers in particular, not to approach the *bad Brothers* by creating posts on the CD forum and sending private MSN messages to the *CCs*. Aaron, 33 years old, said:

Some *CCs* do not read the posts and our precautions on the CD forums. They stop visiting the forum once they have created a post. They just passively wait for the *Brothers* to add and contact them through MSN. In such case, there is no way that I can help them. It is startling how some *CCs* do nothing to protect themselves in such a risky business. As *Brothers*, the best that we can do is to warn the *CCs* and send kind reminders to them to pay attention to our warning posts.

Other than warning messages, *Brothers* have created a *bad Brothers list*, online banners, and webpages that include *bad Brothers'* photos, contact information, and the *bad deeds* that these *bad Brothers* had done, including, but not limited to, having sex with *CCs* without paying, having unsafe sex without *CCs'* consent, stealing, not showing up on the prearranged CD date, and being rude to the *CCs*. The *bad Brothers list*, banners, and websites are being circulated throughout the CD forum. Besides revealing the identities of the *bad Brothers*, *Brothers* have also created 'working guidelines' for *CCs*. The guidelines contain information on what *CCs* should be aware of in the CD field, including the general CD information, psychological preparation, and practical knowledge that *CCs* ought to know before they enter into the CD world. Here, the stereotype of 'men are the protectors, women are the protected' is reinforced. In addition, three *Brothers* in this study had helped *CCs* to find employment outside the commercial sex industry so that the girls could leave the CD field and start anew.

Another common approach to protect the *CCs* is to offer them financial assistance. 19 *Brothers* in this study claimed that they had *lent* money to the *CCs* without any expectation of any sexual favor in return. The offering of money was seen as an act of benefaction rather than an act of a purchase. The *Brothers* consider themselves as a benefactor rather than a stereotypical licentious client and that's why the *Brothers* generally consider themselves different from, and more respectable than, conventional clients. More importantly, lending money to *CCs* is a way for some *Brothers* to extend their commercial sexual relationships to conventional interpersonal relationships. Take the case of Jeremy, 28 years old, for example:

Jeremy: Several *CCs* treat me as a friend. They would call me out for dinner once in a while.

Cassini: Do you have to pay them for these dinner dates?

Jeremy: No! If I paid them, then it would be a *PTGF-Brother* relation, not a friendship. But having said that, if I knew they needed money, I would just give them. They might just need one or two thousand dollars to survive for the rest of the month.

In a sense, the offering of such financial help outside the CD context is a way to win the *CCs'* trust and friendship. However, the authenticity of this kind of friendship can be called into question because of the involvement of money. Did the *CCs* meet Jeremy outside the CD context because they genuinely considered him to be a friend, or because they knew that he would offer them money? The issue of authenticity is a complex one, which will be explored in more detail in Chap. 7.

At any rate, all the *Brothers* who had received financial request from *CCs* did agree to help, and all of them had offered financial help to *CCs* more than once despite none of their previous loans having been returned. In other words, *Brothers would lend* money to *CCs* even in light of the high probability that the loan would not be repaid, and the possibility that the *CCs* would flee from the *Brothers* after they receive the money. Jerry, 30 years old, divulged:

> Several *CCs*, with whom I had traded, told me that they urgently need some money, so, I lent money to them. Deep down in my heart, I was aware that there was a huge chance that they were exploiting me economically… but what if one of them really needed the money? So, I lent the money to them anyways. Not surprisingly, none of them returned the money. Some of them had even disappeared afterwards. It's all right because at least I know who treats me as a friend, and who does not.

Similarly, the case of Leon, 43 years old, also illustrates how some *Brothers* would offer unconditional financial help to *CCs*: 'A CC who had already withdrawn from the CD field called me and said she could not afford to pay her last debt installment. So, I decided to help her and clear her debt.' Since this girl was no longer in the CD field, Leon did not expect her to repay him with sexual favors and nor did he expect her to return the money. Theo, 30 years old, also reported that he had helped a CC economically without any expectation of sexual and/or financial return:

> There was one time a CC called and asked me if I could trade with her because she urgently needed money to pay for her rent. She called me because I was her only customer. Unfortunately, I was very busy at work and

couldn't spare the time to trade with her. Since I did not want her to trade with other people, I just paid the rent for her without trading, not even meeting her.

From Theo's narrative, one reason why he offered financial assistance to the *CC* was to prevent her from having CD dates with other clients. Sanders (2008, p. 106) argued that male clients are somewhat vulnerable 'in terms of their economic generosity towards sex workers to whom they were particularly attached'. Echoing *Brothers*' behavioral pattern and sentiment, male clients in Sander's (2008) study perceived the act of solving sex workers' financial problems as a way to maintain an amicable relationship with them, although men were aware of their vulnerability in being economically and/or emotionally exploited and manipulated by the sex workers. In a similar vein, *Brothers* perceive their financial assistance not only as a way to solve *CCs*' financial difficulties, but also as a way to broadcast their charms, such as reliability, financial capability, and generosity, which might attract *CCs* to interact and form an interpersonal relationship with them outside the CD context.

Through protecting and assisting *CCs*, *Brothers* are able to manifest their superior financial and social capitals (e.g., introducing 'normative' jobs to the *CCs*), which affirm and polish their hegemonic masculinities. *Brothers* normally enjoy assuming this guardian role as it gives them an opportunity to experience being in a dominating social position. Michael, 32 years old, proudly explained why some *CCs* called him 'pa pa' and some *Brothers* referred him as a 'social worker':

> It is probably because I always concern about the *CCs*' well-being and take care of them. The *CCs* need help; however, there are just too many *CCs* out there. There is no way I could protect all of them. All I can do is to protect those *CCs* who are around me.

It is not uncommon for *Brothers* to take pride in their ability to protect the *CCs*. In one comment, Aaron, 33 years old, revealed:

> For me, the best thing about CD is that some *CCs* would come to me for advice when they are in trouble. For example, a *CC* came to me for advice when she found out that she was pregnant, and a few days ago, another *CC* called me before she attempted to commit suicide. I talked to her and comforted her for almost two hours. I feel good when the *CCs* seek my advice and ask for my help when they have trouble. That means they trust me. Some *CCs* still keep contacting me even after they've withdrawn from CD.

For these *Brothers*, the ultimate pleasure of protecting *CCs* is derived from the feeling of being needed and respected. It confirms their self-worth and social role as men; thus through CD, men can reassure their masculinity in a modern risk society where gender relationship is increasingly democratic and hegemonic masculinity is more difficult to achieve.

Besides assisting individual *CCs*, *Brothers* also protect the reputation of CD and *CCs* as a whole by drawing and maintaining a clear line between CD and conventional prostitution, and between *CCs* and sex workers. *Brothers* generally do not regard *CCs* as sex workers but as 'normal young girls or schoolgirls,' said Andrew, 26 years old. However, despite CD participants' conceptual distinction between *CCs* and sex workers, many outsiders do not differentiate *CCs* from sex workers. Occasionally, some outsiders would raise questions on the CD forum regarding traditional sex workers/sex work. This type of questions was regarded as a threat to the integrity of the CD community. Thus, the inquirers were often despised. Drawing from the data of my cyber-ethnography, the following are some typical *Brothers'* responses to defend the uniqueness of CD and *CCs*, as opposed to prostitution and sex workers respectively:

- Here is not a place for discussing sex work/sex workers.
- If you want to discuss sex workers, please leave this forum, bye.
- You are in the wrong place, asking the wrong question.

All *Brothers* in this study believe that being a *CC* is only a temporary and fleeting role that does not define the girls as sex workers. Some *Brothers* do not even consider the girls to be *CCs*, not to mention sex workers. The girls' identity as young girls or schoolgirls has overridden their identity as *CCs*. The youth of the *CCs* also has special meaning and value for many *Brothers*. For them, youth symbolizes innocence and purity, and *Brothers* do put effort to accentuate and protect this unique characteristic of *CCs*.

While all *Brothers* protect *CCs* and the CD world in their own ways in a more private setting, some *Brothers* take a more official and public role to safeguard the social order of the CD community. For example, because of his credibility and his long history in the CD field, Kent, 41 years old, have been appointed as an administrator of the CD forum by the founder of the forum. Kent takes the administrative role voluntarily and has a strong sense of responsibility to protect the *CCs* as well as the

CD community. However, since Kent is married, he has to put some considerable effort to prevent his wife from discovering his CD involvement:

> I cannot go to the CD forum when I am at home because I want to avoid any chance that my wife may find out my CD participation. So, I go to work an hour or two earlier every morning to read and organize new posts that were being created during the previous night. I have to keep myself up to date about what is going on within the CD community, such as who the newcomers are, who violates the CD rules, and the relationships amongst CD participants. I try my best to ensure that the virtual CD community is safe and ordered.

In addition to his role as a client, Kent acts as a gatekeeper of the CD community. He is highly respected by the other CD participants and is regarded as one of the six most respectable *Brothers*, namely the 'Six Big *Brothers*', in the CD community. Because of his reputation, he is often approached by new *CCs* and *Brothers* for help in respect of CD issues. I surmise that this is one of the reasons that he take pride on and enjoy being a gatekeeper.

DISCUSSION

This chapter focuses on the process of becoming a *Brother* and the *Brothers'* subjective view of what it means to be a *Brother*. The three stages of the process of becoming combine to shape *Brothers'* CD experiences, motivate and sustain *Brothers'* CD involvement, shape the *CC–Brother relationships*, and reinforce their masculinity.

Like other kinds of commercial sexual exchanges, the process of CD assumes its own symbolic meaning which extends beyond physical ones. While the relationship between a conventional sex worker and a client generally remains static as a buyer-and-seller relationship in a restricted commercial and physical context, a *CC–Brother* relationship is more dynamic and can take place in an unbounded social context including the cyberspace. *Brothers* take tremendous pleasure in having non-commercial and non-sexual relationships with *CCs*.

The process of CD, exploration, actualization, and protection, provides psychological satisfaction and a new life experience to many *Brothers*.

Becoming a *Brother* involves a learning process. *Brothers* learn the culture and operation of CD by exploring the virtual CD community and interacting with online CD participants. Many of them then continue to learn the details of CD through actualizing CD dates. They learn from their actual experiences, their mistakes, as well as direct interactions with *CCs*. After the *Brothers* have become an 'expert' in CD, some of them will take on 'a guardian' role to look after, take care of, and protect the *CCs*, from which *Brothers* generate another kind of emotional satisfaction and a recognition of their masculinity.

Brothers believe that they are more honorable than all other men who purchase conventional sex based on the premise that they are more than just 'paying customers'. Here, Demetrious' (2001) conceptualization of 'internal hegemony,' that is, 'the social ascendancy of one group of men over others' (p. 341), is useful to understand *Brothers'* experience. However, when applied to the CD context, the 'others' does not include *all* men in general, but only men who purchase sex. Conventional clients are subordinated to *Brothers* in terms of not only their socio-economic status, but also the emotional intensity of their relationships with sex workers. *Brothers* often emphasize that their relationships with *CCs* go well beyond a mere economic client–sex worker model. They believe that they are 'helping' *CCs*, not only financially, but also psychologically. Sometimes, they see themselves as a friend, a counselor, a social worker, an advisor, or even a 'pa pa' to *CCs* because they listen and offer advice to *CCs*, and try to solve their problems. Many *Brothers* have felt content when they could 'help' the *CCs* because it strengthens their masculinity. In Hong Kong society, where women's social status and role are rising, being a *Brother* can restore traditional masculinity and their superior role as a man.

To conclude, being a *Brother* means more than just being a client. It means being a reliable, wise, capable man who is able to protect and help vulnerable *CCs*. It gives a sense of satisfaction and affirmation of their masculinity that the *Brothers* may not able to achieve outside the CD realm. The opportunity to perform various masculinities is one of the incentives that keeps the *Brothers* continuing their CD involvement.

The process of becoming a *Brother* is therefore, a vibrant, complicated, social learning process and interaction, in which *Brothers* construct, maintain, redefine, and strengthen their self-identity and masculinity. It is part of the voyage of their reflexive project of the self. Yet we are reminded that the emotional intimacy and guardian role, while an avenue for expressing masculinity, creates other ambiguities related to the issues of trust and authenticity.

Bibliography

Albert, A. E., Warner, D. L., & Hatcher, R. A. (1998). Facilitating Condom Use with Clients During Commercial Sex in Nevada's Legal Brothels. *American Journal of Public Health, 88*(4), 643–646.

Belza, M. J., Fuente, L. d. l., Suárez, M., Vallejo, F., García, M., López, M., . . . Bolea, Á. (2008). Men Who Pay for Sex in Spain and Condom Use: Prevalence and Correlates in a Representative Sample of the General Population. *Sexually Transmitted Infections, 84*(3), 207–211.

Browne, J., & Minichiello, V. (1995). The Social Meanings Behind Male Sex Work: Implications for Sexual Interactions. *The British Journal of Sociology, 46*(4), 598–622.

Demetriou, D. Z. (2001). Connell's Concept of Hegemonic Masculinity: A Critique. *Theory and Society, 30*(3), 337–361.

Faugier, J., & Cranfield, S. (1995). Reaching Male Clients of Female Prostitutes: The Challenge for HIV Prevention. *AIDS Care, 7*(1), 21–32.

Lau, J. T. F., Siah, P. C., & Tsui, H. Y. (2002). Behavioral Surveillance and Factors Associated with Condom Use and STD Incidences among the Male Commercial Sex Client Population in Hong Kong – Results of Two Surveys. *AIDS Education and Prevention, 14*(4), 306–317.

Leonard, T. L. (1990). Male Clients of Female Street Prostitutes: Unseen Partners in Sexual Disease Transmission. *Medical Anthropology Quarterly, 4*(1), 41–55.

Monto, M. A., & Hotaling, N. (2001). Predictors of Rape Myth Acceptance among Male Clients of Female Street Prostitutes. *Violence Against Women, 7*(3), 275–293.

Peng, Y.-W. (2007). Buying Sex: Domination and Difference in the Discourses of Taiwanese Piao-ke. *Men and Masculinities, 9*(3), 315–336.

Pitts, M. K., Smith, A. M. A., Grierson, J., O'Brien, M., & Misson, S. (2004). Who Pays for Sex and Why? An Analysis of Social and Motivational Factors Associated With Male Clients of Sex Workers. *Archives of Sexual Behavior, 33*(4), 353–358.

Sanders, T. (2008). *Paying for Pleasure: Men who Buy Sex*. Portland: Willan Publishing.

Ward, H., Mercer, C. H., Wellings, K., Fenton, K., Erens, B., Copas, A., & Johnson, A. M. (2005). Who Pays for Sex? An Analysis of the Increasing Prevalence of Female Commercial Sex Contacts among Men in Britain. *Sexually Transmitted Infections, 81*(6), 467–471.

Xantidis, L., & McCabe, M. P. (2000). Personality Characteristics of Male Clients of Female Commercial Sex Workers in Australia. *Archives of Sexual Behavior, 29*(2), 165–176.

CHAPTER 6

Why Do Girls Engage in CD?

In the past, many people have believed that girls are forced into or kidnapped to sell sex against their will, held captive or maltreated by ruthless individuals or vicious members of triad societies (Lethbridge, 1978). However, in recent times, media reports have suggested that many girls sell their sexuality voluntarily (Anonymous, 2012a, 2012b; Chan, 2011). Although the general public is aghast to see how underage girls, high school students, college students, and young women are willingly flocking to sell sex through CD, the social milieu that has facilitated girls to take part in CD has often been overlooked. While the emergence and growth of the phenomenon of CD are blamed on a decline in social morality, girls who engage in CD are blamed for their incurable laziness (Ho, 2003). Rather than earning money through *proper* jobs, which usually requires *hard work*, these young girls choose to earn quick and easy money through CD, which requires no educational qualifications, few special aptitudes, technical skills, or apprenticeship. The general public is even more disturbed if the girls' motive to take part in CD is not because of dire financial problems or survival needs, but for materialistic desires and the pursuit of a consumption-driven lifestyle (Ueno, 2003). In a survey on 2966 secondary school students' attitudes toward the issue of CD in Hong Kong, 87% and 47% of respondents believed that the major reasons for girls to take part in CD were, respectively, to obtain money for the consumption of luxury goods and to receive lavish presents from their

© The Author(s) 2018
C. S. K. Chu, *Compensated Dating*, Gender, Sexualities
and Culture in Asia, https://doi.org/10.1007/978-981-10-6974-1_6

clients (Ng, Leung, & Yau, 2009). Based on these beliefs, girls' voluntary participation in CD has become an indication of moral decay as well as a symbol of materialism amongst adolescents in Hong Kong.

Despite these popular beliefs, materialistic desires and the *decline in morality* can hardly be regarded as sufficient reasons to explain girls' initiation in CD. As such, it is necessary to hear the narratives of the girls. Nevertheless, like most other people who sell sex, girls who provide CD tend to avoid the public gaze because commercial sexual activities are still heavily scrutinized and stigmatized in the general society. Compare to street prostitutes, and sex workers in one-woman brothels and massage parlors, CD providers are comparatively more difficult to identify because they are not located in a specific venue, street, or apartment; and unlike some forms of call girls who usually gather together and wait for their agent to allocate 'jobs' for them upon clients' requests, CD providers work individually without a designated workplace or gathering place. As such, CD providers are largely hidden from society unless they are caught by the police. Fortunately, during my online and offline ethnography, I was able to conduct in-depth interviews with 12 *CCs* and interact with numerous other *CCs* who are generally hidden from the public gaze. Based on these interviews and ethnographic data, this chapter reveals how girls' voluntary CD engagement is related less to materialism or morality, and more to the transformation of intimacy and the increasingly fragmented society in late modernity.

MATERIALISTIC DESIRES

Some *CCs* consider CD as a lucrative part-time job, offering a way to earn easy, good, and quick money. Money obtained from CD is regarded as *easy* because the activity does not require any academic qualifications. In addition, since one of the characteristics of CD is its amateur nature, the girls are not expected to provide professional services, thereby work experience or knowledge is not a concern. In other words, as long as a young girl is willing to *rent out* her time, body, and sexuality, then she can enter into the world of CD simply by a click of a mouse. Furthermore, perhaps due to the lack of knowledge of its underlying risks, a recreational dimension is added to CD. Thus, some adventurous and curious adolescents might regard CD as simply fun or an exciting adventure. As Joey, 16 years old, described: 'I can earn money while having fun and enjoying sex. I really couldn't ask for more!' Meanwhile, CD money is perceived as *good* because the reward is huge but the workload is low compare to the limited jobs that are available to adolescents. The money is also considered as *quick* because the working hours are short. Take, for example, the case of Rose, 19 years old. She exclaimed: 'I once received HKD10,000 for a CD session. It only took me an hour!' Before Rose engaged in CD, she worked as a salesperson in a fashion boutique, earning around HKD6,500 a month. Thus, what she could earn in an hour through CD was already more than one month's salary working in that boutique. As one can imagine, CD can appear to be very appealing to girls who are looking for jobs but have low skill, working experience, and education.

For only two girls in this study was their initiation into CD partly related to materialistic desires: 'I first started CD because I wanted to buy a mobile phone,' said Bella, 20 years old. Rose, 19 years old, offered a similar explanation:

> I didn't have a job, but there were a lot of things that I wanted to buy. Even if I had a job, I wouldn't spend my earnings from hard work on luxury goods. Anyways, at that time, I really needed money, so I went on the Internet and typed 'CD' (in Chinese) in the search engine. A CD forum appeared. Immediately, I registered myself in the forum and created a post. That's how I started CD. I earned HKD80, 000 in just two months but I didn't save any money because I had spent all the money on shopping and plastic surgery—getting my nose and chin jobs done.
>
> When I was having sex with my clients, I was thinking about what to buy after the CD encounter. I used to be very thrifty, but now I have become a squander. In the past, I need to think for a long time before I could decide to buy a piece of clothing because I didn't have much spending money, but now, if I see something nice, I will just buy them without hesitation. I feel very good about it.

Similar to Rose, Joey, 16 years old, continued her CD practice because of its resulting consumption power although it was not her initial reason to engage in CD (it was plastic sexuality, which will be discussed in the next section):

> I spent the proceeds from CD on brand name fashions and bags, mobile phones, and at karaoke clubs, bars, and restaurants for hanging out with friends. So, money is very important. In the past when I saw an expansive designer bag, I would think: 'It's just an ordinary bag. It's nothing special.

I don't need any luxury goods.' But now, I believe having luxuries and brand name goods are quite important. It's an identity. So, I have to obtain more money. For me, CD is an occupation. Once I have started CD, I just can't stop it. It is really hard to stop doing it because money is very important for me now and through CD, I can earn money very easily and quickly.

For these young girls, they needed the money not for necessity, not for the luxury goods per se, but for a sense of self-worth and security that the power of consumption and luxury goods render. It was also about social status as the proceeds from CD could finance a relatively luxurious lifestyle, which otherwise could not be achieved. Rose, 19 years old, described her way of life after she involved in CD:

I haven't taken the buses or subway for a long time; I just take a taxi wherever I go now. I can also able to afford to dine in nice or at least proper restaurants now. I used to have a sales job in a fashion boutique. I had to work for long hours, but I got paid minimally. The salary would never be able to support the lifestyle that I am having now. So, it's really hard for me to go back to a normal job.

In spite of the *ease* of earning *quick* and *good* money, it cannot give a sufficient explanation of why an increasing number of girls have been engaging in CD in recent years. The following sections look beyond this ostensible motive and explore some recent changes in the society that have precipitated girls' involvement in CD.

Plastic Sexuality

In present-day modernity, sex is no longer confined in marriage for procreation purposes, but has become more flexible and non-marital for recreational purposes (Bauman, 2003; Giddens, 1992). Perhaps, the effects of plastic sexuality are more strongly felt by women as plastic sexuality has caused a more drastic change in women's sexual expression and practice than that in men. As Giddens (1992, p. 9) pointed out that in the past:

Virginity on the part of girls prior to marriage was prized by both sexes. Few girls disclosed the fact if they allowed a boyfriend to have full sexual intercourse—and many were only likely to permit such an act to happen once formally engaged to the boy in question. More sexually active girls were disparaged by the others, as well as by the very males who sought to 'take advantage' of them.

While the concept of chastity was predicated on women but not for men in the past, women are now encouraged to enjoy their sexual autonomy and celebrate their sexualities. This was something which historically has been suppressed and denied to the majority of women living in patriarchal societies (Travis S.K. Kong, 2006). Doris, 26 years old, described how sex is no longer male-oriented, and how women can assert their sexualities in the twenty-first century:

> If the sexual skills of my partner were bad, I wouldn't enjoy the sex even if he were very good-looking. However, I would not enjoy the sex either if he had very good sexual skills but bad looking. In other words, my sexual enjoyment depend on multiple factors. In fact, I don't always enjoy the sex with my boyfriend... When he had sexual need, he would request to have sex with me. But if he simply inserted his penis into my body without kissing me, I would be very furious and said: 'It's not only about your sexual needs; it's about my pleasures as well. If I don't get excited, how could I climax?'

Apparently, female sexualities are no longer evolved around reproduction and male pleasures; women's own sexual pleasures have become increasingly important and they are not afraid to assert it: 'I have great sexual appetite, so I am enjoying CD,' said Crystal, 20 years old. Roberts (1992) suggested that this new sexual autonomy of women implies that they have the right to sell their sexuality and it is in this sense that the 'whore is dangerously free.' Joey, 16 years old, supported this claim:

> I did not have an urgent need for money when I first began CD. But since I had already lost my virginity, I felt like having sex is not a big deal anymore. Moreover, I had already had lots of casual sex and one-night stands when I hung out with my peers in karaoke clubs, bars, parties, etc. before I entered into CD. So, when I inadvertently encountered a CD forum online. I thought: 'Sex is what I have always been doing; however, I received no money after casual sex! In contrast, in CD, I can have sex and earn money at the same time. Isn't it better than one-night stands where I don't receive any practical compensation?' CD is a fun way to earn money! Needless to say, having sex with money is better than having sex without money. So, I seldom engage in non-commercial casual sex after I have started CD. If I want sex, I just look for a *Brother* instead of a (non-commercial) sexual partner at a bar or a karaoke club.

In late modernity, sex has lost its previous association with the responsibility and commitment of a relationship. Marriage or even love is no longer viewed as a precondition for sex. As such, there is now a plethora of sexual possibilities, one of which is selling sex. Candy, 20 years old, said:

> I have engaged in countless casual sex. I probably have had more than 20 non-commercial sexual partners. Hourly motels are just everywhere. When a guy approached me in karaoke clubs or bars and I felt he was quite good-looking, we could just go to next building (a motel) and have sex. To be honest, it almost always happened. Sometimes, I did not really like the guy. But since we had already got into the room, I would just do it anyways. Now, I think it's not worth it. I would rather engage in CD than in casual sex with no compensation.

For some girls, even sexual or emotional attraction is not a precondition for sex. Rose, 19 years old, said:

> My oldest client is 93 years old. He is several decades older than me... of course I wasn't attracted to him and didn't enjoy the sex with him, but none of these matter. It was just sex.

Similarly, Ruby, 22 years old, expressed:

> For me, whether my sexual partner is fat or thin, tall or short, it's just the same. I behave the same way with all men. So, I don't think CD is a hard thing to do. Even when I had sex with an overweight client, I didn't have any negative feeling but of course, I didn't have positive feelings either. I just worried that he would have a heart attack during our sex because of his weight.

Traditional sex workers have carried out tremendous emotional labor and techniques to separate private sex and work sex, and to maintain an emotional distance from their clients (Brewis & Linstead, 2000; McKeganey & Barnard, 1996; O'Connell Davidson, 1995). To maintain the boundary between work sex and love sex, some sex workers establish a body exclusion zone, which means that only specific parts of their bodies are allowed to be accessed by clients while others are reserved for loved ones. Sanders (2005) argued that creating physical boundaries and retaining certain sexual behaviors and responses for private relationships are necessary in distancing themselves physically, personally, and internally from their clients. One of her respondents said: 'I think you have to have something saved for your partner' (Sanders, 2005, p. 150). In fact, all sex workers in her study unanimously adopted this emotion-management technique and had a clear distinction between what can be commodified and what cannot be available for sale, especially if the sex workers are in a serious intimate relationship. Nevertheless, *CCs* in this study did not report having body exclusion zone nor sex acts that are performed exclusively in private sex and not in work sex. For them, sex work is truly ordinary 'work' and has nothing to do with 'love':

> [The] heterosexual act of penetration carries no meaning at all; likewise, to be fondled by a man effects no erotic significance either. In contrast with the passionate sex she enjoys with her lover, sex at work is completely insignificant and meaningless—except in terms of monetary gains, of course. In this sense, for her, sex work has little to do with sex. (Ho, 2000, p. 286)

Instead of disassociating work sex from private sex, it appears that *CCs* dedicated most of their emotional effort in the creation of the so-called *girlfriend experience (GFE)*. Numbing their emotions in work sex seems to be an easy task for many *CCs* who claimed that they drew a very clear line between love and sex. Moreover, for some *CCs*, sex is just sex. They do not even differentiate between work sex and private sex: 'my feelings when having sex with my clients are very similar to that with my boyfriend. In fact, I don't have any particular feeling when having sex,' said Rose, 19 years old. This sexual attitude, along with the disassociation between sex and love, have predisposed many girls to enter into CD.

Many *CCs* believe that work sex is very similar to, if not the same as, private sex. This is because modern sex in an intimate setting is characterized by plastic sexuality and the sexual autonomy of women. Such transformations have not only challenged male hegemonic masculinity, but also changed the ways individuals practise sex and form intimate relationship in late modernity. Modern intimate relationships are becoming more and more egalitarian, flexible, and open. They only work if each party 'gains sufficient benefit from the relation to make its continuance worthwhile' (Giddens, 1992, p. 63). Instead of 'everlasting love', intimate relationships have become more fragile, insecure, and fluid as the traditional gendered roles are being defied such that women, especially young women, are more reluctant to sacrifice their self-fulfillment for the cultivation of a monogamous relationship. Lily, 22 years old, exemplified:

I have been jumping from one relationship to another relationship. I changed my boyfriends frequently. I do not want to get into a serious relationship. I am still young. I want to play around.

As illustrated by Lily's narrative, not only sex can be recreational, but so can couple relationships. Modern relationships are formed for the purpose of individual self-fulfillment rather than for external criteria, such as marriage, households, kinship or survival as it was in the past (Giddens, 1992). The CCs confirmed Giddens' (1992, p. 63) perspective that modern love or confluent love 'is not necessarily monogamous, in the sense of sexual exclusiveness,' they even showed that it is not necessarily monogamous, in the sense of emotional exclusiveness. Two CCs were having a romantic relationship with a married man at the time of the interview: 'I knew my boyfriend was married from the very first beginning, but who cares, as long as he treats me well and I am having a great time with him,' said Gloria, 28 years old. Meanwhile, Ruby, 22 years old, reported:

I am in a relationship with this man, but I can't tell people that 'this is my boyfriend' because he is married. Besides him, I am also having a relationship with another guy. Since he lives in Macau, it's easier for me to maintain both relationships simultaneously.

Apparently, monogamy is neither a necessity nor a requirement for modern relationships and love, at least for these young women. Plastic sexuality and the diminishing importance of monogamy, in both senses of emotional and sexual exclusiveness, therefore have created less burden for women to engage in CD.

TECHNOLOGICAL ADVANCEMENT

Besides the transformation of intimacy, the evolution of the information technology along with the explosive growth of Internet access and usage in recent years have also contributed to the social changes in the way individuals understand and practise intimacy and sexuality. The effects of the 'triple A engine' (see Chap. 4) of the Internet have created an unprecedented opportunity for individuals to explicitly express their sexual self, engage in sexual discourse, obtain erotic text, images, and video, and, last but not least, acquire and provide commercial sex services (Fisher & Barak, 2000). In the following, I will illustrate how new technologies are closely intertwined with the changes of individual sexual attitudes and practices, and how these technological advancements have encouraged girls to take part in CD.

Sex is one of the most frequently searched-for terms on the Internet, which has helped to spread the notion of CD swiftly (Spink, Wolfram, Jansen, & Saracevic, 2001). Of the 12 *CCs* whom I have interviewed, six of them searched for CD on the Internet intentionally. Others reported that they have been accidentally exposed to online sex sites, CD information, or CD forums while they were surfing the Internet or through spam mail, pop-up advertisements, unsolicited links, or communication from other online users, and that was how they started the journey into CD. CD information and advertisements recruiting girls to become 'part-time lovers' with the connotation of commercial sex exchange can be found in various local online discussion forums and magazines. Guidelines on how to engage in CD can also be found in cyberspace. Therefore, despite the public discourse that CD is morally wrong, dangerous, and even fatal, the practice of CD did not subside. On the contrary, it appears that CD has even intensified because of the help of the Internet and various forms of information technology.

The use of the Internet for any activity that involves sexuality for the purpose of entertainment, leisure, exploration, sexual arousal, education, support, business, maintaining relationships, and/or seek sexual or romantic partners is known as online sexual activities (OSA) (Boies, 2002). Cooper, David, Griffin-Shelly, and Robin (2004) suggested that the ubiquitousness of OSA has given rise to the next sexual revolution. CD can be seen as one of the emerging OSA in this new sexual age as CD negotiation relies on online communications rather than traditional face-to-face solicitation. This new negotiation method not only reduces any embarrassment that might occur in conventional offline settings, but also deconstructs the structural and normative constraints that are usually associated with the entrance of, and participation in, conventional forms of sex work. For instance, sex workers in one-woman brothels need to rent an apartment in order to run their business. CD does not pose such a prerequisite. *CCs* can solicit and negotiate with various clients simultaneously, safely, freely, and anonymously in cyberspace. With the help of the Internet, the physical barriers of entering into the traditional forms of commercial sex are dissolved in CD. Girls simply have to create a post on an online forum to kick off their pathway to selling sex. Some people may argue that the postings on the CD forums are not very different from the advertisements created by call girls and other commercial sex providers in newspapers or magazines. However, although the contents of them might be similar, the online forums allow synchronous direct interactions between the clients and the girls whereas the traditional forms of advertisements do not. Moreover, online forums enable girls to seek clients actively rather than just waiting for clients' solicitation passively. Online communication thus facilitates the growth and ease to enter in the commercial sex market on the parts of girls as well as men.

Besides expanding the commercial sex market, the recent development and burgeoning growth of various social networking/dating phone applications have also transformed the formation of modern intimate relationships and further facilitate the practice of plastic sexuality. For example, WeChat, a social networking phone application launched in 2000, has become increasingly popular in Hong Kong, Taiwan, and Mainland China. WeChat claims itself as 'the new way to connect'.[1] In addition to communicating with your own friends, WeChat allows users to connect and communicate with strangers through the functions of 'shake' or 'look around'. By shaking your phone, WeChat matches the user with other users who are also shaking their phones concurrently, and by clicking the 'look around' function, a user can view a list of other users who are within 3 km geographically. Through WeChat, users can solicit other individuals conveniently and efficiently. It also accelerates the transformation of the nature of an encounter from a virtual one to a physical one as the 'strangers' are just nearby. Because of the ease of soliciting strangers, WeChat has become a popular way for individuals to form intimate and/or sexual relationships. Many *CCs* in this study had used WeChat and other similar social networking phone applications to meet the opposite sex, to form romantic relationships, and to seek casual sexual partners. Drawing on my fieldnotes, the following script describes how Joey, 16 years old, formed interpersonal/intimate relationships through WeChat:

> At the end of our interview, Joey told me that she was going to meet a boy, whom she just knew this afternoon through WeChat. It would be their first time to meet. Since the place that they would be meeting was near to where we were, and I had never experienced or witnessed how an intimate relationship could be developed through this social networking site, I asked if I could go with her. She agreed. She said she was not particularly nervous or excited about the meeting because she had met other boys in this way for many times.

[1] WeChat official website. http://www.wechat.com.en/.

After we arrived at the designated location, Joey whispered to me: 'I think it's him, the guy in front of us.' I wondered how she knew it because they had never met before. Joey showed me a picture on her phone: 'He sent me a photo of himself.' Joey then went behind him, tapped his shoulder from the back, and quickly came back besides me. The 'stranger' turned around, spotted us, and then walked towards us. We introduced each other. Then we departed. Joey went with the stranger and would be joining his friends for karaoke.

Undoubtedly, new technologies have opened a plethora of new opportunities for young girls to form multiple intimate relationships and engage in sexual adventurism in easier and easier ways:

> if sexual adventurism (in the form of sex with multiple partners or sex with strangers) is experienced as the latest in-thing instead of a life-and-death matter for girls—then it is little wonder that *enjo-kosai* and other forms of teenage sex work would be taken rather lightly by teenage girls. It is simply another form of sexual exploration, and with tangible as well as sizable profits (Ho, 2003, p. 330)

I agree that it is this social milieu of plastic sexuality in modern times that has encouraged girls to involve in CD.

While living in an era of technological revolution, we are also living in a late modern society that is characterized by fragmentation with fewer institutional controls and family obligations, leaving individuals with increased personal freedom. Yet it also means that we are facing a rising trend of family breakdown such that we are fully responsible for ourselves without the emotional support and security from the stable and strong family ties of the past, underlying considerable changes in the construction of the self. CD emerges as a new avenue to experience the self in a modern society that is fused with new kinds of risks and uncertainties.

In Hong Kong, according to the Census and Statistics Department (2016), while the number of registered first marriages of both parties have been falling from about 17 per 1000 population in 1981 to about 9 in 2000 and then increasing to about 14.2 in 2015, the divorce rate has risen rapidly, from 2062 in 1981 to 20,075 in 2015, meaning that the divorce rate in 2015 was almost ten times that recorded in 1981. These trends reflect substantial changes in the meaning of marriage, from a stable institution based on cultural norms and kinship for financial well-being and reproductive necessity to a self-reflexive project based on individual choices, and mutual emotional and/or sexual attractions for personal satisfaction. While marriage is a romantic union of two souls, divorce is a separation between two self-responsible individuals. Both are personal choices, which individuals have more freedom and less moral burdens to make.

Unfortunately, if children were involved, the impact of the breakdown of couple relationships would have underlying impacts on their children. In Hong Kong, the number of single parents with child(ren) aged under 18 living with the same household had increased continuously over the past decade, from 61,431 in 2001 to 81,705 in 2011 according to the Census and Statistics Department (*Thematic Household Survey Report No. 52*, 2013). Widom and Ames (1994) argued that the absence of one or both parents is a major precursor for adolescents to sell sex, probably because of the absence of family stability and security at a very young age. In this study, seven *CCs* come from a single-parent family. Part of the reason that these girls engage in CD is that they feel like they have no one to rely on in a fragmented family and thus, they have to depend on themselves emotionally as well as financially. Take the case of Rose, 19 years old, as an example:

> I have not seen my father since he divorced my mother many years ago. My mother has a job and she works very hard. She is having a harsh life. The only way I can do to make her life easier is to stop asking her for money and support myself financially.

Other girls began CD due to their desire to be independent because of an unstable home. Crystal, 20 years old, said:

> My parents divorced when I was very young. I lived with my mother, but her boyfriend often came to our place. So, I really wanted to move out. I need money. CD appeared to be a good option for me.

Gloria, 28 years old, described how the demise of an intact family and the emergence of new family types in modern society, including but not limited to single-parent family and stepfamily, had led to her desire to leave home: 'My mother passed away when I was a kid. Then my father remarried and that was why I always ran away from home in the past. I wanted to move out so desperately.'

The insecurity of the family might lead girls to seek emotional security and financial support externally, such as from other *CCs*. Lilly, 22 years old, who comes from a single-parent family, expressed:

> Despite the agent squeezed half of my proceeds from CD, I decided to work for her because there were other girls working together with me. We always gathered together while waiting for the agent's call. I could share my happiness and sadness with them. I was indeed happy at that time.

Similarly, Candy, 20 years old, who has never seen her father, began her pathway into commercial sex at the age of 15 for both emotional and financial reasons:

> My relationship with my mother was very bad, so I often ran away from home, but she didn't blame me because I had already started to support her financially. My mother knows that I have been selling sex because I was arrested once during the time when I was working under an agent. From time to time, she would express that she does not want me to work as a *CC*, but there is no choice, for her and for me. I need to help paying for the rent and my little brother's tuition.

Despite the need to be financially independent at a young age because of dire family circumstances, some may argue that it does not sufficiently justify their CD practice. In response to this critique, Bella, 20 years old, who has started to run away from her fragmented home since 14 years of age, said:

> When a young girl has reached a life situation where she does not even have the money to take a bus or to buy a loaf of bread, all she can do is to use her body and sexuality to exchange for money. Otherwise, she would just wait around to die. I was in such situation when I first started CD.

Due to an increasingly trend of the fragmented family, a growing number of adolescents will grow up without the family as a source of support, and some of them have to fend for themselves. With limited education or work skills, *regular* employment in a knowledge-based economy like Hong Kong, creates further challenges. Some adolescents may therefore perceive CD as a way to gain financial and personal autonomy.

Although a broken family is a major precursor for adolescents to sell sex, it should be noted that not all girls who involve in CD come from broken families. Four *CCs* in this study come from well-functioning, intact families. However, due to the increasing individualization of modern societies and the growing number of working mothers, the parent–children relationship might not be as strong as it was in the past (Jamieson, 1987): 'The relationship with my parents is very poor. Once, I got home, I would just go to my room and shut the door,' said Bella, 20 years old. The weak parental ties and low level of attachment to the family may expose adolescents to more opportunities to commit the sale of sex because these adolescents have less family constraints and enjoy more individual freedom; they are growing up in an open enabling environment with more opportunities to explore their self and sexuality that might not be possible under close parent surveillance (Gray, 1973). Joey, 16 years old, is one of them:

> My parents gave me a lot of freedom. I mean, not that they want to, but they cannot always keep an eye on me because both of them have to work. I go out five nights a week and sometimes, I stay overnight elsewhere and do not return home until the next morning either because I have to work (engage in CD) or just hang out with friends on the street or at karaoke clubs. By the time I return home, they have already left for work, and when they come home from work, I have already gone out again. We seldom see each other; it is not unusual that we do not see each other for a week. The relationships with my parents are very distant. We do not fight, but we do not talk either. At the beginning, my parents would still asked: 'when will you come back home?' But gradually, they have stopped asking; probably they know that they cannot control me.

The exceptional freedom that Joey enjoys allows her to take part in CD without parental constraints. She said that if her parents have showed more concern, she might not be able to participate in CD so easily. Jenny, 19 years old, confirmed Joey's sentiments:

> I am not allowed to return home too late at night, but if I ask my parents' permission in advance, I can return home around 11 p.m. So, I am not always being able to go on a CD date. One *Brother* always dates me; however, I am not able to go to the date even if I want to because of my parents' surveillance.

Compared to Joey, Jenny, who has far less individual freedom and a higher degree of expressed parental concern, participates in CD less frequently. Their cases seem to support Lee and Shek's (2013) claim that inadequate family support is a motivating factor for girls to engage in CD whereas family mutuality (e.g., mutual support, love, and concern among family members) is a protective factor that decreases the probability of girls' CD participation. In other words, due to the lack of emotional dependence and protection, forming an intimate relationship with another individual may be vital in recreating psychological stability and ontological security for adolescents in an increasing fragmented family and disembedded society. By participating in CD, girls may develop a sense of self-assurance and obtain the love, affection, and attention that they may not necessarily receive in the realms of their family life.

The Consequences of Plastic Sexuality and Modernity

The transformation of intimacy and sexuality has led to various consequences, including but not limited to, the younger age of first sexual intercourse, increasing prevalence and acceptance of premarital sex, and the higher number of sexual partners, all of which predispose girls to engage in CD voluntarily. Katy, 28 years old, elucidated:

> Since you have already lost your virginity, you can have sex more frequently or have sex for money. You have already started it (sexual activity)! I mean either you don't do it (have sex) at the first place, or you go to the extreme and sell sex frequently. Staying in between the two extreme is very foolish.

All of the *CCs* in this study share Katy's belief that since they have already lost their virginity to someone who is not their husband, it no longer matters if they continue to have more sex with other people because their future husband can never be 'the one and the only one'. Such beliefs predispose them into CD as well as other casual sex.

Given the underlying implication of first sexual intercourse, it should be a matter of concern that there is a universal trend of an earlier age of sexual initiation in all modern societies (Ho, 2003). According to a report published by the Family Planning Association of Hong Kong (*The Report on the Youth Sexuality Study 2006*, 2009), there was an increasing prevalence of adolescents having premarital sex. The percentage of Form 3 to Form 7 adolescent students having premarital sex had risen during the period between 1991 and 2006. The rates were 0.2, 4.5, 6.7 and 8.3% for female students and 1.2, 5.6, 8.7 and 14.1% for male students in 1991, 1996, 2001 and 2006 respectively. The rates of adolescent endorsing premarital sex had also dramatically increased. The rates were 26.3, 41.5, 42.1, 43.5% for girls and 45.8, 49.4, 51.3, and 53% for boys in 1991, 1996 2001 and 2006 correspondingly. By inference, the actual practice and the acceptance rate of premarital sex amongst adolescents will continue to climb.

Although the earlier age of first sexual intercourse might be seen as a sign of sexual freedom and the flexibility of sexuality, it is also found to be linked with higher possibilities of selling sex. The connection is more robust in girls than in boys. For example, James and Meyerdings (1978) indicated that their female subjects who had a history of selling sex had their first sexual intercourse at an earlier age than the general population. Pedersen and Hegna (2003) also suggested that amongst adolescents who had a history of selling sex, those who had their first sexual intercourse at a younger age had a higher number of commercial sex incidents. In the context of CD, although not all girls involved in CD engage in sexual intercourse with clients, many of them do sell various forms of sexual favors and make use of their female sexuality to exchange for money. All except for one girl in this study had their first sexual intercourse below the age of 16, which shows support to the proposition that premarital sex at an earlier age may link with an increased possibility to initiate CD or commercial sex exchange in general.

Although Jenny, 19 years old, does not have prior sexual experience before she involved in CD, she adopts the notion of plastic sexuality and perceives sex to be a recreational activity rather than an activity connected with love and marriage. Jenny initiated CD because she wanted to explore her sexuality: 'I engaged in CD not because of money. I didn't have any financial pressures. I was just bored. It doesn't matter to me whether my first sexual partner is my boyfriend or not,' said Jenny. Indeed, her first sexual partner was her client. Jenny's case illustrates that the connection between sex and love is gradually dissolving and that modern sexuality is increasingly plastic, predisposing at least some girls to engage in CD and normalize their CD behaviors.

Given the dissociation between sex and love, adolescents' sexual attitudes have changed radically in modernity. While it has been regarded in the past as a deviant act to charge money for sex, the notion has now been reversed: it is unwise to have sex without compensation as Jenny expressed: 'there is no reason to have sex for free. It's a logical and natural thing to charge a man for sex.' Although Jenny's perception is hardly likely to be representative of all *CCs*, it is illuminating how the transformation of intimacy and sexuality have led some girls to take part in CD. Similarly, Candy, 20 years old, justified her CD practice by contributing to the practice of plastic sexuality in non-commercial setting in modern times:

> I don't see any problem in engaging in CD. Nowadays, (non-CD) girls have lots of casual sex too. They just pick up sexual partners in Lan Kwai Fong (a clubbing area in Hong Kong). So, there is no difference between what we are doing and what they are doing. They (non-CD girls) are even cheaper than us, because they offer themselves for free.

Making use of their female sexuality for money is now framed by some girls as nothing to be ashamed of. Rather, it has become normalized as a rational choice. The new female sexual autonomy and plastic sexuality seem to have created a new channel to economic resources for teenage girls and young women in a society where economic possibilities for them are limited.

Nevertheless, plastic sexuality has at the same time created a context of an environment that is favorable to breed risky sexual behaviors which might lead to potentially devastating health and social consequences. While essentially any individual can practise plastic sexuality, it has particularly significant health consequences for women, especially adolescent girls and underage girls, who might be unable to refuse to have unprotected sex. The negative impacts of plastic sexuality are likely to be magnified for these individuals because they tend to have unprotected sex more frequently and, therefore, are more susceptible to unintended pregnancy and hence abortion, or even worse, illegal abortions, which might harm their psychological and/or physical well-being. The condition may be exacerbated if the girls do not have adequate sexual health knowledge to protect themselves.

Adolescents in Hong Kong remain to demonstrate a low level of sexual knowledge despite the rising trend of sexual initiation at an earlier age, and the prevalence of premarital sex and the notion of sex as a recreational activity (Ip, Chau, Chang, & Lui, 2001). This might be because formal sex education programs that cover sensitive and controversial issues about sexuality are not fully implemented in Hong Kong, which may further intensify the negative social effects of the practice of plastic sexuality amongst adolescents. The Family Planning Association (in its *Report on the Youth Sexuality Study 2006*, 2009) stated that although there had been an improvement in the general sexual knowledge of adolescents in Hong Kong from 1996 to 2006, they still held some false beliefs about sexual health. In a survey of 4,116 Form 3 to Form 7 students, only a small proportion of respondents correctly answered the statements: 'Chance of pregnancy is slim 2 weeks before menstruation' and 'Pregnancy can occur with extravaginal ejaculation'. In another telephone survey of 1,038 randomly selected young people between 15 and 29 years of age, 40% of the respondents reported that they did not use condoms during vaginal intercourse (Ip et al., 2001). These figures highlight that mistaken sexual health beliefs and unsafe sexual practice are not uncommon among young people in Hong Kong. When the effects of these false beliefs and practice are commingled with that of plastic sexuality, the consequences will be aggravated. Some of the most serious consequences are felt by the females: unintended pregnancy and abortion.

Because of unprotected sex, casual sex, and inadequate sexual health knowledge, four *CCs* had experienced unwanted pregnancies and all of them had performed illegal abortions in unauthorized clinics, either in Hong Kong or Mainland China. Joey, 16 years old at the time of interview, got pregnant *accidentally* when she was 15 years old:

> Even today, I am still not sure who got me pregnant because I had unprotected sex with my boyfriend, multiple casual sex partners, and clients in the same period of time. All of them could possibly cause my pregnancy. I only had unprotected sex during my 'safe period', which means seven days before and after my menstruation cycle. But to my surprise, I still got pregnant!
>
> After I found out I was pregnant, I looked online for places where I could get an abortion in Hong Kong. I was supposed to get it done within the first two months of my pregnancy, but the doctor said: 'oh, you are not 16 yet. I cannot perform an abortion for you because it's too risky.' So, the abortion got postponed until I found a doctor in Mainland China who was willing to perform an abortion for me even if I was underage. I was already three-month pregnant at that time. The experience was extremely painful and awful.
>
> The doctor gave me a pill and she inserted something into my vagina. Then, I was asked to lie on bed for about six hours to wait for the fetus to die. That six hours were really painful and were the longest six hours in my life. No one attended me during this period of time. I was left alone in the room. I was so upset and despaired that I called my friend and cried.

Despite the miserable and depressed experience, Joey claimed that the incident had not disturbed her psychologically. Yet it did have negative consequences for her physical health as she sometimes felt pain around her abdominal area, which she thought was caused by the abortion.

Like Joey, Candy, 20 years old, who had undergone two abortions, reported that she was unsure who caused her first pregnancy when she was 15 years old:

> I could not tell whether it was my boyfriend or my client who impregnated me the first time. I had unprotected sex with my boyfriend and a regular client at that time. That client only traded with me. He had a wife and he never engaged in casual sex. I believed that he didn't have STDs. Moreover, I thought I could not get pregnant so easily at the age of 15! So, I agreed to have unprotected sex with him. Anyhow, after I got pregnant, my agent took me to an illegal clinic in Hong Kong to get an abortion.
>
> I got my second abortion when I was 16, but this time, I knew it was my boyfriend who impregnated me. He said he would marry me and start a family with me. So, I didn't plan to get an abortion at the very first beginning. Nonetheless, he started to ignore me and had sex with other girls soon after I was pregnant. Then, I thought: 'if the baby wouldn't have a father, I should not give birth to it because it would not grow happily without a father.' Moreover, I could not support the baby financially on my own and if I had a baby at such a young age, my life would be over. When I decided to get an abortion, I was already almost five months pregnant. So, I actually went through the process of a natural birth. The doctor used some tools to suck the fetus out from my vagina. I literally saw the bones of the fetus. When I saw the whole body of it, I felt pity for it and I regretted it too. I literally apologized to the baby.

In spite of Candy's claim that the abortions had no negative impact on her psychological and physical health, she admitted missing the babies and said that she had begun self-harming after the abortions: 'I have a lot of scars on my arms,' she said. Although Candy was unable to articulate precisely why she had developed the habit of cutting her arms and that there are various reasons for adolescent girls to inflict self-injury, in the particular case of Candy, based on her personal histories, I construe that the self-injury served as her defense mechanism against her emotional pain and inner homelessness from her fragmented family life (she comes from a single-parent family, has never seen her father, and has a poor relationship with her mother), volatile intimate relationships, the loss of her infants, her CD involvement, and other uncertainties in her life that she had lost control.

The increased likelihood of unwanted pregnancies due to the combined effects of plastic sexuality, unprotected sex, and misconceptions about sexual health knowledge seem to have a concomitant consequence: the transformation of the meaning of abortions. In the past, abortion had challenged the primary social values of 'family' and 'motherhood' if abortion was not performed for a medical reason (Railsback, 1984). Even if the decision was made by the pregnant woman, and/or her spouse and her physician, it was still a painful and serious decision for many women in the past (Ehrlich, 2003). Nonetheless, the CCs seem to take the act of abortion lightly and have few doubts about the decision of having an abortion. Doris, 26 years old, said:

> I had been pregnant and performed abortions for four or five times. The first time I had an abortion was 14 or 15 years of age and the last time I had an abortion was last year (25 years old). I am not worried that the abortions will have any negative effects on my health because the fact that I had been pregnant for so many times reflects that my reproductive health is still very good.

For these young women like Doris, an abortion was their only logical resolution for several reasons. First, all the pregnancies were unintended and they perceived sexual behaviors as recreational/commercial rather than reproductive. Gloria, who was 28 at the time of the interview and who had gone through two abortions by the age of 22, described her reaction towards her third pregnancy at the age of 28:

> We had unprotected sex every day during our Shenzhen vacation. My boyfriend didn't use a condom because it was my safe period and we thought I would not have a chance to get pregnant during safe period. Both of us were shocked when we found out that I was pregnant.

For Gloria, the highlight of the vacation was being able to enjoy sex with her boyfriend every day; reproduction had never come across her mind. So, when her boyfriend asked her how to deal with the pregnancy, she firmly and instantly said: 'get an abortion as soon as possible for sure!'

Another major reason that abortion appeared to be the only sensible option for these young women is that some of them were underage when they got pregnant. Three out of four *CCs* who were pregnant had their first pregnancy below the age of 16. Continuing their pregnancy would reveal not only their illicit sexual behaviors, but also the identity of their sexual partners who would be prosecuted for sex with a minor according to Hong Kong law. As such, abortion appeared to be the lesser evil from the underage girls' perspective.

Moreover, since their pregnancies were not within a marital relationship or would not lead to marriage, continuing their pregnancy seemed to be an illogical decision as Candy succinctly put it: 'being a single mother at a young age would mean that my life would be over'. Thus, in light of the likely life course of being a young single mother, they decided to have an abortion. But even if it is not because of the hardship of single parenthood, raising a child is too harsh for these young women as they lack family, social, and financial support. Doris, 26 years old, believed that she is not financially equipped to have a child:

> If I get pregnant with my boyfriend in the near future, I will definitely get an abortion again because it's not the right time for me to bring a child into this world yet. I want my child to grow up in a financially sufficient environment, but I do not have such financial readiness now or in the next couple of years.

Accordingly, the transformation of sex and intimacy in modernity alters not only the way individuals perceive and practice sex, but also the symbolic meanings and practice of abortions. Many girls generally share Candy's sentiment that abortion 'is a common and logical practice. A lot of girls have had it!' Such a perception is dangerous and should be corrected by implementing a more comprehensive program of sexual education at school and society in general.

DISCUSSION

Money might seem to be an easy and immediate answer for why girls engage in CD, but their CD practice cannot simply be explained in terms of materialism; it must be considered in context, with the organization of CD (i.e., the resemblance between CD and conventional intimate relationship), the change in social institutions (i.e., increasing trend of divorce rate and the emergence of new types of family), the transformation in social conditions (i.e., plastic sexuality and an increasingly individualized and fragmented society), and the economic conditions (i.e., limited productive opportunities for young girls who are living in a highly materialistic culture) in the twentieth century.

Under the traditional code of female sexuality, women were pressured to conform to virginity, domesticity, and monogamy for the purpose of reproduction such that there was a great demarcation between the sexual conduct of women who sell sex and women who do not. This demarcation has gradually dwindled as the meanings and practice of sexuality and intimacy have transformed to being more flexible, recreational, non-marital, non-monogamous, volatile, and even emotionally indifferent. Clearly, the principles of the notion and practices of plastic sexuality are not consistent with traditional moral principles of Chinese societies. Hence, there are moral panics, tensions, and controversial behaviors and attitudes resulting from the effects of the transformation of intimacy and plastic sexuality. CD practice is one of them.

Since most of the girls in this study had already been practicing plastic sexuality and having multiple casual sexual partners prior to their commencement of CD, CD behaviors have brought about only a few changes in their sexual behavioral pattern, and thus it was an easy decision and transition for them to take part in CD. CD appeared to be especially appealing to these girls as it provides financial rewards for something that they had always been doing. In other words, their existing practice of plastic sexuality had directly inclined their entrance into CD.

The transformation of intimacy has also led some girls to enter into CD in a less direct way. In late modernity, marriage and family are no longer the solid institutions they used to be because of the precarious nature of modern intimate relationships, which could end at any time as the result of individual decisions. Moreover, even if the intimate tie is not broken, the relationship, including the parent–child relationship, is less intense and stable because of the influence of the Western notion of individualization. The increasing fragmentation of the modern family implies that the ideology that family is the 'haven in a heartless world' has been increasingly called into question (Jamieson, 1987). The absence of family security as a source of emotional support has created a sense of inner homelessness for the girls such that they have to seek emotional comfort and security from external sources such as CD. As illustrated by the CCs, the increased individualization, weak parental ties, and low attachment to the family seem to have increased girls' probability to initiate and perpetuate their CD practice. In the absence of the support of a stable family, many girls must become financially independent. In light of the limited job opportunities and economic resources for adolescent girls, the fragmented family and the notion of individualization do facilitate adolescents to involve in CD because it is they, rather than their parents, who are responsible for taking care of themselves.

The adverse effects of plastic sexuality are exacerbated when they are combined with inadequate levels of sexual health knowledge. One of these negative consequences is unintended pregnancy. I conjecture that if there is more unintended (adolescent) pregnancy, then there is likely to be more (illegal) abortions because the involved minors or women are not ready for motherhood yet, due to their comparatively young age, life circumstances, financial situations, unstable relationship, and concerns about their future and the well-being of their potential child. Abortion, whether legal or illegal, certainly increases the risk of women's sexual and psychological health.

In conclusion, although plastic sexuality, individualization, and the fragmentation of modern society are not in themselves the causes of girls' involvement in CD or adverse public health since the majority of female adolescents and young women affected by them do not engage in CD, the effects of plastic sexuality, modern relationships, radical individualization, and a fragmented society do designate the contexts of an environment that is favourable to the development of CD behavior.

BIBLIOGRAPHY

Anonymous. (2012a, February 29). A 16 Years Old Girl Quits School to Engage in CD (in Chinese). *The Sun*.

Anonymous. (2012b, February 21). College Female Student Engaged in CD; Send Nude Photos to Attrach Clients (in Chinese). *Oriental Daily*.

Bauman, Z. (2003). *Liquid Love: On the Frailty of Human Bonds*. Cambridge: Polity Press.

Boies, S. (2002). University Students' Uses of and Reactions to Online Sexual Information and Entertainment: Links to Online and Offline Sexual Behaviour. *The Canadian Journal of Human Sexuality, 11*(2), 77–91.

Brewis, J., & Linstead, S. (2000). 'The Worst Thing is the Screwing' (1): Consumption and the Management of Identity in Sex Work. *Gender, Work & Organization, 7*(2), 84–97.

Chan, C. T. (2011, February 12). A Girl Sentenced to 12 Months of Probation Order for CD (in Chinese). *Sing Pao*.

Cooper, A., David, L. D., Griffin-Shelley, E., & Robin, M. M. (2004). Online Sexual Activity: An Examination of Potentially Problematic Behaviors. *Sexual Addiction & Compulsivity, 11*(3), 129–143.

Ehrlich, J. S. (2003). Grounded in the Reality of their Lives: Listening to Teens Who Made the Abortion Decision Without Involving their Parents. *Berkeley Women's Law Journal, 18*, 61–180.

Fisher, W. A., & Barak, A. (2000). Online Sex Shops: Phenomenological, Psychological, and Ideological Perspectives on Internet Sexuality. *CyberPsychology & Behavior, 3*(4), 575–589. https://doi.org/10.1089/109493100420188.

Giddens, A. (1992). *The Transformation of Intimacy: Sexuality, Love and Eroticism in Modern Societies*. Standford, CA: Stanford University Press.

Gray, D. (1973). Turning-Out: A Study of Teenage Prostitution. *Journal of Contemporary Ethnography, 1*(4), 401.

Ho, J. C.-J. (2000). Self-empowerment and 'Professionalism': Conversations with Taiwanese Sex Workers. *Inter-Asia Cultural Studies, 1*(2), 283–299.

Ho, J. (2003). From Spice Girls to Enjo Kosai: Formations of Teenage Girls' Sexualities in Taiwan. *Inter-Asia Cultural Studies, 4*(2), 325–336.

Ip, W.-Y., Chau, J. P., Chang, A. M., & Lui, M. H. (2001). Knowledge of and Attitudes Toward Sex among Chinese Adolescents. *Western Journal of Nursing Research, 23*(2), 211–223.

James, J., & Meyerding, J. (1978). Early Sexual Experience as a Factor in Prostitution. *Archives of Sexual Behavior, 7*(1), 31–42.

Jamieson, L. (1987). Theories of Family Development and the Experience of Being Brought Up. *Sociology, 21*(4), 591–607.

Kong, T. S. K. (2006). What it Feels Like for a Whore: The Body Politics of Women Performing Erotic Labour in Hong Kong. *Gender, Work & Organization, 13*(5), 409–434.

Lee, T. Y., & Shek, D. T. (2013). Compensated Dating in Hong Kong: Prevalence, Psychosocial Correlates, and Relationships with Other Risky Behaviors. *Journal of Pediatric and Adolescent Gynecology, 26*(3 Suppl), S42–S48.

Lethbridge, H. (1978). Prostitution in Hong Kong: A Legal and Moral Dilemma. *Hong Kong Law Journal, 8*, 149–173.

McKeganey, N., & Barnard, M. (1996). *Sex Work on the Streets: Prostitutes and Their Clients*. Buckingham\Bristol: Open University Press.

Ng, W.-Y., Leung, P.-Y., & Yau, G.-S. (2009). 'Secondary School Students' Attitudes and Knowledge towards Compensated Dating': Findings. from Hong Kong Association of Sexuality Educators, Reserachers & Therapists Limited. http://www.hkasert.org.hk/Survey of compensated dating(Revised).pdf

O'Connell Davidson, J. (1995). The Autonomy of 'Free Choice' Prostitution. *Gender, Work and Organization, 2*(1), 1–10.

Pedersen, W., & Hegna, K. (2003). Children and Adolescents Who Sell Sex: A Community Study. *Social Science & Medicine, 56*(1), 135–147. https://doi.org/10.1016/s0277-9536(02)00015-1.

Railsback, C. C. (1984). The Contemporary American Abortion Controversy: Stages in the Argument. *Quarterly Journal of Speech, 70*(4), 410–424.

Roberts, N. (1992). *Whores in History: Prostitution in Western Society.* London: Grafton.

Sanders, T. (2005). 'It's Just Acting': Sex Workers' Strategies for Capitalizing on Sexuality. *Gender, Work & Organization, 12*(4), 319–342.

Spink, A., Wolfram, D., Jansen, M. B. J., & Saracevic, T. (2001). Searching the Web: The Public and Their Queries. *Journal of the American Society for Information Science and Technology, 52*(3), 226–234.

The Report on the Youth Sexuality Study 2006. (2009). Hong Kong: The Family Planning Association of Hong Kong.

Thematic Household Survey Report No. 52. (2013). Hong Kong: Census and Statistics Department.

Ueno, C. (2003). Self-determination on Sexuality? Commercialization of Sex among Teenage Girls in Japan. *Inter-Asia Cultural Studies, 4*(2), 317–324.

Widom, C. S., & Ames, A. M. (1994). Criminal Consequences of Childhood Sexual Victimization. *Child Abuse and Neglect, 18*(4), 303–318.

CHAPTER 7

More than Bounded Authenticity

One common myth about commercial sex is that it is only delimited by the mode of a business-like contract, where sex is seen as a commodity or a product for exchange, and where the provider–client relationship is completely devoid of any kind of deeper emotional interaction or reciprocity (Elizabeth Bernstein, 2007, 2010; Egan, 2003; Hoigard & Finstad, 1992; Huff, 2011; Peng, 2007; Ratliff, 1999; Sanders, 2008a). In fact, commercial sex can exist in alternative modes that involve more dynamic and interpersonal relations, where, in addition to sex, companionship, comfort, and a sense of mutual and authentic sensuous experience can be purchased and sold (Elizabeth Bernstein, 2010; Sanders, 2008a). Another related myth is that clients seek out commercial sex entirely for sexual release and physical pleasure (Campbell, 1998; Monto, 1998; O'Connell Davidson, 1998). Nevertheless, the truth is that many clients, particularly those involved with escort and indoor prostitution, desire more than sexual gratification and a commodified experience. These clients look for companionship, a more private conversation, and a more emotionally rewarding and reciprocal intimacy connection, namely *girlfriend experience* (*GFE*). Although *GFE* replicates aspects of a non-commercial romantic relationship, it is very distinct from an unbounded, conventional private intimate relationship because the seemingly genuine emotions are restricted by temporal and financial constraints (Holzman & Pines, 1982; Milrod & Monto, 2012; Milrod & Weitzer, 2012). Bernstein (2001) described this nature of *GFE* as bounded authenticity.

© The Author(s) 2018
C. S. K. Chu, *Compensated Dating*, Gender, Sexualities
and Culture in Asia, https://doi.org/10.1007/978-981-10-6974-1_7

One of the appeals of bounded authenticity is that it allows men to cultivate emotional and sexual intimacies safely because it is restricted by time and contextual parameters. Bounded authenticity is safe in the sense that the emotional and physical intimacies are contained in the commercial context and would not normally transgress into men's normative world due to the bestowal of payment (Bernstein, 2001). The apparently authentic emotional and physical connections are expected to terminate once it is outside the commercial and temporal peripheries. Terry, 35 years old, said:

> What happens in CD stays in CD. Everything returns to normal once a CD encounter ends. My private life and the relationship with my wife remain the same as if the passionate moment with the CC had not happened.

The *GFE* with sex model not only emulates the idealized notion of a romantic relationship, but also frees men from the emotional attachment and commitment that are normally attached to a conventional relationship. Men can suspend their disbelief and freely enjoy the *mutuality* of passions during the limited time in a commercial context. Once they are out of the financial contract, everything is back to normal such that husbands can go back to their wives, boyfriends can go back to their girlfriends, and men can resume their normal life without any emotional burdens and responsibilities. As pointed out in previous chapters, this is a major reason why some men prefer commercial sex to extramarital affairs, which usually come with emotional obligations and are therefore, more likely to disrupt their original relationships and personal life (Campbell, 1998).

While many clients of conventional prostitution seek commercial sex because of its bounded authenticity, *Brothers* in CD desire more than bounded authenticity. They want their relationships with *CCs* to transgress the bounded commercial milieu into their normative world. Compared to traditional provider–client relationships, *CC–Brother* relationships are more likely to extend beyond a bounded commercial context due to an intense sentiment of *GFE*, which creates a confusion between authentic and fake emotions, the intersection of the CD world and the normative world, as well as the effects of the virtual CD community and cybercommunications amongst CD participants. Instead of discussing how bounded authenticity can be derived or how a commodified sexual encounter can be experienced as an authentic intimate, non-remunerative, mutual, and romantic encounter through the control of the service providers' emotional labor skills and cynical performance within the commercial boundaries, which have already been considerably explored (e.g., Earle & Sharp, 2007; Lever & Dolnick, 2010; Sanders, 2005a, 2008b; Sijuwade, 1995), I will illustrate how *Brothers* desire more than a limited, yet real and reciprocal erotic connection, and how *CC–Brother* relationships can transform from bounded, seller–buyer relationships to unbounded, genuine interpersonal relationships, close friendships, and even conventional romantic relationships, through the narratives of both *Brothers* and *CCs*. In addition, this chapter reveals how online relationships in virtual CD communities can transform into offline friendships. I propose that despite CD being a site for commercial sex exchange, it is also a site where conventional social and romantic relationships can be developed. For some CD participants, CD actually expands their interpersonal network.

Girlfriend Experience Revisited

The fantasy of *GFE* is pervasive amongst *Brothers*. All *Brothers* in this study prefer CD to conventional prostitution such as that experienced in one-woman brothels or massage parlors because CD is a very specific form of commercial sex that is designed and enacted to be experienced as a conventional romantic encounter. *CCs* often demonstrate a sense of caring, consideration, and romance that *Brothers* prefer and perceive as the highlight and benchmark for the quality of their CD experience (Sanders, 2008b). Jerry, 30 years old, said: 'CD is not only about sex. It involves love such as talking sweetly, caring for each other, flirting, etc... as if a romantic date in a normal relationship.' *Brothers* would hold hands with *CCs* when they were strolling along the street after their CD encounter or on the way to the hotel. Derrick, 35 years old, deemed the act of holding hands as more intimate and more emotionally pleasurable than sexual acts:

> People don't usually hold hands with someone they just met... I mean it's common for individuals to have sex with someone they just met at a bar, but they don't usually hold hands with their one-night stand partners or prostitutes on the street. Holding hands is an expression of emotional intimacy and mutual connection. I wouldn't hold a girl's hand on the street if I were not emotionally connected with her even though I might have already had sex with her.

Jack, 28 years old, who was in a long-term conventional relationship at the time of interview, also expressed that his pleasure in CD lied on its romantic elements and emotional connection with *CCs*:

> There was one CD encounter that was especially memorable. It wasn't the sex. After the sexual encounter with Janice (a *CC*), we went to have dinner in a pretty nice restaurant, and then she suggested going to the Victoria Park. So, we went there. Strolling in the park with Janice reminded me of the 'dating feeling'. It was like dating with my girlfriend for the first time. It was so sweet. I haven't had such feeling for a long time. I was really happy and she was happy too.

Such a romantic quality plays a crucial role in differentiating CD from conventional prostitution, and in generating *Brothers's* pleasure, which stems less from erotic compulsion or sexual connections than from emotional attractions and psychic communication. Many *Brothers* desires for experience that simulates the essence of romantic love (Giddens, 1992). Ben, 32 years old, summarized men's desires of *GFE*:

> Being able to date a *CC* who delivers *GFE* is every *Brother's* dream. This *CC* is not particularly pretty, yet she shows lots of care and love for me. I like her not because of her appearance or her sexual skills, but because of her ability to behave like my girlfriend.

While the element of romance is crucial in creating *GFE*, passionate sex or girlfriend sex would accentuate *Brothers'* pleasures emotionally and physically. Many *Brothers* felt that the sex that they received in CD was genuine and mutual, yet many *CCs* relegated aspects of their emotional display during CD sex to acting, which is very different from their experience in private sex. Doris, a 26-year-old *CC*, said:

> I had no love for my clients, so I could have sex with them in a very professional way in the sense that I tried my best to satisfy their sexual requests and preferences. Yet the sex with all *Brothers* followed more or less a standardized procedure: I first had shower with them, then kiss and hug them, performed fellatio, and lastly vaginal sex. The sex with *Brothers* usually involved only three basic sexual positions, but the sex with my boyfriend was not standardized and involved a lot more different sexual positions and foreplays. It's just a completely different story.

All *CCs* mentioned that fellatio usually took place before penetrative sex and that they would perform fellatio even if the *Brothers* did not request it. While some *Brothers* perceived such an act as a sign of mutual and passionate sex, the *CCs* revealed that it was simply their strategy to shorten the length of vaginal sex and at the same time to create a sense of *GFE* to please the *Brothers*. Lily, 22 years old, explained:

> I usually put more effort on fellatio and perform it for a relatively longer period of time. The clients enjoyed it a lot. What they didn't know was that in that way, they would be already sexually excited when they began to penetrate me. They would ejaculate soon after the penetration. I would rather perform fellatio for a longer period of time followed by a quick session of vaginal sex than a lengthy period of vaginal sex.

Fellatio had different practical and symbolic meanings for *Brothers* and *CCs*. For the *Brothers*, fellatio satisfies their sexual fantasy and, more importantly, gives them a sense of feeling that the *CCs* were willing to submit to them. For the *CCs*, however, fellatio is a mechanism to reduce their workload as fellatio is regarded as a less demanding task than vaginal intercourse, and that fellatio can expedite the entire CD session. Some *CCs* might also try to find sexual pleasures during sex with clients. Joey explained in our interview: 'initially, I didn't enjoy the sex with clients. But now, instead of hoping the clients to ejaculate quicker and finish the sex as soon as possible, why not enjoying it?' Doris also said: 'even though I seldom experienced orgasm during sex with clients, I could still find excitement in it'. Their narratives show that *CCs* are not passive sexual objects, controlled entirely by men; rather, they are active agents, who are able to assert their sexual agency to create *GFE* and to direct the CD sexual script in a way that they want it. In a sense, *CCs* even manipulate male sexuality and emotions.

Although *GFE* is largely a performance on the part of the *CCs*, some *Brothers* do believe that the emotions expressed by the *CCs* are sincere and that the *CCs* are equally experiencing emotional and sensual closeness along with sexual pleasures: 'I am sure that this *CC* had true feelings for me and enjoyed having sex with me. She said I am her only client,' said Peter, 36 years old. Such assumptions about mutuality are known as the authentic delusion of mutuality (Sanders, 2008b) or the myth of mutuality (Plumridge, Chetwynd, Reed, & Gifford, 1997). Plumridge et al. (1997) argued that the belief of emotional mutuality is an essential ingredient of men's own pleasure, based on the central premise that sex or a romantic interaction ought to be a mutually satisfactory affair.

While some *Brothers* experience *GFE* as an authentic mutual pleasure, others are not overwhelmed and disguised by the myth of mutuality. David, 30 years old, appropriately described: 'I am paying for an unreal relationship.' Similarly, Andrew, 26 years old, said: 'I treat the *CC* as my girlfriend and she treats me as her boyfriend during our *CD* encounters, but we both understand that our relationship is not a real one. Everything ends when the CD encounters end.' In other words, some *Brothers* do suspend their disbelief temporarily and enjoy the interaction as *genuine* mutuality, even though both the *Brothers* and *CCs* are aware of its inauthenticity. They do understand that no matter how authentic the feelings seem to be within the CD context, it is merely a performance. Yet the *Brothers* still enjoy such kind of performed emotions. Sanders (2008b) has referred this state as the authentic-fake delusion of mutuality.

I argued that the authentic-fake delusion of mutuality is not only created by *CCs'* emotional work, but also by *Brothers'* active engagement in the construction of such sentiment. Johnny, a 40-year-old *Brother*, who was aware that *GFE* is not real, illustrated my point that *GFE* is a dynamic performance of a romanticized version of an ideal encounter that rarely exists in non-commercial settings by both *Brothers* and *CCs*:

> Relationships aren't always sweet. In normal relationships, couples argue. Girls easily get mad and men become discontented with their girlfriends and relationships. But in CD, *Brothers* don't expected to be irritated by *CCs* because we don't pay to be treated badly. We expect *CCs* to be tender, subservient, and happy. *GFE* in CD only imitates the romantic aspects and excludes the troublesome elements of a conventional relationship. It is an unrealistic experience constructed by the acting of the *CCs* and the imagination of the *Brothers*.

Johnny succinctly reiterated Egan's (2003, p. 115) notion that the heterosexual relation in a commercial context is distinct from other non-remunerative 'contexts in which women may challenge their male partners more overtly and even reject them outright'. As Johnny pointed out, *GFE* in CD is not a reflection of the reality of a conventional relationship but an enactment of men's romantic fantasy of a *perfect* relationship – one that is exclusive of stresses and conflicts and one that is only infused with romantic elements in which men take the dominant role and women assume the subordinate role. Sexual service providers, whether exotic dancers or *CCs*, 'are paid not to challenge the customers directly... Thus, (the girls) must appear to the customers as their fantasy object in an unproblematic way' (Egan, 2003, p. 116). In this sense, *GFE* in CD is a reinforcement and reconstruction of male desire for a hegemonic heterosexual relationship that they may be unable to achieve in non-commercial contexts.

Importantly, *Brothers* revealed that *GFE* is not simply a service unilaterally provided by *CCs* and which *Brothers* unilaterally enjoy; rather, it is a reflexive and dynamic experience that requires the performance and efforts of both *CCs* and *Brothers*. *Brothers* do not just passively receive *GFE*, but they actively make an effort to enact *GFE* to be experienced as an authentic-fake delusion of mutuality (Sanders, 2008b).

Brothers who experience the myth of mutuality and *Brothers* who experience the authentic-fake delusion of mutuality differ in their ways of achieving *GFE*. On the one hand, *Brothers* who believe in emotional mutuality generally try to please *CCs* by showing care to them on the premise that the *CCs* would return their affections: 'If you treat the *CCs* nicely, the reward that you will get back from them is unimaginable,' said Terry, 35 years old. These *Brothers* might prepare gifts for their *CCs* to express their care and affection. For instance, on their CD dates, Phillip, 37 years old, baked a cake for a *CC*; Eric, 39 years old, brought a novel by his *CC's* favorite novelist; Derrick, 35 years old, brought chocolates; Rooney, 28 years old, brought cosmetics, and so on. The major purpose of these actions was to win the heart of their *CCs* in the hope that the *CCs* would genuinely like them and thus, provide the *holy grail of GFE*. By contrast, *Brothers* who are aware that *GFE* is only a performance usually use their financial power to increase the likelihood that the *CCs* would perform *GFE* accordingly. Kent, 41 years old, elucidated:

> If I pay the *CC* before the sexual encounter, she may only provide some standard services because I have already paid. I mean, since the payment has already been made, the *CC* does not have any incentive to do particular things to please me, but I want more than just standard services! In contrast, if I don't pay the *CC* in advance, she would try her best to please me. If she can give me *GFE* and I am happy, I will probably give her more tips. In this sense, she will benefit more too, right? It's a win—win situation. So, I never pay at the beginning of a CD encounter. I always pay at the end of it.

Concisely, *Brothers* who are aware that *GFE* is artificial and that it only takes place with the precondition of monetary compensations tend to use their financial power to generate their fantasies and desires whereas those who believe *GFE* is genuine tend to use their personal charms and care to win the girls' *authentic* affections.

Interestingly, the myth of mutuality or the authentic delusion of mutuality and the authentic-fake delusion of mutuality are not necessarily incompatible. Theo, 30 years old, described how these two conditions could be experienced simultaneously:

> I understand that there is a ninety-nine percent chance that the affections that the *CCs* show to me are fake, yet there is still a one percent chance that the affections are genuine. I choose to believe this one percent.

Theo was aware that the seemingly genuine *GFE* is most probably a performance on the part of the girls; in this case, Theo was experiencing the authentic-fake delusion of mutuality. Concurrently, however, he was also experiencing the myth of mutuality as he believed that *GFE* is not exclusively a performance; it could possibly be genuine as well. Theo's case illuminates that rather than developing a bipolar imagery of 'the myth of mutuality' and 'the authentic-fake delusion of mutuality' – an either/or situation, we should understand *Brothers'* sentiments along a continuum of these two sentiments.

Is GFE *Always Pleasurable?*

Numerous *Brothers'* accounts have shown that romance and intimacy – whether authentic or illusionary – play an essential role in their pleasure in paying for CD. Yet it is not uncommon for men to experience disappointment and some negative feelings after a passionate CD encounter. Supporting Sanders' (2008b) findings, 22 *Brothers* in this study felt a sense of emptiness after a CD encounter. Cyrus, 42 years old, revealed:

> After having sex with the *CCs*, of course I felt very good and relaxed. But once we were apart, I felt empty because I was being left alone again. I realized that the passion was not real; it was only a trade.

Once the CD encounter was over, the feeling of inner-self emptiness hit Cyrus again. Ryan, 33 years old, also expressed that the experience of emotional fallout after a CD encounter is not uncommon for *Brothers*, especially those who are single and do not have a source of emotional support in their conventional personal life:

> When I went out with a *PTGF*, I undoubtedly enjoyed the *GFE*. I felt like she was treating me as her boyfriend. The emotional connection was so intense and real, yet a *PTGF* session usually lasted for two hours only. After sharing a meal or watching a movie, the time was almost up. I felt empty when the *CC* left. I was a little bit frustrated that I was not able to form a real relationship.

Although *GFE* offers emotional fulfillment and satisfies *Brothers'* yearning for a passionate interaction in general, it is only momentary. The intense, yet ephemeral relations may leave some *Brothers* longing even more for a conventional intimate relationship.

To counteract the emotional tensions and frustrations resulting from CD encounters, Ben, 36 years old, described how he prolonged his encounters with the *CCs* such that their passionate interactions would not end so abruptly and thus, alleviated his emotional fallout:

> After the sexual encounter, especially a passionate one, I would feel empty and down because I could sense that the *CCs* detached their emotions more quickly than I did. Their affections for me could be gone just in an instant. Recently, I have engaged in CD only with familiar *CCs* because they are more willing to go to a movie with me, dine with me, and allow me to send them back to their homes after the sexual encounter and thus, my upset feelings and emptiness are not as strong. Withdrawing emotions every time after having sex immediately is actually very excruciating. So now, if I just want to fulfill my sexual needs, I would rather watch pornography, which doesn't involve any emotions.

While emotional fallouts from a bounded and fleeting CD encounter decrease the desire of some *Brothers* such as Ben to enter into new CD relations or even lead them to withdraw entirely from CD, the emotional frustrations also encourage some *Brothers* to transform their commercial relationships into non-commercial relationships such that longer-lasting and more emotionally stable relationships can be developed.

Like the sex worker–client relationships in traditional forms of prostitution, *CC–Brother* relationships can transform to interpersonal or even romantic relationships (Sanders, 2005b; Warr & Pyett, 1999). In the case of traditional sex worker–client relations, such transformation is more likely to happen if sex worker–client interactions start to occur outside of the initial strictly commercial setting such that the relationship cannot be clearly defined as commercial or non-commercial (Sanders, 2008b). Some sex workers in Sanders' (2005a) study reported that after they started 'dating' a client, their sexual encounter had changed from a mercantile one to a non-mercantile one, and their relationship had altered from a business contract to a romantic relation. Some of these initially commercial relationship had even led to marriage (Sanders, 2008b). Since the physical and/or emotional intimacies in commercial encounters are not necessarily rigidly bounded in temporal, physical, and economic settings, we have to rethink whether commercial intimacies are inevitably counterfeit and bounded.

While clients in Sanders' (2008b) study used an expression of 'fidelity' to describe the non-commercial relationships that they had developed with particular sex workers, *Brothers* are more likely to use the term 'friendship', echoing the *clients* in Bernstein's (2010) study, to describe their relations with *CCs*. They prefer the term 'friendship' because it symbolizes a deeper emotional connection than that in a strictly commercial provider–client relation. *Brothers* often use the concept of 'friendship' to highlight the non-commercial and non-sexual aspects of their relations with *CCs*. Johnny, 40 years old, stated:

> I seldom have sex with *CCs* now. Now, I only date the *CCs* to chat, as some of them have already become my friends. Some *CCs* don't really have an urgent need for money and they would consider me as their friend rather than client. In some instances, after talking with the *CCs* on the CD forum or MSN for a while, I could even date some *CCs*, whom I had never traded with or met, just for drinks or dinner. I didn't have to pay them because I am their friend not their client.

In traditional forms of commercial setting, although genuine friendships could be developed between sex workers and their regular clients as they knew each other, Earle and Sharp (2007) argued that interpersonal relationships and non-commercial encounters are unlikely to be common because they found no instances of such in their own research. Nonetheless, in the context of CD, it is not uncommon for *Brothers* and *CCs* to meet for non-commercial and non-sexual reasons, and to form genuine mutual friendships that are experienced by both parties. In other words, while a crossed-boundary relationship is an exceptional case in conventional sex worker–client relationships, it is not unusual in *CC–Brother* relationships. This difference is perhaps one of the major qualities that sets CD apart from traditional forms of commercial sex and makes CD so unique and valuable for CD participants, especially the *Brothers*. The following sections describe why it is not uncommon for *CC–Brother* relations to transgress the commercial restrictions and how such transgressed relations are formed.

Crossing the Commercial Boundary

Many *Brothers* revealed yearning for, and enjoyment of, spending time with *CCs* outside the temporal and sexual constraints of a CD encounter. *Brothers* wish to engage in activities that are not supposed to take place in a commercial sexual CD script. Don, 40 years old, said: 'I always ask the *CCs* if they want to eat with me before or after the business (sexual encounter). I always try my best to keep her company as long as possible.' Likewise, Andrew, 26 years old, commented: 'I want to know more about the *CCs* because there is always a possibility that I can develop a more personal and deeper relationship with them.'

Confirming Bernstein's (2001) suggestions that some clients are proud of their ability to date and befriend sex workers outside commercial settings, during our interviews, many *Brothers* showed delight and pride in being able to transform their relationships with *CCs* from a bounded, commercial, erotic context into an unbounded, non-commercial, social context, from not only their enthusiastic expressions and attitudes, but also their eagerness to share instances of crossed-boundary activities and relationships with me and other CD members. Some *Brothers* share their non-commercial and non-sexual activities with *CCs* on the CD forum in writings and some share photos, such as their romantic dinners or the places that they have visited, on their Facebook pages.[1] In response to these photos and non-commercial encounters, other *Brothers* commonly express jealousy or their yearnings

---

[1] Besides the CD forums and MSN, some *Brothers* and *CCs* use Facebook to connect and communicate with each other. To protect the identity of the involved *CCs* and *Brothers* in the non-commercial gatherings, the photos on Facebook don't usually show the faces of the involved parties, but only the food, the restaurant, etc. A description of the photo and the feelings of the involved parties are usually included as well.

to engage in crossed-boundary activities and relationships with *CCs*. Apparently, the ability to transcend the restricted commercial relationship boosts *Brothers'* ego because it shows that they can still be desirable to *CCs* without paying them. The fact that they are not providing any financial benefits to the *CCs* for their companionship render unique satisfaction to men as they can obtain for 'free' what other *Brothers* must purchase (Ratliff, 1999).

The online CD forum and other online communicative platforms have drastically transformed the relationships between *CCs* and *Brothers*. Online communications enable the formation of personal relationships that focus on the value of the conversation itself without finding each other as potential commercial sex partners or clients (Ben-Ze'ev, 2004). Ben, 36 years old, elaborated on how the relationships that were built over the virtual CD community could go from online to offline:

> A few days ago, I just had dinner with several *CCs* whom I had never traded and met before. The way I befriend with the *CCs* through the CD forum is just like the way online users make friends with each other through online chatrooms or dating sites. CD forum is no different from other online social networking site. Some people think that meeting friends offline is more *real* and *reliable*, but I believe that online relationships can be stronger and more satisfying. For me, the cyberspace is a very good channel to meet new friends. Because the CD forum is anonymous and the people in the other side of the computer cannot see me, I could engage in a deeper talk with them and even expose some very personal matter that I wouldn't expose in person. Some of my online relationships with the *CCs* have moved to offline and we have become friends rather than having trading relationships.

Cybercommunication functions to normalize *CC–Brother* relationship because it mirrors aspects of a conventional heterosexual social relationship. The anonymous nature of cyberspace also enables self-disclosure, which facilitates genuine friendships, and pure relationships to develop between *Brothers* and *CCs*. Thus, virtual communications in the CD community are as important and as real as offline interactions – both construct social relations, reinforce group identity, and maintain friendship. The following fieldnotes from Gloria's birthday party in a karaoke room exemplifies how the behaviors and activities in the online and offline worlds merge together and how the two arenas constantly interact with and transform each other:

While we were chatting, playing, and singing, Phillip suddenly mentioned something about *cbox* (the instant interactive chat box on the CD forum). And then all of a sudden, everyone became very quiet and was immersed in their phones. At the beginning, I didn't know what was happening. But I soon realized that they were all connected to the CD forum and chatting in *cbox* with their phones.

Although they were physically together in the 'real' world, for a while they were completely immersed in the virtual CD world, communicating with each other as well as other CD participants online. Since everyone was communicating in *cbox*, I was compelled to communicate with them in *cbox* with my phone as well. Then, an interesting thing happened: they started to talk to me in the virtual community, yet no one said a word to me in the physical world. This situation probably had lasted for ten minutes. Then gradually, they withdrew themselves from the *cbox* one by one.

I think the scenario was quite interesting. Even though they could communicate with each other offline, they chose to communicate online in *cbox*. I believe this is because in *cbox*, they could interact not only amongst themselves, but also with other CD participants. They wanted to share their living moments not only with offline CD members, but also with online CD participants. For instance, although everyone had already said 'Happy Birthday' to Gloria offline, all of us said it once again in *cbox*, as if we didn't say it before, as an implicit way to let other CD members know that it was Gloria's birthday. As expected, our actions had led many other online users to send birthday wishes to Gloria who seemed to be very happy about it.

Constantly connecting with the larger virtual CD world appears to be very important to them. The virtual community really means a lot to them.

Griffiths (2001), Korzenny (1978), and Walther and Burgoon (1992) pointed out that emotional intimacy tends to develop faster in the virtual world than in the offline world. This is because online interactants can connect and communicate with each other at any time they wish regardless of their geographic location. The intimacy that may take weeks or months to develop in an offline setting may take only hours or days to develop in an online setting. Ben-Ze'ev (2004) further built on this notion that individuals may experience a higher level of intimacy and affection with their online partners than their offline partners because cyber-relations are free from any physical, social, or structural constraints. This may explain why *CC–Brother* relationships can be intensified in a very short period of time as they often communicate online, which allows

CCs and *Brothers* to establish a certain level of intimacy and familiarity even before they actually meet in the physical world. Thus, they do not have to waste time on getting to know each other or establishing a connection in offline settings as they have already done so online. Moreover, due to virtual interactions, it is likely that the emotional connection in the initial CD encounter is stronger than that in conventional prostitution, in which prior communication is usually absent.

Online communication serves to facilitate the development of crossed boundary relationships not only between *Brothers* and *CCs*, but also amongst *Brothers* and amongst *CCs*. Gloria, 28 years old, revealed:

> Once in a while, some *CCs* with whom I was not acquainted would contact me via the CD forum, probably because of my popularity and reputation in CD. They usually asked me some questions about CD. Some of them even requested to talk to me on the phone or even in person. I do not mind talking with them on the phone. Based on our phone conversations, if I feel like we can become friends, I will most probably meet them. However, I usually don't meet with those who are too young because we cannot 'click'.

> Hebe (a 23 years old *CC* with whom I met and socialized during my offline ethnography but didn't have a chance to conduct a formal interview) and I got together once in a while. When we met, we talked about the *Brothers* and other *CCs*; we also shared our CD experiences. You know, Jason (a *Brother* in his 30s with whom I met and socialized with during my offline ethnography but didn't have a chance to conduct a formal interview) was actually my client, but his penis is so long that I felt like hell when having sex with him. I can't stand it. So, when he requested to trade with me again, I referred Hebe to him. It turned out that Hebe likes Jason a lot because he is so handsome. She said Jason is her favorite client.

Indeed, it is not uncommon for *CCs* to become friends and refer clients to each other. A major benefit of socialization amongst CD participants is that it serves to relieve their psychological burdens as it provides an opportunity for them to talk about their CD experiences, whether good or bad, which cannot be discussed with their non-CD friends. As such, friendship amongst CD participants is actually an important source of emotional support for them. Rooney, 28 years old, described how his genuine friendships with several *CCs* and *Brothers* were valuable to him:

Cassini:	What is the best thing about CD since you have involved in it?
Rooney:	It has to be getting to know Phillip (a 40-year-old *Brother*), who is a very close friend of mine now and is my best friend within the CD circle, Gloria (a 28-year-old *CC*), Greta (a 24-year-old *CC*, who wasn't being formally interviewed but was being observed in my cyber-ethnography and offline participant observation). Four of us have become very good friends.

The friendships that I form in CD differ from those I form outside CD. There is no better or worse because they belong to different categories and cannot be comparable. The topics and interests that I share with my *non-CD* friends are different from that of my CD friends. My friends outside CD do not know my CD involvement, so I cannot be completely honest with them. There is a side of me that they do not know about. In contrast, in front of Phillip, I can talk about almost everything freely. I can talk about my CD experiences, my relationships with the *CCs*, and of course we talk about work too.

A sense of solidarity have developed between Rooney, Phillip, and other *Brothers* and *CCs* because they belong to the same group where familiarity espoused from common experience prevail; the secretes of their CD involvement can be shared and kept securely within the group (Goffman, 1959). On the positive side, such aspects of solidarity within the CD community can lead to the development of trusting relationships and create new networks for emotional support for CD participants. However, on the negative side, it leads CD participants, especially *CCs*, to depend more on the newly found CD sphere and less on the non-CD world because maintaining non-CD social networks and making new friends outside CD can sometimes be very difficult. Gloria, 28 years old, explained:

I have been trying to avoid socializing with my ex-colleagues and ex-classmates recently because they always wonder how I can survive (financially) without having a job during all these years. I lied to my friends, even to my brother. I told them that I had a boyfriend and he supported me financially. But I think even my brother has gotten suspicious because he has never seen my 'boyfriend'.

I don't have too many friends outside the CD circle now because I seldom meet them. You know, I always go to work [CD] and I can't pick up the phone when I am working. Last time when I gathered with my friends, one of them questioned: 'You said you are unemployed, but strangely, you always didn't pick up the phone when we called you. What have you been so busying at?' Shall I lie to them that I have a job? But what kind of job? I really can't think of one. So, in order to avoid these difficult questions from my friends, I have just stopped going to the gatherings altogether.

After her narration, Gloria and I had further discussed several plausible ways that she could explain to her friends and family about how she didn't have to work but could still support herself financially. But here is the catch: Gloria did not want to lie. Hence, social withdrawal seems to be the best strategy to prevent the risk of disclosure of her CD involvement and lying. This isolating strategy was also adopted by six other CCs and other sex workers elsewhere (Sanders, 2005b).

Katy, 28 years old, explained why making new friends outside the CD circle could be difficult and how CD has affected her personal life:

What I get in CD is a lot of money, quick money. But what I have lost in CD is friends. I no longer want to make new friends. I am scared of the way people look at me, their gazes. So now, I avoid going to places where there are a lot of people. Moreover, I do not know how to communicate with strangers who are not in the CD circle anymore. Like the other day, I went to a fashion boutique and then the sale lady approached me and talked to me. I was so frightened that I wanted to flee immediately.

On the one hand, the difficulty of making new non-CD friends and maintaining existing non-CD friendships have isolated some CCs from friends outside the CD network. On the other hand, these difficulties have compelled them to make friends with members in the CD sphere exclusively. Ultimately, the only people left in the CCs' personal social network would be the CD members, who would also become their only source of social and emotional support. Take Gloria's case, for example: three years in a role, Gloria spent and celebrated her birthdays with *Brothers* and CCs instead of non-CD friends. It was quite apparent that her friendship with CD participants had already been stronger and closer than that with her friends outside CD. Such social and emotional dependence on the CD network make it even more difficult for Gloria and other girls, who have already immersed themselves in the CD community, to withdraw from CD in the future if they want to.

Although the interpersonal relationships with other CCs and *Brothers* could provide emotional support to individual CD members, it is not without cost to maintain them. Sometimes, they have to do something that is against their wish. For example, Doris, a 26-year-old *CC* and a friend of Gloria, had asked Gloria for a favor to engage in a 3P CD session with Doris and a *Brother*. Gloria told me that she did not want to do it despite the higher than usual financial rewards because it pertains to higher sexual risk (in a 3P session, the *Brother* usually wouldn't change the condom in between the vaginal intercourses with different girls). So, even though the *Brother* is relatively more protected, the *CCs* are not. The *CCs* are exposed to potential STDs via the fluids on the outer surface of the condom (if one of the *CCs* has STDs, then the other *CC* may be infected, given that the *Brother* uses the same condom to have vaginal intercourses with both *CCs*). Nevertheless, since Gloria did not want to jeopardize her friendship with Doris, she agreed, not once, but several times. This case illustrates how the relationship that extends beyond the bounded context of CD could affect individuals' behavior both outside and as inside CD.

The Intersecting of the CD and Non-CD Worlds

For some CD participants, both *Brothers* and *CCs*, their CD world and non-CD worlds have increasingly merged together because they constantly engage in activities that are outside the bounded commercial CD context with other CD members. Fifteen *Brothers* and six *CCs* reported that they had gathered with other *CCs* and *Brothers* as a group of friends during their leisure time for non-commercial and non-sexual purposes, just as any other groups of friends would have socialized in a conventional setting. I was invited to some of their social gatherings, including dinners, drinks, karaoke, birthday parties, mahjong, and barbeques. While some involved individuals were acquainted with all participants, some individuals knew only a few participants. More interestingly, although some CD participants had already known each other for a long time online, they might have never met offline before the social event. Therefore, at each of these social occasions, some *Brothers* and *CCs* might be meeting in person for the first time. For example, at the end of the interview with Wendy, a 26-year-old *CC*, she invited me to join her dinner with four *Brothers*. I agreed, so she text-messaged the *Brothers* to see whether they would mind if I join. They agreed to let me join the gathering. Since Wendy would be bringing a newcomer (me) to the dinner, a *Brother* also asked if he could bring another newcomer (a *CC*) along to the dinner. Again, everyone agreed. So, the numbers of people who joined the dinner had now increased from five people to seven people

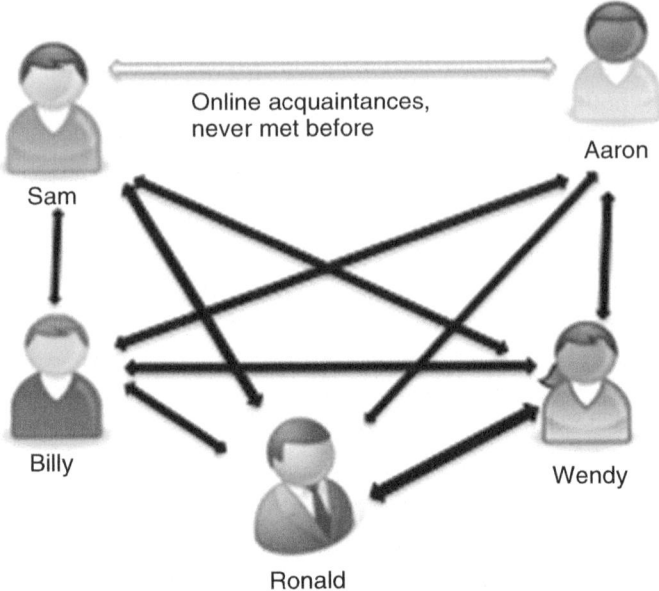

Fig. 7.1 Original group: Except Sam and Aaron, who had only met online but never offline, the rest of the group had met each other offline previously

(refer to Figs. 7.1 and 7.2). Situations like this always happened. More often than not, unacquainted *Brothers* and *CCs* would be introduced to an existing CD network through the introduction of at least one involved group member during a social gathering, and new friendships would develop subsequently. Through these social gatherings, *Brothers* and *CCs* could befriend individuals who normally would not exist in their own social network as Jack, 28 years old, said: 'CD opens my eyes. I meet all sorts of people from different social backgrounds through CD.' In this light, CD has actually expanded individuals' social interpersonal network in additional to their sexual network.

The first non-commercial and non-sexual social occasion amongst CD participants that I joined was a karaoke evening. There were more than ten *Brothers* and *CCs*, but I was acquainted with only two of the *Brothers*. Even though it was Jack, 28 years old, who invited me to the event, it was also his first time to attend such social gathering among CD members. Like me, he had never met most of the people who attended the karaoke

Winnie, a *CC*
introduced by Billy

I was introduced by
Wendy

Sam   Aaron   Ronald

Fig. 7.2   Final group: Billy introduced Winnie, a *CC*, to the group. Wendy introduced me to the group. New friendships were formed

occasion; like Wendy, however, Jack did seek the group's consent to my
participation before taking me to the event. Both Jack and I were a little
nervous about the gathering because we had never been to one before.
When we entered the karaoke room, some *Brothers* and *CCs* were already
singing karaoke and some playing finger-guessing games or dice games.
After we introduced ourselves, it did not take too long for us to mingle
into the group. As time passed, a few more *Brothers* and *CCs* joined us
while some left. The event was seemingly an ordinary social gathering.
Except for one pair of *Brother* and *CC* who exhibited intimate behaviors
like conventional couples, all other *Brothers* and *CCs* did not flirt nor show
particular signs of physical intimacy even though some of them did engage
in CD and did have commercial sexual contacts previously.

As the research progressed, my CD network expanded and I was being
invited to increasingly more non-commercial and non-sexual social gatherings by different *CCs* and *Brothers*. Some *CCs* and *Brothers* could only
attend breakfast, lunch, or early dinner gatherings either because they
could only meet CD participants during office hours when their legitimate
partners were not monitoring their whereabouts, or because they had
to return home at a certain time due to the close watch by parents or

legitimate partners. From my ethnographic observations, there are two major types of CD social gatherings. One type involves a relatively large group of people who might be unacquainted with each other, like my first karaoke event. The other type involves only a few *CCs* and *Brothers* who are very familiar with each other and would therefore engage in more personal and deeper conversations. Normally, in the former type of gatherings, girls do not have to pay and all the *Brothers* share the bill. Every participant seems to acknowledge such informal normal, albeit it is not articulated explicitly. When I first attended the CD social gathering, I was unaware of this custom, so I asked Crystal, a 20-year-old *CC,* how much I should pay. According to my fieldnotes, Crystal gave me a stern gaze, signaling me to remain silent and then whispered to me: 'The *Brothers* are going to settle the bill. Put back your wallet!' By contrast, in the second type of close-group gatherings, men and women usually share the bill equally. Such action seems to be an expression of their genuine friendship in which monetary elements are uninvolved and no one intends to take advantage of anyone. It is a symbolic way to reflect that their relationship is found on authentic friendship and not on money.

Some CD participants who have already quitted buying and selling CD services would keep interacting with existing CD participants online and offline. Take, for example, the case of Wendy and Aaron, who have successfully transformed their commercial *CC–Brother* relationship into a non-commercial, genuine cohabiting relationship. Although both of them claimed that they had stopped providing and purchasing sexual services in CD, they still actively participated in the virtual CD community and regularly met with other active and non-active *Brothers* and *CCs* in physical settings. They even brought their toddler to these gatherings and jokingly discussed some possible online CD pseudonyms for their toddler (I knew it because I was in several of their gatherings). Although Wendy and Aaron had stopped providing and purchasing CD, the CD sphere, and their friendships with past and current CD participants, still constituted an important part of their normative personal life and social network.

While for some participants, their world has become a hybrid of the CD sphere and the non-CD sphere, some participants do not wish their CD world to fuse with their normative non-CD world. Some CD members are reluctant to develop interpersonal relationships and engage in activities that are outside the strictly commercial boundary of CD. When I asked Doris, a 26-year-old *CC,* whether she had ever hung out with *Brothers* outside the CD context, she said:

No, absolutely not although many clients did ask me if I could go out and dine with them. For example, a client suggested: 'Whatever you want to eat. We can even go to a very luxurious restaurant.' I rejected all such requests because I wouldn't get any money from dining with them. I would have to spend two or three hours to dine with a client, but in these two or three hours of time, I could probably engage in CD and make HKD 2,000 or 3,000 dollars. I don't provide *PTGF* service anymore, but if I do, I charge HKD 500 for an hour. I mean, don't waste my time! I told my clients directly that if they want to see me, they have to trade with me. They can choose not to have sex with me, but they have to pay the same amount of money.

While Doris would not hang out with clients outside the professional boundary, Rose, 19 years old, would, but only for the sake of other social benefits:

I normally do not hang out with clients outside CD and I seldom dine with them after our CD encounters, even many of them want to, except for one client who is extraordinarily rich. Like one afternoon, he took me to a very high class Chinese restaurant. As we were heading to the VIP room, many people recognized him and everyone addressed him respectfully as '老爺, 老爺' (pronounced as '*lo yeah, lo yea*' in Cantonese, literally means 'my lord, my lord'). We had shark fins and other expensive dishes. The food was really delicious. The bill was over HKD3,000!

As illustrated by her narrative, Rose was willing to socialize with her client outside the commercial context not because she wanted to develop a crossed-boundary relationship, but because she could obtain social benefits that are not accessible in her ordinary life. In this sense, CD, as she put it, 'has widened her horizons'.

Romantic Relationships

Supporting the findings of Sanders (2005b, 2008b), Warr and Pyett (1999), and Peng (2007), five *CCs* and 19 *Brothers* in this study have developed genuine romantic feelings for their clients and *CCs*, respectively. Amongst them, four girls and 11 men have successfully transformed a bounded, commercial *CC–Brother* relationship into an unbounded, non-commercial intimate relationship. Some of them have even developed into a cohabiting relationship and one of them has resulted in marriage.

Once again, the virtual CD community and online communications have expedited the development of romantic feelings, especially on the part of men. Virtual relationships not only serve as an important source of comfort and companionship for men (Alvin Cooper & Sportolari, 1997), but also enable intense emotions to be generated as Peter, 36 years old, reported:

> I fell in love with Bonnie (a CC) after dating her (a CD encounter). In fact, I knew that I would fall in love with her even before we met because when I chatted with her online, I had a very special feeling and connection with her. We had chatted through MSN for about a week before we met. That's why we were already very intimate and emotionally connected on our first date.

In their study of an online community of regular clients of Internet Sexual Service Providers, Milrod and Monto (2012) stated that clients frequently admit, on various discussion boards, to be falling in love with providers and attempting to establish relationships that go beyond the commercial-sexual arrangements. A similar discourse exists in the CD virtual community. While Taiwanese clients 'use a mocking term, *seasickness*, to describe the dizzy feeling of being in love with a prostitute' (Peng, 2007, p. 327), CD participants used a special term, *sunken boat* (沉船), to describe the condition of falling in love with a CC. This term is not in common use in conventional everyday discourse, but is widely used in the context of CD. To 'sink' for someone means to fall in love with them. The term is not used exclusively to describe client being in love with a CC, but can also be used to describe a CC being in love with a *Brother*; it is more frequently used, however, in the former scenario because *Brothers* seem to be more likely to form an emotional attachment with a CC than vice versa. This is probably because clients tend to inflate and exaggerate the sexual and emotional connection that the CCs do not experience (Sanders, 2008b). As discussed previously, the seemingly authentic *GFE* that the *Brothers* felt is likely to be a performance only.

While some CD participants express their love to a CC or a *Brother* during their usual discourse on the instant chatroom of the CD forum, some share their *sunken boat* experiences and feelings in a special section on the messageboard, which is literally known as the 'sunken boat experience sharing section', in which some *Brothers* created personal *sunken boat diaries* (沉船記) to share their processes and consequences of falling in love with various CCs.

There are several *sunken boat* conditions to describe different levels of emotional attachment. From the lowest to the deepest level of emotional attachment, they are as follows: *floating; water leaking into the boat; half-floating, half-sinking;* and *sunken boat*. These four conditions illustrate the emotional tensions, complexity, and dynamics of *CC–Brother* relationships. *Floating* is a neutral stage during which a *Brother* is not emotionally attached to the *CCs*. It is not a desirable stage because *floating* implies that the *CC–Brother* relationship is only a superficial one with very few emotional connections. *Water leaking into the boat* means that a *Brother* has developed genuine emotional feelings for a *CC*, yet the feelings are controllable and can be withdrawn easily. The condition is just like a water leakage, which could be halted; the water that has already been leaked into the boat would evaporate or could be poured out easily. There can be several leakages simultaneously, which means that a *Brother* can be in a stage where he has developed feelings for several *CCs* concurrently. Like confluent love, romantic relations between *CCs* and *Brothers* are not necessarily monogamous. The third situation is *half-floating, half-sinking*, which is regarded as the most desirable condition because the emotional attachment is deep enough to mirror an authentic romantic emotional connection, yet the *Brother* can still maintain his sensibility and a sense of self such that the emotional feelings would not disrupt his conventional personal relationships and private life. Kent, 41 years old, elaborated:

> I would say I am *half-floating, half-sinking* with this *CC*, which means that I have strong emotions for her, but I wouldn't sacrifice my family because of her. At least, I still go back to my wife. I am still aware that I have to be responsible for my family, which is definitely the most important thing for me.

The final condition is *sunken boat,* which is characterized by intense emotional attachment. *Sunken boat* means completely falling in love with a *CC*; a *Brother* in this stage would want to develop a genuine, non-commercial romantic relationship with the *CC* outside the CD context. The stage of *sunken boat* ought to be avoided because as Alex, 32 years old, puts it: 'it is uncontrollable, risky, and irreversible. It puts you in a state of vulnerability'. Interestingly, Alex's description of *sunken boat* was strikingly similar to Giddens' (1992) description of passionate love, which is filled with strong emotional connection and sexual compulsions. Passionate love tends to threaten ordinary life, and is regarded as dangerous. Likewise, in the stage of *sunken boat*, a *Brother* is over-emotionally attached to a *CC*. Such condition is dangerous in the sense that it could affect his primary conventional relationships. Leon, 43 years old, elaborated the impacts of his *sunken boat* experience:

> My intense relationship with this *CC* had almost caused my wife to divorce me. Although I was in love with this *CC* and I didn't have any romantic feeling for my wife anymore, I did not want a divorce for the sake of our kids. I did not want to create a big fuss. So, I begged her to stay (in the marriage). It wasn't easy but she agreed at the end. We are fine now.

Other *Brothers* who have been married or in a relationship also confessed that they had thought of divorcing their wives or breaking up with their girlfriends because they were in the stage of *sunken boat*, but they ultimately did not do so either because their love for the *CC* was not reciprocated or because they realized that the mutuality was only an delusion. Only one *Brother* ultimately divorced his wife because of a *sunken boat* situation. Aaron, 33 years old, recalled:

> I was actually in a marriage when I met Wendy (a *CC*). You know, many *Brothers* seek CD because they are divorced or in an unhappy relationship. Basically, if we meet a *CC* who is the right girl, we would really pour our heart to her. That is why so many *Brothers* entered into the stage of *sunken boat*. When I met Wendy, I felt that we really clicked. She felt the chemistry between us too. So, we started dating. It didn't take long for me to realize that she is the one. So, I divorced my wife although she was pregnant at that time, and I moved in with Wendy.

In Aaron's case, although his condition of *sunken boat* did not create obvious negative emotions for himself and the involved *CC*, it inevitably jeopardized his existing legitimate relationship, the well-being of his pregnant wife, and their unborn child. That is why *sunken boat* is a condition that shall be rationally avoided by *Brothers*. Cyrus, 42 years old, explained:

> My relationship with this *CC* has lasted for two years already. I love her but I cannot sink. If I sink, my family will break. So, I always remind myself that I cannot move one step further with her. If I don't have a wife, I think I would totally sink for this *CC*. I don't think I could control myself because my love for her is so strong and it will just grow stronger. But, I have a family. I can't sink because I know the consequence will be detrimental.

To prevent oneself from falling into the condition of *sunken boat*, some *Brothers* would avoid dating the same *CC* repeatedly. Alex, 32 years old, gave the following advice to the *Brothers*:

> In order to avoid sinking completely and 'die' in the end, I suggest the following to the *Brothers*, especially the young and newbies who fall in love easily and become out of control easily.
>
> First, do not take the passion with *CC* so seriously. Take it easy and take it as if it is a joyful game. Otherwise, both the *Brother* the *CC* will get hurt.
>
> Second, *Brother* can enjoy and devote oneself to the game, but he should be able to free himself once the game is over. I mean, if a *Brother* decides to sink, sink only for a short period of time. Plan ahead and give a deadline for the relationship.
>
> Third, use the BRAIN instead of the PENIS to think. *Brothers* should maintain their ability to resist temptations from any *CCs* including those who look like angels. Always control the passion and emotion with cautions.
>
> If a *Brother* always keeps these rules in mind, then he can enjoy the experience of *sunken boat* safely. Otherwise, don't play this game.

Basically, *sunken boat* is a situation where a *Brother* (or a *CC*) desires the bounded authenticity to go beyond the commercial context or the bounded authenticity has already extended to the *Brother's* and/or *CC's* normative life. The sentiment in *sunken boat* is different from that in bounded authenticity because the former is not a situation devoid of the complications of a non-remunerative conventional intimacy. *Brothers* who are in the condition of *sunken boat* desire more than paying to experience a bounded *GFE* or the authentic-fake delusion of mutuality, rather, they desire to develop an unbounded non-commercial, genuine, and romantic relationship with the *CCs*. They desire to transcend their identity of 'clients' in the commercial category to 'boyfriends' or 'close and trusted friends' in the conventional category. Although *sunken boat* can be risky, it is sometimes perceived as a privileged status as it implies that the *Brother* is a passionate man who is different from stereotypical lecherous customers.

For *Brothers* who are already in a conventional relationship, the condition of *sunken boat* is no difference from having an extramarital affair, which undeniably affects *Brothers'* primary and legitimate relationships. Hence, the condition of totally sunk is not encouraged, particularly for those *Brothers* who cannot bear its possible negative consequences on their conventional relationships and emotional life. While being completely sunk is not preferred, the circumstances of *water leaking* and *half-floating, half-sinking* are desirable. Ivan, 36 years old said:

> CD is fun only if you get wet. If you only float on the surface of the sea and don't get yourself wet, then you are missing the essence of CD as you are not immersing in it. That is the reason why I always get myself wet partially.

Not all *Brothers* have the ability to get into the situation of *water leaking, half-floating, half-sinking,* or *sunken boat* even if they want to. Victor, 34 years old, expressed disappointedly: 'This year, I don't have a boat to sink for. It's my failure.' Such an expression means that he felt a bit frustrated that he was unable to fall in love with any *CC* this year. The implication is that being able to *get wet* or emotionally involved with *a CC* represents a status, an identity, and an emotional capability of the *Brothers*.

While the process of *sunken boat* and establishing a crossed-boundary relationship can be recreational and pleasurable for some *Brothers*, it can also be highly problematic for both *Brothers* and *CCs* if it is only 'a self-serving interpretative schema' instead of a mutual relationship (Plumridge et al., 1997, p. 178). Sanders (2008b) pointed out that some clients would experience a range of uncomfortable and negative emotions, such as embarrassment, anxiety, and emptiness due to 'falling in love' or futile emotions for individual sex workers that were unreciprocated. *Brothers* in this study also reported various negative feelings, including being cheated, regret, loss, confusion, and despair often after they realized that the emotional attachment was only one-sided. The *special* relationship that they thought they had developed with the *CC* often left them in frustration after they found out that it was merely their own fantasy. Ivan, 37 years old, described his despair:

> I had a very intense relationship with this girl whom I had traded with more than ten times. I believe that we had developed a mutually trusted relationship. She always said she treats me as if I am her husband. It's hard not to *sink* for her. So, when she asked if she could borrow some money from me, I agreed without hesitation. She always asked me to make love with her, but at the same time she would ask me to lend her some money after the sex. I had lent forty thousand dollars to her in total. Luckily, I had good buddies like Jack (a 28 years old *Brother*) to caution me that the girl is not really into me, but only after my money. So, I tried not to lend money to her to see whether she would still treat me like 'her husband'. It turned out that she

disappeared after I rejected lending money to her. I felt like I was being cheated. After that incident, I never trust any *CC* anymore. Even now, I am still hurt, not financially but emotionally!

Like Ivan, some *Brothers,* who are confused about the seemingly genuine emotions that the *CCs* display, may use some tactics to test whether the *CCs'* affections are true or not. Sam, 32 years old, is one of them:

> I was in a *sunken boat* condition with this *CC*, who had just reached 18 years old and had almost become my girlfriend. We had a very close relationship. I had even met her parents when I went to her apartment to fix her computer.
>
> I lent some money to her and told her: 'I don't expect you to return the money but just do not disappear and do not flee away.' Originally, I really wanted to help her unconditionally; the money didn't matter to me, but finally I decided to take this as an opportunity to verify whether this girl is truly in love with me or not. So, it was very simple. I used HKD 4,000 to test her integrity. Disappointedly, I couldn't get in touch with her after I lent her the money. Was I too naïve? Anyways, I had to wake up. To be honest, I was very upset that she disappeared, partly because she didn't keep her promise, and partly because I felt like she had been playing with my feelings. Although I was aware that most of the emotions in the CD world are fake, I was still very disappointed that she lied to me.

Similarly, some *Brothers* expressed negative emotions due to the deep feelings that they had developed for *CCs*. Take, for example, the case of Jack, a 28-year-old *Brother* with a long-term girlfriend. He admitted that he had been in a *sunken boat* condition with three *CCs* previously and that he was in a non-commercial romantic and sexual relationship with a *CC*, Lenka, at the time of the interview. He had visited Lenka's home and met her parents. Jack and I had been keeping in touch after the formal interview through social gatherings amongst CD participants, online communications, and phone conversations. According to my fieldnotes, he had experienced an emotional breakdown due to the death of Lenka:

> It was 1 p.m. Jack just called me. He was crying and sounded very upset. He told me that Lenka committed suicide three days ago. He blamed himself for her death because Lenka asked him whether he would marry her; she also asked Jack that between his long-term girlfriend and Lenka, who would he choose; he said he would choose his girlfriend. Lenka was not happy with his answer.

Jack told me that marrying Lenka did cross his mind, but since other *CCs* had cheated him in the past, he was scared of having a committed relationship with a *CC*. Moreover, due to Lenka's complicated family background, it was impossible for Jack's family to accept her.

A few days before Lenka had committed suicide, she requested to meet Jack, but he refused her because he was at work. Jack said: 'if I had seen her and talked to her that evening, she would probably be fine now and it (her suicide) would not have happened.' He told me that he had been crying every day since her death.

Jack sent me an Internet link about the news of Lenka's death. The news didn't mention that she was a *CC*, probably because her family members did not know that she was one. He continued to cry.

Although we cannot be sure that whether Jack's crossed-boundary relationship with Lenka had anything to do with her suicide, the emotional attachment undoubtedly had created an emotional burden for Jack.

In other cases, the emotional attachment between *Brothers* and *CCs* had posed greater risk on the sexual health of both parties as it increased their tendency and desire to engage in unprotected sex:

When there is a strong chemistry between the *CC* and me, the sex just happens naturally. In such situation, I don't bother using a condom. (Theo, 30 years old)

During that romantic moment, nothing came across my mind... not the condom and not the age of the girl... I just wouldn't think of those things. I simply wanted to enjoy a good time with her. (Ben, 32 year old)

I kissed every inch of her body. I made love with her. I did not use the condom... it's a way to express my love for her and to assert that she is mine. (A *Brother*, who was in a *sunken boat* condition with a *CC*, wrote on the forum)

Apparently, unprotected sex is a way for some *Brothers* to reflect their passionate love, their desire to sexually conquer or possess the *CCs*, and/or the authenticity of their sexual relations.

Interestingly, unprotected sex is also a way for *CCs* and other sex workers to express the authenticity of their love; nevertheless, not to their clients, but to their private romantic partners. In Warr and Pyett's (1999, p. 294) study of 24 female sex workers in Melbourne, most of the women with private partners did not use condoms in their relationships because 'not using condoms enabled them to experience their private relationships as qualitatively different from the sex they engaged in through work'; otherwise, their private sex would be experienced as if it was work sex. Similarly, all *CCs* reported a tendency to not use condoms with their private partners because the absence of a condom was considered as a symbolic way to express their trust and love for their partners. Bella, 20 years old, said: 'the only difference between sex with *Brothers* and sex with my boyfriend is that I use condom with *Brothers* but don't with my boyfriend'. In the same vein, Candy, 20 years old, explained the reason why she used a condom with clients, but not with her boyfriend: 'my boyfriend and I take our relationship seriously. He said he would marry me and have a family with me'. Both cases reveal that in a non-commercial romantic relationship, a condom is not necessary, or even, inappropriate as it is a negation of genuineness. Having sex with a condom signifies that the sex is mechanical and sterile whereas having sex without a condom breaks down the wall that separates one person from another. To use or not to use a condom is a rational choice as well as an emotional choice. Nevertheless, while both *Brothers* and *CCs* use condoms as a symbolic tool to differentiate between passionless and passionate sexual encounters, the ways they apply it are striking different. On the one hand, *Brothers* desire to have unprotected sex with a particular *CC* because they want to declare that their relationship is not merely a commercial one but an emotionally involved one. On the other hand, *CCs* desire to have protected sex with *Brothers* and unprotected sex with their private partners because they wish to maintain and reinforce a clear distinction between an emotionally indifferent commercial *CC–Brother* relationship and an emotionally involved private relationship. Despite the divergent reasons and contexts for unprotected sex, both *Brothers'* and *CCs'* practices expose themselves as well as their private partners to higher risks of STDs. In addition to STDs, the practices also expose *CCs* to higher risk of unwanted pregnancy.

While some occasions of unprotected sex in *genuine CC–Brother* relationships were enacted with the *CC's* consent, some were not, especially if the *Brothers'* affections were unrequited. Peter, 36 years old, admitted that he had forced unprotected sex on a *CC*:

> I was in a deep *sunken boat* condition with this *CC*, but she had clearly expressed that she had no romantic feelings for me. In one of our CD encounters, I took off the condom in the middle of our sexual intercourse without her knowledge. I just did not want any barrier (the condom) between us. I love her so much that I wanted to feel her and be completely intimate with her. She was so mad afterwards that she refused to pick up my calls and see me again.

However, since I was so in love with her, I always checked her online time, kept track of the *Brothers* whom she had dated, called her, text-messaged her, and emailed her numerous times daily. She was so scared of me that she had to change her online account and online name, and close down her online blog. Despite all her effort to avoid me, I did find my way to keep track of her. Ultimately, she had to ask another *Brother* to ask me to stop disturbing her.

Peter's unreciprocated love for the *CC* caused him to force unprotected sex on her. Apparently, his online stalking and compulsive behaviors of attempting to connect with the *CC* outside the CD context had created enormous psychological burdens for the *CC* as well. This case reveals that although the intense emotions and crossed-boundary relationships can be enjoyable for some CD participants, they can also lead to unwanted and negative side effects to other CD participants and the partners in their private lives.

DISCUSSION

This chapter has elaborated the concept of bounded authenticity, which is a commercial and counterfeit emotion that is enacted to be experienced as a romantic and genuine emotion on the part of men. The seemingly genuine emotion expressed by *CCs* and sex workers in general is merely a performance (Lever & Dolnick, 2010; Sanders, 2008b; Sijuwade, 1995). They are paid to render this counterfeit intimacy. Bounded authenticity is desirable for men because its commercial nature guarantees that the authenticity and relation do not transgress to the clients' normative world and this is why Bernstein (2001, p. 398) had pointed out that the major advantage of commercial sex 'is a clear and bounded nature of the encounter'. Yet this chapter has shown that some *Brothers* desire more than bounded authenticity and that they wish to transgress the temporal, sexual, and commercial boundary. As such, CD is not only a site for commercial sexual transaction, but also a conventional heterosexual social scene, in which *CC–Brother* relationships are constructed as complex and dynamic interpersonal relationships rather than simple and static seller–buyer relationships.

The transformation of a commercial *CC–Brother* relationship to a normative interpersonal relationship, genuine friendship, or even an authentic romantic relationship is facilitated by the effects of online communication, the merging of the CD world and non-CD world, and the confusion between *GFE* and authentic intimacy. In some cases, however, the desire of crossed-boundary relationship and over-emotional attachment in CD relationships can lead to tremendous emotional burdens and sexual risks on the *Brothers* and the *CCs*, as the higher level of emotional attachment tends to lead to a higher tendency of unprotected sex and frustrations, especially when the emotions are unrequited.

The bounded commercial CD relationship can grow to become non-bounded romantic relationship as well as genuine friendships. In the context of CD, it is not uncommon for CD participants to move their friendships from online to offline, and integrate their CD world with non-CD world. For some CD participants, CD is a site for commercial sex as well as a platform to expand their interpersonal network. My ethnography shows that CD participants often gather together for non-commercial and non-sexual social purposes, even after they have withdrawn from CD. The relationships amongst CD participants are, therefore, not necessarily commercial or sexual ones, but can also be an unbounded, non-remunerative, and non-sexual social relationships. The various forms of crossed-boundary CD relationships, which mirror aspects of conventional interpersonal relationships, therefore serve to decrease the commercial and sexual nature of CD and normalize their involvement in CD.

While the crossed-boundary friendships allow CD participants to create a sense of solidarity and psychological support for each other, they can also further isolate CD participants, particularly *CCs*, from the non-CD world as they rely more on the CD social network and less on the non-CD ones. As their normative world and CD world have gradually merged into one, the clear boundary that differentiates their professional life and personal life become blurred. One consequence of this condition is that the CD world will ultimately become a primary and an indispensable part of the CD participants' social network and emotional support, which would perpetuate their CD practice.

BIBLIOGRAPHY

Ben-Ze'ev, A. (2004). *Love Online: Emotions on the Internet.* Cambridge, NY: Cambridge University Press.

Bernstein, E. (2001). The Meaning of the Purchase: Desire, Demand and the Commerce of Sex. *Ethnography, 2*(3), 389–420.

Bernstein, E. (2007). Buying and Selling the Girlfriend Experience: The Social and Subjective Contours of Market Intimacy. In M. Padilla, J. Hirsch, M. Munoz-Labboy, R. Sember, & R. Parker (Eds.), *Love and Globalization: Transformers of Intimacy in the Contemporary World.* Nashville: Vanderbilt University Press.

Bernstein, E. (2010). *Temporarily Yours: Intimacy, Authenticity, and the Commerce of Sex*. Chicago: University of Chicago Press.

Campbell, R. (1998). Invisible Men: Making Visible Male Clients of Female Prostitutes in Merseyside. In J. E. Elias, R. N. Vern, L. Bullough, V. Elias, & G. Brewer (Eds.), *Prostitution: On Whores, Hustlers, and Johns* (pp. 155–171). New York: Prometheus Books.

Cooper, A., & Sportolari, L. (1997). Romance in Cyberspace: Understanding Online Attraction. *Journal of Sex Education and Therapy, 22*(1), 7–14.

Earle, S., & Sharp, K. (2007). *Sex in Cyberspace : Men Who Pay for Sex*. Hampshire: Ashgate Publishing Limited.

Egan, D. R. (2003). I'll be Your Fantasy Girl, If You'll be My Money Man: Mapping Desire, Fantasy and Power in Two Exotic Dance Clubs. *Journal for the Psychoanalysis of Culture and Society, 8*(1), 109–120.

Giddens, A. (1992). *The Transformation of Intimacy: Sexuality, Love and Eroticism in Modern Societies*. Standford, CA: Stanford University Press.

Goffman, E. (1959). *The Presentation of Self in Everyday Life*. New York: Anchor Press/Doubleday.

Griffiths, M. (2001). Sex on the Internet: Observations and Implications for Internet Sex Addiction. *Journal of Sex Research, 38*(4), 333.

Hoigard, C., & Finstad, L. (1992). *Backstreets: Prostitution, Money and Love*. University Park: The Pennsylvania State University Press.

Holzman, H. R., & Pines, S. (1982). Buying Sex: The Phenomenology of Being a John. *Deviant Behavior, 4*(1), 89–116.

Huff, A. D. (2011). Buying the Girlfriend Experience: An Exploration of the Consumption Experiences of Male Customers of Escorts. *Research in Consumer Behavior, 13*, 111–126.

Korzenny, F. (1978). A Theory of Electronic Propinquity Mediated Communication in Organizations. *Communication Research, 5*(1), 3–24.

Lever, J., & Dolnick, D. (2010). Call Girls and Street Prostitutes: Selling Sex and Intimacy. In R. Weitzer (Ed.), *Sex for Sale: Prostitution, Pornography, and the Sex Industry* (2nd ed., pp. 187–204). New York\London: Routledge.

Milrod, C., & Monto, M. A. (2012). The Hobbyist and the Girlfriend Experience: Behaviors and Preferences of Male Customers of Internet Sexual Service Providers. *Deviant Behavior, 33*(10), 792–810.

Milrod, C., & Weitzer, R. (2012). The Intimacy Prism: Emotion Management among the Clients of Escorts. *Men and Masculinities, 15*(5), 447–467.

Monto, M. A. (1998). Holding Men Accountable for Prostitution The Unique Approach of the Sexual Exploitation Education Project (SEEP). *Violence Against Women, 4*(4), 505–517.

O'Connell Davidson, J. (1998). *Prostitution, Power and Freedom*. Cambridge: Polity Press.

Peng, Y.-W. (2007). Buying Sex: Domination and Difference in the Discourses of Taiwanese Piao-ke. *Men and Masculinities, 9*(3), 315–336.

Plumridge, E. W., Chetwynd, J. S., Reed, A., & Gifford, S. J. (1997). Discourses of Emotionality in Commercial Sex: The Missing Client Voice. *Feminism and Psychology, 7*(2), 165–181.

Ratliff, E. A. (1999). Women as 'Sex Workers,' Men as 'Boyfriends': Shifting Identities in Philippine Go-Go Bars and Their Significance in STD/AIDS Control. *Anthropology & Medicine, 6*(1), 79–101.

Sanders, T. (2005a). 'It's Just Acting': Sex Workers' Strategies for Capitalizing on Sexuality. *Gender, Work & Organization, 12*(4), 319–342.

Sanders, T. (2005b). *Sex Work: A Risky Business.* Cullompton: Willan Publishing.

Sanders, T. (2008a). Male Sexual Scripts: Intimacy, Sexuality and Pleasure in the Purchase of Commercial Sex. *Sociology, 42*(3), 400.

Sanders, T. (2008b). *Paying for Pleasure: Men who Buy Sex.* Portland: Willan Publishing.

Sijuwade, P. O. (1995). Counterfeit Intimacy: A Dramaturgical Analysis of an Erotic Performance. *Social Behavior and Personality: An International Journal, 23*(4), 369–376.

Walther, J. B., & Burgoon, J. K. (1992). Relational Communication in Computer-mediated Interaction. *Human Communication Research, 19*(1), 50–88.

Warr, D. J., & Pyett, P. M. (1999). Difficult Relations: Sex Work, Love and Intimacy. *Sociology of Health & Illness, 21*(3), 290–309.

CHAPTER 8

Conclusion

This book sheds light on the phenomenon of CD and explores the subjective experiences of CD participants by drawing from four major data sources, including formal in-depth interviews with 30 male clients (*Brothers*) and 12 female CD providers (*CCs*), informal online, face-to-face, and phone conversations with CD participants, cyber-ethnography of a major online CD forum, and offline ethnography in multiple types of non-commercial and non-sexual social gatherings with various groups of CD participants. From these data, the book has focused on the emerging social phenomenon of CD as a way of examining some of the complex forms of intimate relationships in contemporary Hong Kong society. In particular, the book has tried to show how plastic sexuality, modern intimacy, and other social changes (i.e., the new female sexual and financial autonomy, the transformation of family structures, individualization, the fragmentation of society, the advancement of information technology, the development of cyberrelationships and personal insecurities in a risky society that is full of uncertainties) have created a favorable milieu for the emergence and soaring of CD practice, which is conventionally understood as a form of deviant intimacy and a form of *bad sex*. In accounting for the lived experiences of *Brothers* and *CCs*, as well as their reasons and processes of engaging in CD, this book illuminates how CD practices is intertwined with the transformation of the overarching gender pattern in late modernity.

© The Author(s) 2018
C. S. K. Chu, *Compensated Dating*, Gender, Sexualities
and Culture in Asia, https://doi.org/10.1007/978-981-10-6974-1_8

CD: A FORM OF PROSTITUTION OR A REFLECTION OF PLASTIC SEXUALITY?

According to conventional moral codes, CD is a variant of (teenage) prostitution because, more often than not, it ultimately involves financial payment in the form of cash or goods and services with an economic value to take sexual advantages of young women. However, from the vantage point of a majority of CD participants, CD is not a form of prostitution. Their perception is based on the premise that the organization of CD resembles conventional modern intimate sexual scripts and differs substantially from the commercial sexual script of prostitution. The practice of CD and modern intimacy resemble each other twofoldly. First, CD incorporates conventional script of courtship, which creates a feeling of *girlfriend experience* (*GFE*) and a sense of mutuality. The intense emotional intimacy, whether authentic or counterfeit, confuses CD relationships with confluent love and passionate love in modern intimacies. Such confusion creates an illusion for some *Brothers* and *CCs* that they are romantic lovers rather than participants in a commercial transaction. The frequent and dynamic interactions inside and outside of a strictly commercial and sexual contract also make CD less like traditional forms of prostitution and more like conventional intimate relationships. Rather than a monetary transaction involving a commodity, the sex and money involved in CD are projected as an altruistic or affectionate exchange. As such, the *GFE* in CD downplays the pecuniary business nature, as occurs in prostitution, and highlights the reciprocal feature, as is played out in conventional modern relationships. Another reason that the distinction between CD relationships and non-commercial relationships is becoming progressively ambiguous is that the unique features that used to characterize only commercial relationships can now be found in non-commercial modern intimate relationships. Today, the sexual scripts in modern relationships can be as non-reproductive, recreational, casual, non-monogamous, non-marital, or even, emotionally indifferent as those found in commercial relationships. *CC–Brother* relationships may be fleeting, but so too are many modern intimate relationships, given that they only work 'until further notice' (Giddens, 1992). The heightened commercialization in conventional courtship rituals (i.e., romantic dinner, and the giving of flowers and gifts) also makes it more difficult to demarcate between CD script and the script in mainstream modern intimate relationships. Alongside the *GFE* offered in CD, CD relationships and modern non-commercial relationships therefore resemble each other. While the former mirrors the romantic quality of the latter, the latter mirrors the economic, recreational, and non-monogamous elements of the former. The effects of the transformation of sex and intimacy in modernity and the essential nature of CD combine to enable CD participants to normalize their CD behaviors. For CD participants, CD is an innocuous dating activity that is no different from other conventional dating activities. Ben, a 36-year-old client, gave a concise description of this perception: 'CD relationships are just the same as conventional interpersonal relationships.'

Several other features of CD also make it more like modern intimate relationships and less like prostitution. While sex is almost always expected to take place in traditional acts of prostitution, sex is neither taken for granted, nor indeed desired, by all *Brothers*. Despite the money exchange, sex in the context of CD has to be negotiated, depending on the *mood* of a particular CD context and the *chemistry* between the involved *Brother* and *CC*, just like the situation in a conventional sexual script of modern relationships. In other words, sex is not a precondition for CD and the money is often regarded as a gift, a favor for *vulnerable* girls, an expression of affection, or a financial responsibility to a *girlfriend* rather than a payment for sex. Such conception and practice remove the sexual and, more importantly, the commercial aspects of *CC–Brother* relationships, which further differentiate CD from prostitution, and draw CD and non-commercial romantic relationships closer.

Many CD participants conceptualize CD as a variant of modern relationships rather than a form of prostitution because, in contrast to sex worker–client relationships, CD relationships are unbounded. *Brothers* and *CCs* often engage in non-commercial and non-sexual activities, including, but not limited to, strolling on the streets, chatting on phones, having romantic dinners and overseas vacations, meeting each other's parents and friends, and hanging out with other *Brothers* and *CCs* as a group of friends. All these activities are supposed to take place in conventional interpersonal relationships and courtship rituals, but not in commercial sexual scripts, which are normally restricted inside a bounded milieu in terms of temporal, contextual, social, and economic parameters. By contrast, *CC–Brother* relationships are not confined in these constraints and are more flexible. Moreover, with the help of computer-mediated technology, cybercommunication is ubiquitous amongst CD participants, something which rarely occurs in traditional sex work settings. CD participants form a very tight virtual community in which they closely interact with each other at anytime and anywhere they want. Because of the intense communication, *CC–Brother* relations can often develop into genuine romantic relationships and friendships.

In essence, CD encounters understate the financial and sexual aspects in prostitution whilst emphasizing the emotional and mutual aspects found in conventional relationships. The departures of CD from traditional prostitution and the resemblances between CD and non-commercial relationships serve as CD participants' rationales to justify their CD behaviors as a way to forge modern intimacy and plastic sexuality, rather than as a channel to buy and sell sex. One major advantage of the demarcation between CD and prostitution is that it helps CD participants to reduce the social stigma associated with their CD behaviors.

Yet CD has still aroused much moral concern because it illuminates the growing trend of adolescents having recreational sex at an earlier age. Under the influence of traditional Chinese culture, sex remains a sensitive domain within the educational and parenting systems. Adolescents are expected to be asexual subjects. Adolescents, particularly females, who express sexual interests are regarded as deviant individuals characterized by moral problems and even psychological disorder and crime (Ho & Tsang, 2002). However, this perception is gradually being defied as the concepts of plastic sexuality and modern intimacy have progressively influenced individuals' sexual practice and attitudes. Although the notions affect men as well as women, the impacts are greater for women than men for two principal reasons. First, while men have always enjoyed a higher level of sexual freedom than women such that men are more easily condoned to have multiple sexual partners and recreational sex, female sexuality has always been repressed and restricted to procreative sex, both historically and culturally, in Chinese societies. As such, once sexuality is being liberated for both men and women, women would experience a more drastic change under the transformation of intimacy. In fact, a study conducted by the Family Planning Association among Hong Kong high school students shows that female students exhibit a similar and even more liberal sexual values and behaviors (including the acceptance of homosexuality, bisexuality, cohabitation and pre-marital sex) than their male counterparts, which confirms a huge disparity from traditional expectations of sexual attitudes and practices on the part of women (*The Report of Youth Sexuality Study 2011*, 2011). Secondly, the new female biography—higher access and attainment in education and increased levels of labor force participation—has brought more direct transformations to women's lives than it has to those of men. The changes have brought new sexual autonomy for women, which allows them to assert and explore their sexualities—including the right to use their sexuality in exchange of money or other benefits. The consequences of this are not only limited to sex workers, but affect all women as a group, who are now described as 'dangerously free' (Roberts, 1992, p. 355).

Although a new sexual autonomy of women has gradually emerged in late modernity, it has not yet completely replaced the traditional image of women who ought to ensure their chastity. As such, the whore stigma is still strongly attached to sex workers because of deeply rooted conventional moral codes. In the context of CD, one direct resolution for CD participants to reduce the whore stigma is to disassociate *CCs* from sex workers. The separation of *CCs* from sex workers and thus, CD behavior from prostitution, are important phenomena as they have attracted a number of men, who shun prostitution due to the whore stigma, into CD.

Several distinctive features of *CCs* have helped CD participants to set *CCs* apart from the category of sex workers. First, *CCs* are generally younger, more innocent, and less sexually experienced than sex workers. While engaging in CD is only a transitory phase for *CCs*, such that they can get out of the field whenever they want easily, providing sexual services is an occupation and a relatively long-term practice for sex workers, who cannot get out of the field easily based on the assumption that they have greater structural and economic constraints. Thus, *Brothers* conceive *CCs* as *clean*, amateur, and controllable whereas sex workers as seen as *dirty*, professional, and sometimes manipulative. Because of the professionalism implicated in sex workers and the amateurism implicated in *CCs*, most CD participants hold the myth that sex workers offer merely 'fast food sex' and mechanical sex, whereas *CCs* provide emotional and passionate sex that generates *GFE*. Moreover, CD participants consider *CCs* to more respectable than sex workers because they believe that *CCs* have the power to choose their clients and to refuse clients' sexual requests: If *CCs* do not want to engage in intimate acts with *Brothers*, they can always refuse to do so. By contrast, sex workers usually do not have such power because they are expected to be permanently available for sex and to provide sexual services to clients indiscriminately. In this sense, the notions of coercion and victimization, which are usually found in the discourse of prostitution, are generally absent in the normal CD discourse.[1] Consequently, *CCs* are distinct from sex workers in terms of the power relations with *Brothers* and clients respectively; *CCs* are not as subordinate as sex workers in respect to the *Brothers* and clients accordingly. From the perspective of CD participants, *CC–Brother* relations are a type of reciprocal and egalitarian pure relationship that focus on mutual needs and benefits, rather than imbalanced relationships that focus on men's unilateral enjoyment, or on a despicable form of men's exploitation, oppression, and degradation of women. In fact, all informants in this study believe that *CCs* are just like other non-female sex workers because all women, including those who are not in the sex industry, trade their sexuality for financial, social, and/or emotional support.

Given that CD participants classify *CCs* as being different from sex workers, *Brothers* usually differentiate themselves from conventional male clients. *Brothers* tend to believe that they are better than clients of prostitution based on several rationales. The most crucial factor that renders *Brothers* as more respectable than other clients of prostitution is that the *Brothers* believe that they are searching for a deeper emotional exchange rather than superficial, quick, and physical gratification. While conventional clients seek commercial sex precisely because of its bounded nature, *Brothers* seek CD for its unbounded nature, which means that while conventional clients generally wish to confine the authenticity with sex workers in a commercial context, *Brothers* aim to extend the seemingly authentic, mutual, emotional, and erotic connection from a commercial setting to a non-commercial and normative context. Moreover, because the financial cost of a CD encounter is generally higher than a typical paid sex session with a sex worker in a one-woman-brothel, *Brothers* tend to believe that they are relatively well-educated, well-mannered, well-off, and thus, have a higher socio-economic class than conventional clients

Because of the similarities between *CC–Brother* relationships and modern intimate relationships, and the differentiations between CD and prostitution, *CCs* and sex workers, and *Brothers* and clients, CD is considered

---

[1] I am not arguing that coercion and victimization do not exist in CD. They certainly do. As addressed in Chap. 7, *CCs* might be forced into unsafe sex in some exceptional cases where *Brothers* become overly emotionally attached to the *CCs*. Chapter 1 also mentions that there are CD encounters in which underage girls and young women were being forced into CD, being sexually victimized, and even murdered. However, this book focuses on the cases in which both parties enter into CD voluntarily and the mainstream and hidden CD encounters which are not represented in the Media. The findings of this study show that the discourse of coercion and victimization is not a common theme in normal CD discourse.

as a manifestation of plastic sexuality and a new channel for social networking. This classification can therefore encourage men and young women, including those who have never engaged in commercial sex and even those who condemn the idea of prostitution, to engage in CD.

In addition to the abstract ideological distinctions between CD and prostitution in CD participants' conceptions, one significant factor that propels the emergence and the soar of the CD phenomenon is the advancement of technology, which has significantly increased the ease of accessing CD information and negotiating a CD encounter. Technological evolution has undoubtedly made it easier than ever before to enter into CD and thus, made it more attractive compared to traditional forms of prostitution for both men and girls. Due to the anonymity, affordability, and accessibility of the Internet, CD becomes an attractive and safe way for men, particularly those who have never before engaged in commercial sex, and girls, especially those who are under the surveillance of school and parents, to enter into CD as a way of exploring their sexual self in a relatively hidden way.

The growth in the use of the Internet and the evolution of various information technologies in the past decade has boosted a new kind of intimate relationship: the cyber-relationship. Cybercommunication facilitates the development of intense emotional intimacy and affection between individuals because it deconstructs physical, social, and structural constraints and thus, the cyber-relationship is a critical propellant for the growth of plastic sexuality in late modernity. Cybercommunication not only increases the intimacy amongst CD participants, but also provides justification for CD participants to perceive CD relationships as a variant of modern interpersonal relationships. The platform of cyberspace creates a more clandestine, less rigid, and less business-like relationship in comparison to conventional client–sex worker relationships, and therefore, attracts a group of men and girls who shun prostitution due to the whore stigma, and who want to explore plastic sexuality, but could not in their normative setting due to conventional moral and social constraints, as well as the stigma attached to prostitution.

Another major factor that predisposes men to seek CD is the overarching gender relationship in modern times. Today, the entrenched dichotomy in which men dominate the productive role and the social, political, and economic realms whereas women dominate the reproductive role and the domestic realm no longer holds in Hong Kong. Given the higher level of women's educational attainment and labor force participation rate, the power and status of Hong Kong women in the public sphere have been increasing continuously. Although the rising trend of Hong Kong women's educational attainment and participation in the productive realm put women in a higher socio-economic position than ever before, it does not mean that a true equality of the genders has already been achieved since Hong Kong's social system is embedded in a unique mixture of traditional Chinese values and individualistic values of modernity (Cheung, 1997; Westwood, 1997). Under this distinctive mixed value system, the newly claimed women status might even have introduced new struggles to women, including the disadvantages, barriers, and problems that women face in the male-constructed world of modern industrial capitalistic economic relation (Westwood, 1997). Yet the new female biography and the increasingly prominent social roles of women have inevitably changed the gender structure in Hong Kong. Moreover, marriage can no longer confine women in the domestic sphere, which creates further insecurities for men's paternalistic power. Modern gender relationships and intimate relationships are becoming increasingly egalitarian in a way that men no longer have absolute power and control over women in the public and private spheres. All of these changes have posed tremendous threats to male hegemonic masculinity and have changed the cultural expectation of being a man in late modern Hong Kong society.

To summarize, Hong Kong men have been confronted by a crisis of masculinity as we enter into the period of late modernity from a combination of two major changes (Choi et al., 2012). The first change is the emergence of a new female biography. Women's socio-economic status has greatly improved, which opened up greater life choices and opportunities. The role of women is no longer defined exclusively in relations to men or in the family. They are more independent and have the rights to enjoy and use their sexuality for their own ends. The second concomitant change is the increasingly democratic heterosexual relationship. Although we still have gender inequalities in Hong Kong, the discrepancy has become much less than that in the past. There has been resistance among Hong Kong women to take the traditional subordinate gender role. With a rising portion of women acquiring a new female biography, women desire a more egalitarian relationship with men, socially and privately.

The rising trends of women's power and control in the labor market, gender relationship, interpersonal relationship, and legitimate sexual partnerships have placed hegemonic masculinity at risk and have created a higher demand on man. CD serves as a plausible site for men to relax by temporarily putting aside the demands of the new male role and allowing them to regain and assert their masculinity in *CC–Brother* relationships. Although CD can be seen as an egalitarian relationship in terms of the equal power and freedom between *Brothers* and *CCs* to negotiate a CD relationship, and get in or out of it, *CCs* are expected to play a subordinate and docile role. In other words, CD is a modern egalitarian intimate relationship that is enacted to be experienced as a traditional male-oriented and male dominated intimate gender script. The obedience that *CCs* display is particularly valuable for men because women in modern social and private settings tend to become increasingly fierce; they are no longer subordinates, but competitors to men.

Accordingly, the implication of CD is threefold. First, it serves as a platform for individuals, both men and girls, to cultivate plastic sexuality and modern intimacy. Second, it serves as a way for women to make use of their new sexual autonomy to reflect their selves or to gain financial independence. Finally, it serves as a resolution for men to reconstruct and affirm their masculinity in late modernity.

CULTURAL SPECIFICITY OF CD IN HONG KONG

CD has a unique mixture of modern and traditional values. On the one hand, CD is a reflection of the modern notions of plastic sexuality, individualization, female sexual autonomy, and consumerism. On the other hand, it is an enactment of traditional gender relationships where men are the breadwinners and protectors whilst women are subordinated and dependent. Although the phenomenon of CD began in Japan in the early 1990s, and it has become a growing trend in other Asian countries such as Taiwan, Singapore, South Korea, and some parts of more modernized and prosperous parts of China, including but not limited to Shanghai and Canton provinces, which have undergone rapid economic and social changes in recent decades, there are several aspects that are culturally distinct to CD in Hong Kong. First, the phenomenon of CD is more likely to become normalized among young adults in Hong Kong than those in other East Asian countries because, compared to other East Asian countries, Hong Kong are more exposed to and influenced by the notions of plastic sexuality and pure relationships, probably because of its history of

British colonial rule and its high level of Westernization (Brewer, 1999). In fact, 'both male and female students in Hong Kong had more sexually permissive behaviors and attitudes than their counterparts in Taiwan' (Chang, Tsang, Lin, & Lui, 1997, p. 276). The impacts of plastic sexuality and other Western values, which foster and normalize the practice of CD, are thus relatively more visible and direct in Hong Kong. In particular, young women in Hong Kong are comparatively freer to express their sexuality and exhibit higher levels of plastic sexuality. For example, while Korean girls tend to express negative attitudes toward sex, perceive sex as one means of submitting to their boyfriends and/or to maintain their romantic relationship, feel powerless or inappropriate to resist gratifying male sexual desires, recognize themselves as sex objects without recognizing their own sexual feelings and needs, and are taught to keep silent about their sexual desires (Kong, 2003), girls in Hong Kong tend to take more initiative to explore their sexual desires and attain sexual pleasures (Ho & Tsang, 2002). This implies that young women in Hong Kong have already exhibited attitudes and behavioral patterns that are encouraging to the development of CD behaviors.

Moreover, compared to other countries, Hong Kong has a relatively free and open cyberspace and social platform that is favorable for the expansion of CD. In light of the rising phenomenon of CD, the Japanese government has more stringent police actions to combat CD behaviors, the Taiwanese government has started to regulate online chatrooms and websites for potential CD behaviors, and the Chinese government has extensive Internet censorship on pornography and other sexually-related materials (Jacobs, 2012, p. 901; Yeung, 2012, p. 902; Anonymous, 1997, p. 900). In contrast, under Hong Kong legislation, cyberspace remains a grey area. Unlike China and Taiwan, the cyberspace in Hong Kong is largely unregulated. To date, there are few effective legal regulations and law enforcements against online CD activities (Wong & Cheung, 2012). In consequence, there are several online forums that are publicly available for individuals to freely talk about CD, create CD advertisements, and negotiate CD encounters with few or no legal consequences.

Finally, the demography of people who engage in CD is different from that in other Asian countries such as Korea. While men who seek CD in Korea are mostly married men around their 40s and are addressed as *Uncles* by the girls involved in CD, many men who seek CD are in their 20s to 30s and are referred as *Brothers* by CD participants. Many *Brothers* conceptualize their *CC–Brother* relations as egalitarian friendships or romantic relationships rather than exploitative client–sex worker relationships. Moreover, while girls who took part in CD in Korea are largely *problematic* students, *CCs* in Hong Kong are basically unidentifiable and include *normal* and *good* students from middle-class and intact families (Kong, 2003, p. 211; Ueno, 2003, p. 17). Thus, the CD scenario of Hong Kong diverges from the stereotypical image of CD participants and CD relationships elsewhere.

Instead of the general perception that CD is a form of sexual exploitation of teenage sexuality by male "predators", individuals who have already participated in CD or who are considering the possibility of engaging in CD regard it as a new opportunity to explore their sexuality and/or an easy way to earn quick and good money. Many CD participants normalize CD and consider CD to be a mutually beneficial relationship. As Johnny, a 40 years old *Brother*, put it: 'I get what I want and the *CC* gets what she wants in CD. There is nothing wrong with CD.' Such prevailing perception makes us reconsider the dichotomies between good sex and bad sex, and between conventional relationships and commercial relationships in modernity. Rather than blaming the girls for their "decline of morality" and blaming men for their "predatory" behaviors, an increased understanding of the social milieu that propel them to seek love, sex, emotional and/ or financial supports in CD seems to be more useful, especially if you regard CD as problematic and would like to identify plausible solutions to it.

BIBLIOGRAPHY

Anonymous. (1997, April 4). Tokyo Bill to Outlaw Sex With Youths for Money. *The New York Times*. Retrieved from http://www.nytimes.com/1997/04/04/world/tokyo-bill-to-outlaw-sex-with-youths-for-money.html

Brewer, M. B. (1999). Multiple Identities and Identity Transition: Implications for Hong Kong. *International Journal of Intercultural Relations, 23*(2), 187–197.

Chang, J.-S., Tsang, A. K. T., Lin, R.-H., & Lui, P.-K. (1997). Premarital Sexual Mores in Taiwan and Hong Kong. *Journal of Asian and African Studies, 32*(3-4), 265–285.

Cheung, F. M. (1997). *Engendering Hong Kong Society: A Gender Perspective of Women's Status*. Hong Kong: Chinese University Press.

Choi, S. Y. P., Au, W. W. T., Wong, A. W. C., Liong, M. C. C., Wong, M. F. Y., Lo, S. K. W., & Chao, K.-C. (2012). *Exploratory Study on Gender Stereotyping and Its Impacts on Male Gender*. Hong Kong: Equal Opportunities Commission.

Giddens, A. (1992). *The Transformation of Intimacy: Sexuality, Love and Eroticism in Modern Societies*. Standford, CA: Stanford University Press.

Ho, P. S. Y., & Tsang, K.-T. (2002). The Things Girls Shouldn't See: Relocating the Penis in Sex Education in Hong Kong. *Sex Education, 2*(1), 61–73.

Jacobs, K. (2012). *People's Pornography: Sex and Surveillance on the Chinese Internet*. Bristol: Intellect Books.

Kong, M.-H. (2003). Material Girls: Sexual Perceptions of Korean Teenage Girls Who Have Experienced 'Compensated Dates'. *Asian Journal of Women's Studies, 9*(2), 67–94.

Roberts, N. (1992). *Whores in History: Prostitution in Western Society*. London: Grafton.

The Report of Youth Sexuality Study 2011. (2011). (T. F. P. A. o. H. Kong, Trans. T. F. P. A. o. H. Kong Ed.). Hong Kong: The Family Planning Assoication of Hong Kong.

Ueno, C. (2003). Self-determination on Sexuality? Commercialization of Sex among Teenage Girls in Japan. *Inter-Asia Cultural Studies, 4*(2), 317–324.

Westwood, R. I. (1997). The Vertical Dimension and Theoretical Accounts of the Sexual Division of Labour at Work. In F. M. Cheung (Ed.), *Engendering Hong Kong Soceity: A Gender Perspective of Women's Status* (pp. 101–156). Hong Kong: Chinese University Press.

Wong, Y.-Y., & Cheung, P.-K. (2012, March 5). The Police Force Considers to Define Online Discussion Forums as Publice Places; Online Compensated dating = Public Solicitation (in Chinese). *Apple Daily*, p. A12.

Yeung, C.-K. (2012). Online Compensated Dating: Violation of Law Even without the Terms of Sexual Intercourse or Obscenity? Retrieved November 1, 2012, from Law Taiwan http://lawtw.com/article.php?template=article_content&parent_path=,1,4,&article_category_id=2235&job_id=166841&article_id=93058

BIBLIOGRAPHY

Ackland, R. (2013). *Web Social Science: Concepts, Data and Tools for Social Scientists in the Digital Age*. London: Sage.

Albert, A. E., Warner, D. L., & Hatcher, R. A. (1998). Facilitating Condom Use with Clients During Commercial Sex in Nevada's Legal Brothels. *American Journal of Public Health, 88*(4), 643–646.

Alvarez, M. R., Sherman, R. P., & VanBeselaere, C. (2003). Subject Acquisition for Web-Based Surveys. *Political Analysis, 11*(1), 23–43.

American Sociological Association. (1999/2008). *Code of Ethics and Policies and Procedures of the ASA Committee on Professional Ethics*. Washinton, DC: American Sociological Association.

Anonymous. (1997, April 4). Tokyo Bill to Outlaw Sex With Youths for Money. *The New York Times*. Retrieved from http://www.nytimes.com/1997/04/04/world/tokyo-bill-to-outlaw-sex-with-youths-for-money.html

Anonymous. (2009, September 5). Addicted to Materialism! Teenage Girls Engaged in CD for the Sake of Gucci Phone Accessories (in Chinese). *Now News*.

Anonymous. (2010a). 61 Years Old Accountant Had CD with over 100 Teenage Girls, Sent to Prison for 56 Months (in Chinese) *Wen Wei Po*. Hong Kong.

Anonymous. (2010b, August 15). Adolescent Girl Engaged in Compensated Dating for the Sake of Playing Online Game (in Chinese). *The Sun*. Retrieved from http://the-sun.on.cc/cnt/news/20100815/00410_096.html

Anonymous. (2011a, September 25). IT Technician Engaged in Compensated Dating with a Twelve-year-old Girl. *Appledaily*.

© The Author(s) 2018

C. S. K. Chu, *Compensated Dating*, Gender, Sexualities and Culture in Asia, https://doi.org/10.1007/978-981-10-6974-1

Anonymous. (2011b). A Nine-year-old Girl Engaged in Compensated Dating Online. Men Welcomed It and No One Stopped It. The Police Force Exclaimed: The Society is Getting Sick! (in Chinese). *Ta Kung Po*, p. A15.

Anonymous. (2012a, March 10). A 14 Years Old Girl Controlled Her 13 Years Old Classmate to Engage in CD (in Chinese). *Sing Pao Daily*, p. A06.

Anonymous. (2012b, March 10). A 14 Years Old Girl Forced Her 13 Years Old Classmates to Engage in CD. *Sing Pao Daily*.

Anonymous. (2012c, February 29). A 16 Years Old Girl Quits School to Engage in CD (in Chinese). *The Sun*.

Anonymous. (2012d, February 21). College Female Student Engaged in CD; Send Nude Photos to Attrach Clients (in Chinese). *Oriental Daily*.

Anonymous. (2012e, December 17). The Trend of Compensated Dating is Growing in the Cantone Province Because of Luxury Goods (in Chinese). *The China Press*.

Apt, C., Hurlbert, D. F., Sarmiento, G. R., & Hurlbert, M. K. (1996). The Role of Fellatio in Marital Sexuality: An Examination of Sexual Compatibility and Sexual Desire. *Sexual & Marital Therapy, 11*(4), 383–392.

Arendell, T. (1997). Reflections on the Researcher--Researched Relationship: A Woman Interviewing Men. *Qualitative Sociology, 20*(3), 341–368.

Armstrong, E. G. (1978). Massage Parlors and Their Customers. *Archives of Sexual Behavior, 7*(2), 117–125.

Assael, H. (2005). A Demographic and Psychographic Profile of Heavy Internet Users and Users by Type of Internet Usage. *Journal of Advertising Research, 45*(01), 93–123.

Atchison, C., Fraser, L., & Lowman, J. (1998). Men Who Buy Sex: Preliminary Findings of an Exploratory Study. In J. E. Elias, V. L. Bullough, V. Elias, & G. Brewer (Eds.), *Prostitution: On Whores, Hustlers and Johns* (pp. 172–203). New York: Prometheus Books.

Bandura, A. (1982). Self-efficacy Mechanism in Human Agency. *American Psychologist, 37*(2), 122–147.

Barnes, C. (1991). *Disabled People in Britain and Discrimination: A Case for Anti-discrimination Legislation.* London: Hurst & Company.

Barry, K. (1988). Female Sexual Slavery: The Problem, Policies and Cause for Feminist Action. In E. Boneparth & E. Stoper (Eds.), *Women, Power and Policy: Towards the Year 2000* (pp. 282–306). London: Pergamon Press.

Barry, K. (1995). *The Prostitution of Sexuality: The Global Exploitation of Women.* New York: New York University Press.

Bauman, Z. (2000). *Liquid Modernity* (Vol. 9). Cambridge: Polity Press.

Bauman, Z. (2003). *Liquid Love: On the Frailty of Human Bonds.* Cambridge: Polity Press.

Beck, U. (1992). *Risk Society: Towards a New Modernity.* Thousand Oaks, CA: SAGE Publications.

Beck, U., & Beck-Gernsheim, E. (1995). *The Normal Chaos of Love*. Cambridge: Polity Press.

Belza, M. J., Fuente, L. d. l., Suárez, M., Vallejo, F., García, M., López, M., . . . Bolea, Á. (2008). Men Who Pay for Sex in Spain and Condom Use: Prevalence and Correlates in a Representative Sample of the General Population. *Sexually Transmitted Infections, 84*(3), 207–211.

Ben-Ze'ev, A. (2004). *Love Online: Emotions on the Internet*. Cambridge, NY: Cambridge University Press.

Berger, C. R. (1979). Beyond Initial Interaction: Uncertainty, Understanding, and the Development of Interpersonal Relationships. In H. Giles & R. N. S. Clair (Eds.), *Language and Social Psychology* (pp. 122–144). Oxford, UK: Basil Blackwell.

Bernstein, E. (2001). The Meaning of the Purchase: Desire, Demand and the Commerce of Sex. *Ethnography, 2*(3), 389–420.

Bernstein, E. (2007). Buying and Selling the Girlfriend Experience: The Social and Subjective Contours of Market Intimacy. In M. Padilla, J. Hirsch, M. Munoz-Labboy, R. Sember, & R. Parker (Eds.), *Love and Globalization: Transformers of Intimacy in the Contemporary World*. Nashville: Vanderbilt University Press.

Bernstein, E. (2010). *Temporarily Yours: Intimacy, Authenticity, and the Commerce of Sex*. Chicago: University of Chicago Press.

Berson, I. R., & Berson, M. J. (2002). Emerging Risks of Violence in the Digital Age. *Journal of School Violence, 1*(2), 51–71.

Boies, S. (2002). University Students' Uses of and Reactions to Online Sexual Information and Entertainment: Links to Online and Offline Sexual Behaviour. *The Canadian Journal of Human Sexuality, 11*(2), 77–91.

Brewer, M. B. (1999). Multiple Identities and Identity Transition: Implications for Hong Kong. *International Journal of Intercultural Relations, 23*(2), 187–197.

Brewis, J., & Linstead, S. (2000). 'The Worst Thing is the Screwing' (1): Consumption and the Management of Identity in Sex Work. *Gender, Work & Organization, 7*(2), 84–97.

Brown, H. (1994). 'An Ordinary Sexual Life?': A Review of the Normalisation Principle as It Applies to the Sexual Options of People with Learning Disabilities. *Disability and Society, 9*(2), 123–144.

Browne, J., & Minichiello, V. (1995). The Social Meanings Behind Male Sex Work: Implications for Sexual Interactions. *The British Journal of Sociology, 46*(4), 598–622.

Buchanan, E. A. (2011). Internet Research Ethics: Past, Present, and Future. In M. Consalvo & C. Ess (Eds.), *The Handbook of Internet Studies* (pp. 83–108). New York: Wiley-Blackwell.

Campbell, R. (1998). Invisible Men: Making Visible Male Clients of Female Prostitutes in Merseyside. In J. E. Elias, R. N. Vern, L. Bullough, V. Elias, & G. Brewer (Eds.), *Prostitution: On Whores, Hustlers, and Johns* (pp. 155–171). New York: Prometheus Books.

Chan, C. T. (2011, February 12). A Girl Sentenced to 12 Months of Probation Order for CD (in Chinese). *Sing Pao.*

Chan, M.-S. (2012, March 3). A Married Engineer Engaged in CD with a Girl under 13 (in Chinese). *Apple Daily,* p. A17.

Chang, J.-S., Tsang, A. K. T., Lin, R.-H., & Lui, P.-K. (1997). Premarital Sexual Mores in Taiwan and Hong Kong. *Journal of Asian and African Studies, 32*(3-4), 265–285.

Chapkis, W. (1997). *Live Sex Acts: Women Performing Erotic Labor.* New York: Routledge.

Cheung, F. M. (1997). *Engendering Hong Kong Society: A Gender Perspective of Women's Status.* Hong Kong: Chinese University Press.

Cheung, F. M., Lai, B. L. L., Au, K.-c., & Ngai, S. S. Y. (1997). Gender Role Identity, Stereotypes, and Attitudes in Hong Kong. In F. M. Cheung (Ed.), *Engendering Hong Kong Soceity: A Gender Perspective of Women's Status* (pp. 201–235). Hong Kong: Chinese University Press.

Cheung, J. C. K., Lee, T.-Y., & Li, J. C. M. (2011). *Family-centered Prevention of Adolescent Girls' and Boys' Prostitution Final Report* (D. o. A. S. Studies, Trans.). Hong Kong: City University of Hong Kong.

Cheung, Y.-W. (2011, August 29). When a Compensated Dating Girl Meets a Social Worker (in Chinese). *Sing Tao Daily,* p. A22.

Choi, S. Y. P., Au, W. W. T., Wong, A. W. C., Liong, M. C. C., Wong, M. F. Y., Lo, S. K. W., & Chao, K.-C. (2012). *Exploratory Study on Gender Stereotyping and Its Impacts on Male Gender.* Hong Kong: Equal Opportunities Commission.

Chung, Y. (2009, July 30). About 15% of Sexual Victims in Hong Kong Met the Suspects on The Internet (in Chinese). *Sina.* Retrieved from http://finance-news.sina.com/sinacn/304-000-106-109/2009-07-30/20581125528.html

Connell, R. W. (1995). *Maculinities.* Cambridge: Polity Press.

Connell, R. W., & Messerschmidt, J. W. (2005). Hegemonic Masculinity: Rethinking the Concept. *Gender & Society, 19*(6), 829–859.

Cooper, A. (1998). Sexuality and the Internet: Surfing into the New Millennium. *CyberPsychology & Behavior, 1*(2), 187–193. https://doi.org/10.1089/cpb.1998.1.187.

Cooper, A., David, L. D., Griffin-Shelley, E., & Robin, M. M. (2004). Online Sexual Activity: An Examination of Potentially Problematic Behaviors. *Sexual Addiction & Compulsivity, 11*(3), 129–143.

Cooper, A., & Sportolari, L. (1997). Romance in Cyberspace: Understanding Online Attraction. *Journal of Sex Education and Therapy, 22*(1), 7–14.

Cornwell, B., & Lundgren, D. C. (2001). Love on the Internet: Involvement and Misrepresentation in Romantic Relationships in Cyberspace vs. Realspace. *Computers in Human Behavior, 17*(2), 197–211.

Coy, M. (2009). 'Moved Around Like Bags of Rubbish Nobody Wants': How Multiple Placement Moves Can Make Young Women Vulnerable to Sexual Exploitation. *Child Abuse Review, 18*(4), 254–266.

Davis, K. (1937). The Sociology of Prostitution. *American Sociological Review, 2*, 744–755.

Demetriou, D. Z. (2001). Connell's Concept of Hegemonic Masculinity: A Critique. *Theory and Society, 30*(3), 337–361.

Department of State, U. S. A. (2014). Trafficking in Persons Report. U.S.A.

Dunphy, R. (2000). *Sexual Politics: An Introduction.* Edinburgh: Edinburgh University Press.

Dworkin, A. (1989). *Pornography: Men Possessing Women.* New York: Plume New York.

Earle, S., & Sharp, K. (2007). *Sex in Cyberspace : Men Who Pay for Sex.* Hampshire: Ashgate Publishing Limited.

Egan, D. R. (2003). I'll be Your Fantasy Girl, If You'll be My Money Man: Mapping Desire, Fantasy and Power in Two Exotic Dance Clubs. *Journal for the Psychoanalysis of Culture and Society, 8*(1), 109–120.

Ehrlich, J. S. (2003). Grounded in the Reality of their Lives: Listening to Teens Who Made the Abortion Decision Without Involving their Parents. *Berkeley Women's Law Journal, 18*, 61–180.

Elliott, A., & Urry, J. (2010). *Mobile Lives.* Oxford, UK: Routledge.

Ellison, N. B., Hancock, J. T., & Toma, C. L. (2012). Profile as Promise: A Framework for Conceptualizing Veracity in Online Dating Self-presentations. *New Media & Society, 14*(1), 45–62.

Ellison, N., Heino, R., & Gibbs, J. (2006). Managing Impressions Online: Self-presentation Processes in the Online Dating Environment. *Journal of Computer-Mediated Communication, 11*(2), 415–441.

Faugier, J., & Cranfield, S. (1995). Reaching Male Clients of Female Prostitutes: The Challenge for HIV Prevention. *AIDS Care, 7*(1), 21–32.

Fisher, W. A., & Barak, A. (2000). Online Sex Shops: Phenomenological, Psychological, and Ideological Perspectives on Internet Sexuality. *CyberPsychology & Behavior, 3*(4), 575–589. https://doi.org/10.1089/109493100420188.

Fox, N., & Roberts, C. (1999). GPs in Cyberspace: The Sociology of a 'Virtual Community'. *Sociological Review, 47*(4), 643–672.

Fricker, R. D. J. (2008). Sampling Methods for Web and E-mail Surveys. In N. Fielding, R. M. Lee, & G. Blank (Eds.), *The SAGE Handbook of Online Research Methods* (pp. 195–216). Los Angeles: SAGE.

Fukuda, A. (2003). *Feminism and Empowerment in Japan: Compensated Dating.* (M.A. MQ83578), Dalhousie University Canada. Retrieved from http://pro-

quest.umi.com/pqdweb?did=766586401&Fmt=7&clientId=17557&RQT=3
09&VName=PQD

Gemme, R., Payment, N., & Malenfant, L. (1989). *Street Prostitution: Assessing the Impact of the Law*. Montreal, Ottawa: Department of Justice Canada.

Giddens, A. (1990). *The Consequences of Modernity*. Cambridge: Polity Press.

Giddens, A. (1992a). Romantic Love and Other Attachments. In *The Transformation of Intimacy: Sexuality, Love and Eroticism in Modern Societies*. Standford, CA: Standford University Press.

Giddens, A. (1992b). *The Transformation of Intimacy: Sexuality, Love and Eroticism in Modern Societies*. Standford, CA: Stanford University Press.

Goffman, E. (1959). *The Presentation of Self in Everyday Life*. New York: Anchor Press/Doubleday.

Gray, D. (1973). Turning-Out: A Study of Teenage Prostitution. *Journal of Contemporary Ethnography, 1*(4), 401.

Greene, J. C., & Caracelli, V. J. (1997). *Advances in Mixed-Method Evaluation: The Challenges and Benefits of Integrating Diverse Paradigms*. San Francisco, CA: Jossey-Bass Publishers.

Griffiths, M. (2001). Sex on the Internet: Observations and Implications for Internet Sex Addiction. *Journal of Sex Research, 38*(4), 333.

Hammersley, M., & Atkinson, P. (2007). *Ethnography: Principles in Practice*. London\New York: Routledge.

Hausbeck, K., & Brents, B. G. (2002). McDonaldiztion of the Sex Industries? The Business of Sex. In G. Ritzer (Ed.), *McDonaldization: The Reader* (pp. 91–106). Thousand Oaks, CA: Pine Forrest Press.

Hine, C. (2015). *Ethnography for the Internet: Embedded, Emobodied and Everyday*. London: Bloomsbury Academic.

Ho, J. C.-J. (2000). Self-empowerment and 'Professionalism': Conversations with Taiwanese Sex Workers. *Inter-Asia Cultural Studies, 1*(2), 283–299.

Ho, J. (2003). From Spice Girls to Enjo Kosai: Formations of Teenage Girls' Sexualities in Taiwan. *Inter-Asia Cultural Studies, 4*(2), 325–336.

Ho, P. S. Y., & Tsang, K.-T. (2002). The Things Girls Shouldn't See: Relocating the Penis in Sex Education in Hong Kong. *Sex Education, 2*(1), 61–73.

Ho, S.-C. (1984). Women's Labor Force Participation in Hong Kong, 1971–1981. *Journal of Marriage and the Family, 46*, 947–953.

Hochschild, A. R. (1983). *The Managed Heart*. Berkeley: University of California Press.

Hoigard, C., & Finstad, L. (1992). *Backstreets: Prostitution, Money and Love*. University Park: The Pennsylvania State University Press.

Holzman, H. R., & Pines, S. (1982). Buying Sex: The Phenomenology of Being a John. *Deviant Behavior, 4*(1), 89–116.

Hookway, N. (2008). 'Entering the Blogosphere': Some Strategies for Using Blogs in Social Research. *Qualitative Research, 8*(1), 91–113.

Huff, A. D. (2011). Buying the Girlfriend Experience: An Exploration of the Consumption Experiences of Male Customers of Escorts. *Research in Consumer Behavior, 13*, 111–126.

Illouz, E. (1997). *Consuming the Romantic Utopia: Love and the Cultural Contradictions of Capitalism.* Berkeley, CA: University of California Press.

Ip, W.-Y., Chau, J. P., Chang, A. M., & Lui, M. H. (2001). Knowledge of and Attitudes Toward Sex among Chinese Adolescents. *Western Journal of Nursing Research, 23*(2), 211–223.

Jacobs, K. (2012). *People's Pornography: Sex and Surveillance on the Chinese Internet.* Bristol: Intellect Books.

James, J., & Meyerding, J. (1978). Early Sexual Experience as a Factor in Prostitution. *Archives of Sexual Behavior, 7*(1), 31–42.

Jamieson, L. (1987). Theories of Family Development and the Experience of Being Brought Up. *Sociology, 21*(4), 591–607.

Janghorbani, M., & Lam, T.-H. (2003). Sexual Media Use by Young Adults in Hong Kong: Prevalence and Associated Factors. *Archives of Sexual Behavior, 32*(6), 545–553.

Jeffreys, S. (2008). *The Idea of Prostitution.* North Melbourne, Australia: Spinifex.

Joinson, A. N., & Dietz-Uhler, B. (2002). Explanations for the Perpetration of and Reactions to Deception in a Virtual Community. *Social Science Computer Review, 20*(3), 275–289.

Jordan, J. (1997). User Pays: Why Men Buy Sex. *Australian & New Zealand Journal of Criminology, 30*(1), 55–71.

Joshua, B. (2009). Police Saddened as Young Girls Lured into 'Compensated Dating'. *South China Morning Post,* p. 3. Retrieved from http://proquest.umi. com/pqdweb?did=1853572941&Fmt=7&clientId=17557&RQT=309&VNa me=PQD

Kappeler, S. (1996). Subjects, Objects and Equal Opportunities. In S. Jackson & S. Scott (Eds.), *Feminism and Sexuality: A Reader* (pp. 300–306). New York: Columbia University Press.

Koken, J., Bimbi, D. S., & Parsons, J. T. (2010). Male and Female Escorts: A Comparative Analysis. In R. Weitzer (Ed.), *Sex for Sale: Prostitution, Pornography, and the Sex Industry* (2nd ed.). New York: Routledge.

Kong, M.-H. (2003). Material Girls: Sexual Perceptions of Korean Teenage Girls Who Have Experienced 'Compensated Dates'. *Asian Journal of Women's Studies, 9*(2), 67–94.

Kong, T. S. K. (2002). The Seduction of the Golden Boy: The Body Politics of Hong Kong Gay Men. *Body & Society, 8*(1), 29.

Kong, T. S. K. (2006). What it Feels Like for a Whore: The Body Politics of Women Performing Erotic Labour in Hong Kong. *Gender, Work & Organization, 13*(5), 409–434.

Koo, L. C. (1985). The (non) Status of Women in Traditional Chinese Society. *Bullentin of the Hong Kong Psychological Society, 14,* 64–70.

Korzenny, F. (1978). A Theory of Electronic Propinquity Mediated Communication in Organizations. *Communication Research, 5*(1), 3–24.

Lai, Y.-k. (2007). Schoolgirls Fail to See Paid 'Dating' as Prostitution: Group. *South China Morning Post,* p. 4. Retrieved from http://proquest.umi.com/pqdweb?did=1364734281&Fmt=7&clientId=17557&RQT=309&VName=PQD

Lam, O.-W. (2003). Why Did Enjo Kosai Anchor in Taiwan but Not in Hong Kong? Or the Convergence of "Enjo" and "Kosai" in Teenage Sex Work. *Inter-Asia Cultural Studies, 4*(2), 353–363.

Lam, Y.-W. (2012). Mediators Take Advantage of Valentine's Day as a Business Opportunity. "Lovers for Rent" to Attract Clients (in Chinese). *Wen Wei Po,* p. A03. Retrieved from http://paper.wenweipo.com/2012/02/12/YO1202120003.htm

Lau, J. T. F., Siah, P. C., & Tsui, H. Y. (2002). Behavioral Surveillance and Factors Associated with Condom Use and STD Incidences among the Male Commercial Sex Client Population in Hong Kong – Results of Two Surveys. *AIDS Education and Prevention, 14*(4), 306–317.

Lee, T. Y., & Shek, D. T. (2013). Compensated Dating in Hong Kong: Prevalence, Psychosocial Correlates, and Relationships with Other Risky Behaviors. *Journal of Pediatric and Adolescent Gynecology, 26*(3 Suppl), S42–S48.

Leonard, T. L. (1990). Male Clients of Female Street Prostitutes: Unseen Partners in Sexual Disease Transmission. *Medical Anthropology Quarterly, 4*(1), 41–55.

Lethbridge, H. (1978). Prostitution in Hong Kong: A Legal and Moral Dilemma. *Hong Kong Law Journal, 8,* 149–173.

Lever, J., & Dolnick, D. (2010). Call Girls and Street Prostitutes: Selling Sex and Intimacy. In R. Weitzer (Ed.), *Sex for Sale: Prostitution, Pornography, and the Sex Industry* (2nd ed., pp. 187–204). New York\London: Routledge.

Liamputtong, P. (2009). *Qualitative Research Methods* (3rd ed.). Australia and New Zealand: Oxford University Press.

Lorde, A. (1991). The Use of the Erotic; The Erotic as Power. In J. Barrington (Ed.), *Intimate Wilderness.* Portland, OR: Eighth Moutain Press.

Lunnay, B., Borlagdan, J., McNaughton, D., & Ward, P. (2015). Ethical Use of Social Media to Facilitate Qualitative Research. *Qualitative Health Research, 25*(1), 99–109.

Maxwell, J. A. (2005). *Qualitative Research Design: An Interactive Approach* (Vol. 41). Thousand Oaks, CA: Sage Publications.

Maxwell, J. A. (2012). *A Realist Approach for Qualitative Research.* Thousand Oaks, CA: Sage Publications.

McKeganey, N. (1994). Why Do Men Buy Sex and What are Their Assessments of the HIV-related Risks When They Do? *AIDS Care, 6*(3), 289–301.

McKeganey, N., & Barnard, M. (1996). *Sex Work on the Streets: Prostitutes and Their Clients*. Buckingham\Bristol: Open University Press.

Milrod, C., & Monto, M. A. (2012). The Hobbyist and the Girlfriend Experience: Behaviors and Preferences of Male Customers of Internet Sexual Service Providers. *Deviant Behavior, 33*(10), 792–810.

Milrod, C., & Weitzer, R. (2012). The Intimacy Prism: Emotion Management among the Clients of Escorts. *Men and Masculinities, 15*(5), 447–467.

Mok, D. (2017, April 3). Compensated Dating Ring that Earned HK$20 Million in Hong Kong Over Last Five Years Busted. *South China Morning Post*. Retrieved from http://www.scmp.com/news/hong-kong/law-crime/article/2084221/compensated-dating-ring-earned-hk20-million-hong-kong-over

Monto, M. A. (1998). Holding Men Accountable for Prostitution The Unique Approach of the Sexual Exploitation Education Project (SEEP). *Violence Against Women, 4*(4), 505–517.

Monto, M. A. (2000). Why Men Seek Out Prostitutes. In R. Weitzer (Ed.), *Sex for Sale: Prostitution, Pornography, and the Sex Industry* (pp. 67–83). New York: Routledge.

Monto, M. A. (2001). Prostitution and Fellatio. *The Journal of Sex Research, 38*(2), 140–145.

Monto, M. A., & Hotaling, N. (2001). Predictors of Rape Myth Acceptance among Male Clients of Female Street Prostitutes. *Violence Against Women, 7*(3), 275–293.

Ng, W.-Y., Leung, P.-Y., & Yau, G.-S. (2009). 'Secondary School Students' Attitudes and Knowledge towards Compensated Dating': Findings. from Hong Kong Association of Sexuality Educators, Reserachers & Therapists Limited. http://www.hkasert.org.hk/Survey of compensated dating(Revised).pdf

O'Connell Davidson, J. (1995). The Autonomy of 'Free Choice' Prostitution. *Gender, Work and Organization, 2*(1), 1–10.

O'Connell Davidson, J. (1998). *Prostitution, Power and Freedom*. Cambridge: Polity Press.

O'Connell Davidson, J. (2003). Eroticizing Prostitute Use. In R. Matthews & M. O'Neill (Eds.), *Prostitution* (pp. 189–224). Aldershot, Hants, UK; Burlington, VT: Ashgate/Dartmouth.

Oseni, K., Dingley, K., & Hart, P. (2017). *Instant Messaging and Social Networks: The Advantages in Online Research Methodology*. Paper Presented at the The 6th International Conference of Educational and Information Technology Cambridge, UK.

Pedersen, W., & Hegna, K. (2003). Children and Adolescents Who Sell Sex: A Community Study. *Social Science & Medicine, 56*(1), 135–147. https://doi.org/10.1016/s0277-9536(02)00015-1.

Peng, Y.-W. (2007). Buying Sex: Domination and Difference in the Discourses of Taiwanese Piao-ke. *Men and Masculinities, 9*(3), 315–336.

Pitts, M. K., Smith, A. M. A., Grierson, J., O'Brien, M., & Misson, S. (2004). Who Pays for Sex and Why? An Analysis of Social and Motivational Factors Associated With Male Clients of Sex Workers. *Archives of Sexual Behavior, 33*(4), 353–358.

Plumridge, E. W., Chetwynd, J. S., Reed, A., & Gifford, S. J. (1997). Discourses of Emotionality in Commercial Sex: The Missing Client Voice. *Feminism and Psychology, 7*(2), 165–181.

Railsback, C. C. (1984). The Contemporary American Abortion Controversy: Stages in the Argument. *Quarterly Journal of Speech, 70*(4), 410–424.

Ramirez, A., Fleuriet, C., & Cole, M. (2015). When Online Dating Partners Meet Offline: The Effect of Modality Switching on Relational Communication between Online Daters. *Journal of Computer-Mediated Communication, 20*(1), 99–114.

Ratliff, E. A. (1999). Women as 'Sex Workers,' Men as 'Boyfriends': Shifting Identities in Philippine Go-Go Bars and Their Significance in STD/AIDS Control. *Anthropology & Medicine, 6*(1), 79–101.

Roberts, L., Smith, L., & Pollock, C. (2004). Conducting Ethical Research Online: Respect for Individuals, Identities and the Ownership of Words. In E. A. Bunchanan (Ed.), *Readings in Virtual Research Ethics: Issues and Controversies* (pp. 156–173). Hershey, PA: Idea Group.

Roberts, N. (1992). *Whores in History: Prostitution in Western Society*. London: Grafton.

Robson, C. (2011). *Real World Research: A Resource for Users of Social Research Methods in Applied Settings*. Chichester: Wiley.

Ronai, C. R., & Ellis, C. (1989). TURN-ONS FOR MONEY Interactional Strategies of the Table Dancer. *Journal of Contemporary Ethnography, 18*(3), 271–298.

Rubin, G. S. (1993). Thinking Sex: Notes for a Radical Theory of the Politics of Sexuality. In H. Abelove, M. A. Barale, & D.-M. Haplperin (Eds.), *The Lesbian and Gay Studies Reader* (pp. 3–44). London: Routledge.

Rubin, S. B. (2002). *Jon Inc.: The Making of Japan's Salaried Men into Clients of High School Prostitutes*. (M.A. MQ69653), University of Alberta (Canada), Canada. Retrieved from http://proquest.umi.com/pqdweb?did=766177711&Fmt=7&clientId=17557&RQT=309&VName=PQD

Salmons, J. (2016). Using Social Media in Data Collection: Designing Studies with the Qualitative E-Research Framework. In L. Sloan & A. Quan-Haase (Eds.), *The SAGE Handbook of Social Media Research Methods* (p. 177). London: Sage Publications.

Sanders, T. (2005a). 'It's Just Acting': Sex Workers' Strategies for Capitalizing on Sexuality. *Gender, Work & Organization, 12*(4), 319–342.

Sanders, T. (2005b). *Sex Work: A Risky Business*. Cullompton: Willan Publishing.

Sanders, T. (2007). The Politics of Sexual Citizenship: Commercial Sex and Disability. *Disability & Society, 22*(5), 439–455.

Sanders, T. (2008a). Male Sexual Scripts: Intimacy, Sexuality and Pleasure in the Purchase of Commercial Sex. *Sociology, 42*(3), 400.

Sanders, T. (2008b). *Paying for Pleasure: Men who Buy Sex*. Portland: Willan Publishing.

Sijuwade, P. O. (1995). Counterfeit Intimacy: A Dramaturgical Analysis of an Erotic Performance. *Social Behavior and Personality: An International Journal, 23*(4), 369–376.

Smalley, S., Contreras, J., Childress, S., Bailey, H., & Sinderbrand, R. (2003). This Could Be Your Kid. *Newsweek, 142*(7), 44–47.

Soothill, K., & Sanders, T. (2005). The Geographical Mobility, Preferences and Pleasures of Prolific Punters: A Demonstration Study of the Activities of Prostitutes' Clients. *Sociological Research Online, 10*(.1). http://www.socresonline.org.uk/10/1/soothill.html

Spink, A., Wolfram, D., Jansen, M. B. J., & Saracevic, T. (2001). Searching the Web: The Public and Their Queries. *Journal of the American Society for Information Science and Technology, 52*(3), 226–234.

Stone, A. R. (1996). *The War of Desire and Technology at the Close of the Mechanical Age*. Cambridge, MA: MIT Press.

Sullivan, E., & Simon, W. (1998). The Client: A Social, Psychological, and Behavioral Look at the Unseen Patron of Prostitution. In J. E. Elias, V. L. Bullough, V. Elias, & G. Brewer (Eds.), *Prostitution: On Whores, Hustlers, and Johns* (pp. 134–155). Amherst, NY: Prometheus Books.

Swader, C. S., Strelkova, O., Sutormina, A., Syomina, V., Vysotskaya, V., & Fedorova, I. (2013). Love as a Fictitious Commodity: Gift-for-Sex Barters as Contractual Carriers of Intimacy. *Sexuality & Culture, 17*, 598–616.

The Report of Youth Sexuality Study 2011. (2011). (T. F. P. A. o. H. Kong, Trans. T. F. P. A. o. H. Kong Ed.). Hong Kong: The Family Planning Assoication of Hong Kong.

The Report on the Youth Sexuality Study 2006. (2009). Hong Kong: The Family Planning Association of Hong Kong.

The Sage Handbook of Qualitative Research. (2011). United States: Sage Publication.

Thematic Household Survey Report No. 52. (2013). Hong Kong: Census and Statistics Department.

Tse, M.-M., & Mak, C.-W. (2011, April 2). A 11 Years Old Boy Enaged in Same-Sex CD Due to Sexual Curiosity (in Chinese). *The Sun*. Retrieved from http://orientaldaily.on.cc/cnt/news/20110402/00176_019.html

Udagawa, Y. (2007). *Compensated Dating in Japan: An Exploration of Anomie and Social Change in Japan*. Missouri: University of Central Missouri.

Ueno, C. (2003). Self-determination on Sexuality? Commercialization of Sex among Teenage Girls in Japan. *Inter-Asia Cultural Studies, 4*(2), 317–324.

Van Gelder, L. (1996[1985]). The Strange Case of the Electronic Lover. In R. Kling (Ed.), *Computerization and Controversy: Value Conflicts and Social Changes* (2nd ed., pp. 533–546). San Diego, CA: Academic Press.

Vanwesenbeeck, I. (2001). Another Decade of Social Scientific Work on Sex Work: A Review of Research 1990–2000. *Annual Review of Sex Research, 12,* 242–289.

Walther, J. B., & Burgoon, J. K. (1992). Relational Communication in Computer-mediated Interaction. *Human Communication Research, 19*(1), 50–88.

Ward, H., Mercer, C. H., Wellings, K., Fenton, K., Erens, B., Copas, A., & Johnson, A. M. (2005). Who Pays for Sex? An Analysis of the Increasing Prevalence of Female Commercial Sex Contacts among Men in Britain. *Sexually Transmitted Infections, 81*(6), 467–471.

Warr, D. J., & Pyett, P. M. (1999). Difficult Relations: Sex Work, Love and Intimacy. *Sociology of Health & Illness, 21*(3), 290–309.

Waskul, D. D. (2003). *Self-games and Body-Play: Personhood in Online Chat and Cybersex.* New York: Peter Lang.

Weatherall, A., & Priestley, A. (2001). A Feminist Discourse Analysis of Sex Work. *Feminism & Psychology, 11*(3), 323.

Westerhoff, N. (2008). Why do Men Buy Sex? *Scientific American Mind, 19*(6), 62–67.

Westwood, R. I. (1997). The Vertical Dimension and Theoretical Accounts of the Sexual Division of Labour at Work. In F. M. Cheung (Ed.), *Engendering Hong Kong Soceity: A Gender Perspective of Women's Status* (pp. 101–156). Hong Kong: Chinese University Press.

Westwood, R. I., Ngo, H.-Y., & Leung, S.-M. (1997). The Gendered Segmentation of the Labour Market. In F. M. Cheung (Ed.), *Engendering Hong Kong Society: A Gender Perspective of Women's Status* (pp. 41–100). Hong Kong: Chinese University Press.

Widom, C. S., & Ames, A. M. (1994). Criminal Consequences of Childhood Sexual Victimization. *Child Abuse and Neglect, 18*(4), 303–318.

Wilson, E., Kenny, A., & Dickson-Swift, V. (2015). Using Blogs as a Qualitative Health Research Tool: A Scoping Review. *International Journal of Qualitative Methods, 14*(5), 1–12.

Wilton, T. (1999). Selling Sex, Giving Care: The Construction of AIDS as a Workplace Hazard'. In N. Daykin & L. Doyal (Eds.), *Health and Work: Critical Perspectives* (pp. 180–197). New York: St. Martin's Press.

Winick, C. (1962). Prostitutes 'Clients' Perception of the Prostitutes and of Themselves. *International Journal of Social Psychiatry, 8*(4), 289–297.

Women and Girls in Hong Kong: Current Situations and Future Challenges. (2012). Hong Kong: Hong Kong Institute of Asia-Pacific Studies, Chinese University of Hong Kong.

Women and Men in Hong Kong Key Statistics. (2016). Hong Kong: Census and Statistics Dpeartment.

Wong, Y.-Y., & Cheung, P.-K. (2012, March 5). The Police Force Considers to Define Online Discussion Forums as Publice Places; Online Compensated dating = Public Solicitation (in Chinese). *Apple Daily,* p. A12.

Xantidis, L., & McCabe, M. P. (2000). Personality Characteristics of Male Clients of Female Commercial Sex Workers in Australia. *Archives of Sexual Behavior,* 29(2), 165–176.

Yeung, C.-K. (2012). Online Compensated Dating: Violation of Law Even without the Terms of Sexual Intercourse or Obscenity? Retrieved November 1, 2012, from Law Taiwan http://lawtw.com/article.php?template=article_content&parent_path=,1,4,&article_category_id=2235&job_id=166841&article_id=93058

Yuen, Y. (2009). The Murder Case of a Teenage Girl Involved in Compensated Dating in Hong Kong was Brought to the Court: The Murdering Process was Revealed (in Chinese). Retrieved Oct 17, 2017, from Society Eastday. http://big5.eastday.com:82/gate/big5/news.eastday.com/eastday/06news/society/s/20090721/u1a4520555.html

Zelizer, V. A. (2005). *The Purchase of Intimacy.* Princeton: Princeton University Press.

Zhang, C.-M. (2011). Online Advertisement Duped Teenagers into CD (in Chinese). *Wen Wei Po.*

Index[1]

A

Abortion, 143–147

Abuse, 22

Actualization, 107, 112–118

Adolescent, 3, 4, 7–9, 49, 50, 80, 99, 128, 129, 138–145, 149, 190

Agent, 13, 14, 20, 106, 128, 139, 145, 157

Anonymity, 26, 27, 35, 96, 100, 193

Anxiety, 66, 94, 116, 178

Armstrong, E. G., 50, 69

Authenticity, 3, 4, 15, 22, 23, 30, 55, 120, 124, 153–183, 192
  bounded authenticity, 4, 15, 153–183

Autonomy, 2, 20, 131, 133, 139, 143, 187, 191, 195

B

Barry, K., 20, 90

Bauman, Z., 21, 61, 130

Beck, U., 4, 61, 65, 73, 93

Beck-Gernsheim, E., 61, 65, 73, 93

Bernstein, E., 4, 15, 22, 31, 81, 153, 154, 162, 163, 182

Blanchard, 81

Blow job (BJ), 52, 64
  See also Fellatio; Oral sex

Bodies, 3, 6, 10, 12, 14, 20, 21, 37, 54, 58, 67, 81, 83, 88, 116, 128, 131, 132, 139, 145, 180

Brothel, 48, 50, 63, 79, 80, 82, 83, 86, 96, 105, 155
  See also One-woman brothel

Brother, 13–15, 28, 31, 33–35, 37–39, 47–73, 77–101, 105–124, 131, 140, 154–164, 163n1, 166–183, 187–192, 196

Brown, H., 66

Buying sex, 50, 85, 89, 99

C

Call girl, 63, 64, 79, 115, 128, 136

Campbell, R., 31, 32, 51, 57, 59, 61, 66, 81, 153, 154

Cbox, 38, 108, 111, 113, 165

[1]Note: Page numbers followed by 'n' refer to notes.

© The Author(s) 2018
C. S. K. Chu, *Compensated Dating*, Gender, Sexualities
and Culture in Asia, https://doi.org/10.1007/978-981-10-6974-1

CC, 13, 20, 52, 80, 106, 128, 154, 187
CC–*Brother* relationship, 16, 21, 23, 70,
    97, 100, 107, 109, 113, 123, 155,
    162, 163, 165, 172, 173, 175,
    181, 182, 188, 189, 192, 195
CD, *see* Compensated dating
CD-Rom, 108
Census and Statistic Department,
    68, 92, 93, 137, 138
Chatroom, 27, 28, 38, 40, 113, 164,
    174, 196
    See also Cbox
Child prostitute, 95, 96
Client, 1–3, 5–9, 13, 15, 20, 21, 23,
    32, 34, 37, 47–54, 57, 59–64,
    66, 73, 79–82, 84, 95, 99, 100,
    105, 106, 109, 110, 112, 115,
    119, 121, 123, 124, 128, 129,
    132, 133, 135, 136, 142, 144,
    145, 153, 154, 156, 157,
    162–164, 166, 173, 174, 177,
    178, 180–182, 187, 189,
    191–193, 197
Client-sex worker relationship,
    193, 197
    See also CC-*Brother* relationship;
        Sex worker-client relationship
Coercion, 5, 6, 191, 192n1
Commercialization, 4, 188
Commercial sex, 7, 10, 15, 20, 23, 31,
    47–49, 51, 53, 54, 56, 59, 60,
    69, 72, 77–84, 86–89, 91, 95–97,
    99, 100, 105, 108, 109, 112,
    113, 119, 134–136, 139, 142,
    153, 154, 163, 164, 182, 183,
    192, 193
    See also Prostitution; Sex work
Commodification,
    7, 22, 64
Compensated dating (CD), 2–16,
    19–40, 47–73, 77, 108
Compensated dating girl, *see* CC

Computer-mediated communication,
    7, 8, 48
Concern Action in Relieving *Enjo-
    kosai* (CARE), 9
Condom use, 29, 58, 105, 144, 146,
    169, 180, 181
Confluent love, 4, 21, 83, 134,
    175, 188
Confucian ideology/value system,
    94, 100, 194
Connell, R. W., 91, 95
Control, 20, 30, 37, 69, 92, 94–96,
    137, 140, 146, 155, 176, 177, 194
Conventional relationships, 21, 51,
    54, 60–63, 65–72, 154, 156,
    158, 176–178, 190, 197
Counterfeit intimacy, 22, 182
    See also Intimacy
Courtship, 62, 73, 82, 84, 188, 189
Crime Prevention Bureau, 10
Curiosity, 79, 80, 99, 117
Cyber-ethnography, 19, 23, 26–31,
    33, 40, 52, 109, 122, 167, 187
    See also Ethnography
Cyber relationship, 187, 193
    See also Online relationship
Cyberspace, 8, 10, 11, 16, 26, 27,
    29, 33, 34, 49, 123, 135, 164,
    193, 196

D
Data analysis, 24, 40
Demography
    clients, 37, 50
    interviewees, 35–37
Destigmatization, 84
Deviant, 6, 28, 34, 59, 66, 72, 78, 85,
    89, 143, 187, 190
Discrimination, 98
Divorce, 54, 68, 137, 138, 147, 176
Drug, 4–6, 39, 117

E

Earl, S., 57, 69, 155, 162
Embarrassment, *see* Negative emotion
Emotion work, 15, 178
    managing emotions, 22, 29
Enjo Kosai, 49, 89, 90, 137
Eroticization, 56–60, 72
Escort, 49, 64, 153
Ethics, 9, 25, 27, 53
Ethnography, 6, 14, 19, 29, 107, 128,
    166, 183, 187
    See also Cyber-ethnography
Exploitation, 4, 20, 90, 192, 197

F

Family Planning Association,
    141, 144, 190
Fantasy, 33, 34, 59, 96, 101, 155,
    157–160, 178
Fast food sex, 81, 191
Fellatio, 51–54, 72, 156, 157
    See also Blow job (BJ); Oral sex
Freshness, 56, 57, 72, 118
Friendship, 40, 80, 120, 155, 162–164,
    166–172, 182, 183, 190, 197

G

Gaining access, 31–35
Gender relationships, 23, 77, 92, 94,
    101, 122, 193–195
GFE, see Girlfriend experience
Giddens, A., 4, 8, 21, 54, 55, 61, 62,
    73, 81, 83, 92, 99, 100, 130,
    133, 134, 156, 175, 188
Girlfriend experience (GFE), 55, 65,
    73, 77, 80–84, 133, 153–163,
    174, 177, 182, 188, 191
Girlfriend sex, 71, 189
    See also Girlfriend experience (GFE)
Guardian, 107, 121, 124
Guilt, *see* Negative emotion

H

Heath consequence, 106, 143
Hierarchy, 47
    of male clients, 91
    of sex, 78
    of sex work, 49
Ho, J., 3, 6, 31, 127, 137, 141
Ho, J. C.-J., 20, 133
Ho, P. S. Y., 190, 196
Ho, S.-C., 93
Hochschild, A. R., 4, 15, 22

I

Illicit
    nature of prostitution, 59
    sex, 51
Illusion, 62, 84, 188
Individualization, 15, 140, 148, 149,
    187, 195
Information technology, 48, 112, 113,
    134, 135, 187, 193
Inner homelessness, 73, 145, 148
Interview
    face-to-face interview, 30, 31,
        34, 37
    in-depth interview, 19, 23, 29,
        31–37, 128, 187
Intimacy
    authentic intimacy, 182
    avoidance of intimacy, 60–66
    counterfeit intimacy, 182
    transformation of intimacy,
        15, 53, 128, 134, 141,
        143, 148, 190
    unbounded relationship, 22

K

Kong, M.-H., 21, 31,
    196, 197
Kong, T. S. K.,
    9, 81, 131

L

Legitimate relationship, 53, 57, 70, 176, 177
Loser image, 69, 91

M

Marriage, 8, 23, 39, 51, 61, 66, 68, 70, 78, 79, 84, 92–94, 130, 132, 134, 137, 138, 142, 147, 148, 162, 173, 176, 194
Masculinity
crisis, 92, 194
hegemonic masculinity, 15, 34, 54, 69, 77, 92, 94–96, 100, 107, 121, 122, 133, 194
Massage parlors, 32, 48, 79, 128, 155
Materialistic desire, 127–130
McCabe, M. P., 50, 105
Milrod, C., 31, 153, 174
Modernity, 4, 7, 15, 16, 20, 21, 23, 29, 52, 53, 73, 84, 91, 96, 99, 100, 128, 130, 132, 133, 141–148, 187, 189, 191, 193–195, 197
Monogamous, 55, 57, 59, 60, 78, 133, 134, 175
Monto, M. A., 31, 153, 174
Moral burden, 60, 79, 90, 99, 138
Morality, 7, 49, 89, 127, 128, 197
Motivation, 15, 50, 51, 72, 83, 106
MSN, 32, 97, 108–114, 117–119, 162, 163n1, 174
Mutuality
authentic delusion of mutuality, 157, 160
authentic fake delusion of mutuality, 158–160, 177
myth of mutuality, 157–160

N

Negative emotion
embarrassment, 178
frustration, 178
guilt, 118
Non-commercial
encounter, 162, 163
partner, 67, 131
relationship, 21–23, 66–68, 73, 95, 161, 162, 188–190
sex, 51, 61, 62, 69, 131
Non-sexual, 5, 39, 87, 89, 115, 123, 163, 169–171, 183, 187, 189

O

Objectification, 21, 60
O'Connell Davidson, J., 59–61, 95, 132, 153
One-woman brothel, 48, 50, 63, 79, 80, 82, 83, 86, 96, 115, 128, 135, 192
See also Brothel
Online relationship, 164
See also Cyber relationship
Online sexual activities (OSA), 3, 135
Oral sex, 63
See also Blow job (BJ); Fellatio

P

Participant observation, 19, 23, 28, 31, 39, 40, 167
Passionate sex, 55, 133, 156, 157, 191
Peng, Y.-W., 60, 62, 64, 71, 86, 87, 95, 115, 153, 173, 174
Performance, 51, 81, 95, 155, 157–160, 174, 182
Plastic sexuality, 4, 54–57, 60, 69, 73, 83–85, 99, 129–134, 136, 137, 141–149, 187–196

Pleasure, 20, 56–59, 61–63, 71, 72, 81, 83, 91, 100, 122, 123, 131, 153, 156, 158, 160

Plumridge, E. W., 157, 178

Police, 3, 5, 9–12, 32, 34, 57, 108, 109, 128, 196

Power, 20, 39, 55, 59, 83, 87, 88, 90–92, 94, 100, 129, 130, 159, 160, 191, 192, 194, 195

Precursor, 15, 138, 140

Predator, 5, 6, 197

Pregnancy, 98, 143–147, 149, 181

Pressures, 51, 64, 65, 95, 142

Private sex, 132, 133, 156, 180, 181

Prostitute, 31, 50, 59, 61, 79, 85, 86, 95, 100, 128, 155, 174
    See also Sex worker

Prostitution, 3, 5, 7, 9, 10, 15, 22, 23, 47, 48, 50, 51, 53–55, 57, 59, 62, 64–66, 71–73, 79–84, 96–100, 108, 112, 115, 122, 153–156, 162, 166, 188–195
    See also Commercial sex; Sex work

Protection, 107, 118–123, 141

Pseudonyms, 28, 61, 172

Psychological
    burden/harm/disorder, 8, 9, 166, 182, 190
    health/well-being/stability, 65, 141, 149
    satisfaction/comfort, 66, 73, 123
    support, 183

Pure relationship, 4, 21, 23, 77, 100, 164, 192, 195

R

Rape, 60

Reciprocity, 22, 90, 153

Regulation, 10, 27, 196

Resistance, 94, 194

Risk
    of engaging in CD, 29, 73
    financial risk, 58
    legal risk, 9, 58

Risk society, 4, 122

Risk-taking, 57, 58

Risky activity, 58

Romantic relationship, 39, 62, 65, 66, 70, 80, 81, 134, 136, 153–155, 162, 173–183, 189, 190, 196, 197

S

Sanders, T., 4, 23, 28, 31, 33, 53, 66, 67, 69, 81, 82, 87, 108, 121, 132, 133, 153, 155, 157–160, 162, 168, 173, 174, 178, 182

Self-identity, 94, 116, 124

Selling sex, 2, 32, 80, 132, 135, 139, 142

Sexual knowledge, 143, 144

Sexually transmitted diseases (STDs), 86, 105

Sexual pleasure, 51, 55, 71, 79, 100, 131, 157, 196

Sexual risk, 169, 183

Sexual script, 51, 52, 59, 64, 157, 188, 189

Sex work, 5, 6, 49, 81–83, 95, 133, 137, 189

Sex worker, 2, 13, 15, 23, 31–33, 39, 49, 51, 52, 54, 59, 60, 62, 63, 66, 69, 80–82, 84–91, 95, 96, 98, 99, 106, 109, 112, 121–124, 128, 132, 133, 135, 162, 163, 168, 178, 180, 182, 191, 192

Sex worker-client relationship, 100, 163, 189
    See also CC–*Brother* relationship; Client-sex worker relationship

Sharp, K., 57, 69, 155, 162
Simon, W., 47, 48
Social gathering, 35, 39, 40, 169–172, 179, 187
Social withdrawal, 168
Stereotypes, 6, 37, 86, 119
Stigma, 7, 29, 34, 53, 79, 89, 97, 99, 115, 190, 193
Street prostitution, 49
Suicide, 121, 179, 180
Sullivan, E., 47, 48, 105
Sunken boat
  floating, 175
  half-floating, half-sinking, 175, 178
  water leaking into the boat, 175
Surveillance, 49, 96, 100, 140

T
Taboo sex, 78, 98
Taiwanese clients, 62, 87, 174
Taiwanese sex workers, 62, 87
Technological advancement, 15, 77, 96, 134–141
Thrill, 51, 53, 54, 56, 57, 88, 115, 116
Trade, 13, 14, 64, 67, 86, 110, 111, 118, 120, 160, 166, 173, 192
Triple A engine, 96, 97, 100, 134

Trust, 2, 34, 35, 38, 39, 109, 120, 121, 124, 179, 181
Tsang, K.-T., 190, 196

U
Ueno, C., 5, 20, 31, 49, 89, 127, 197
Underage, 5–7, 10, 11, 127, 143, 144, 146, 147, 192n1
Unprotected sex, 143–146, 180–183

V
Victimization, 20, 90, 191, 192n1
Virtual community, 26, 28, 29, 97, 165, 174, 190

W
Warning, 10–13, 119
WeChat, 136
Westernization, 91, 196
Whore stigma, 32, 87, 99, 191, 193
Wilton, T., 84, 89
Winick, C., 54

X
Xantidis, L., 50, 105

The manufacturer's authorised representative in the EU is Springer
Nature Customer Service Centre GmbH, Europaplatz 3, 69115 Heidelberg,
Germany. If you have any concerns regarding our products, please
contact ProductSafety@springernature.com

Printed and bound by CPI Group (UK) Ltd, Croydon, CR0 4YY
29/04/2026
02099478-0006